Third Edition

STARTING YOUR

CAREER AS A

FREELANCE

WRITER

Third Edition

STARTING YOUR CAREER AS A FREELANCE WRITER

MOIRA ALLEN

ALLWORTH PRESS
NEW YORK

Allworth Press books may be purchased in bulk at special discounts for sales promotion, corporate gifts, fund-raising, or educational purposes. Special editions can also be created to specifications. For details, contact the Special Sales Department, Allworth Press, 307 West 36th Street, 11th Floor, New York, NY 10018 or info@skyhorsepublishing.com.

22 21 20 19 18   5 4 3 2 1

Published by Allworth Press, an imprint of Skyhorse Publishing, Inc., 307 West 36th Street, 11th Floor, New York, NY 10018. Allworth Press® is a registered trademark of Skyhorse Publishing, Inc.®, a Delaware corporation.

www.allworth.com

Cover design by Mary Belibasakis
Cover photograph by iStockphoto

Library of Congress Cataloging-in-Publication Data

Names: Allen, Moira Anderson, 1959-
Title: Starting your career as a freelance writer / Moira Allen.
Description: Third edition. | New York, N.Y.: Allworth Press, 2018. |
    Includes index. | Includes bibliographical references and index.
Identifiers: LCCN 2017042648 (print) | LCCN 2017049213 (ebook) | ISBN
    9781621535591 (E-book) | ISBN 9781621535508 (pbk.: alk. paper)
Subjects: LCSH: Authorship—Vocational guidance. | Authorship—Marketing.
Classification: LCC PN151 (ebook) | LCC PN151 .A49 2018 (print) | DDC
    808/.02023—dc23
LC record available at https://lccn.loc.gov/2017042648

Print ISBN: 978-1-62153-550-8
eBook ISBN: 978-1-62153-559-1

Printed in the United States of America

TABLE OF CONTENTS

Introduction

This is the book I always wanted to write. As a writer and writing instructor, I have searched in vain for a book that answers the questions writers ask about launching a freelance career. A book that explains, in clear detail, what to do first, what to do next, what to do after that.

It's not that there aren't any books on freelance writing. There are dozens. So why do I think I can write one that covers the topic better than the rest?

The answer is that while I'm a writer, I'm not *just* a writer. I'm also an editor. I've sat on both sides of the desk. I know what it's like to send out queries and submissions and wait for a response—and I also know what it's like to *receive* those queries and submissions, and what makes good ones stand out from the rest. I know how to *get* an acceptance, and I also know what inspires me to *give* one.

Having spent fifteen years as the editor and publisher of Writing-World.com, one of the world's largest websites for writers, I've also answered hundreds of questions from writers about nearly every aspect of the writing business. Consequently, I know what questions writers ask about launching a successful career. (There are, by the way, far more answers to those questions than I can cram into this book; you'll find many more articles to help guide your career, by me and by dozens of other experts, at Writing-World.com.)

This book will guide you through the steps needed to start freelancing and the steps needed to make your career successful. Whether you want to freelance as a sideline to your day job or while taking care of a home and family, or whether you're interested in going "full time" and supporting yourself as a writer, this book will give you the tools you need.

INTRODUCTION

You may want to read this book more than once as you progress in your career. But whether you read it once or a dozen times, there is one even more important thing you must do to become a successful writer. And that is this: put the book down and *start writing*!

—Moira Allen
editors@writing-world.com
www.writing-world.com

CHAPTER 1

So You Want to Be a Freelance Writer

Writing for publication is one of the most rewarding careers I can think of. It offers opportunities for independence, creativity, and the occasional moment of fame. It gives you a way to speak to (and for) others—to entertain, educate, inspire, motivate, comfort, and assist. It gives you a chance to earn an income by doing something you love. It may even give you a chance to change the world—or at least to change a small part of it by giving readers the tools they need to make their lives better. Plus, there's nothing like the thrill of seeing your name in print!

Writing is also one of the easier careers to break into. You don't need any special qualifications—no special degrees or educational background, certification or business license. You can start a career at any age. And thanks to the magic of the Internet, you can launch a writing career from just about anywhere in the world.

At the same time, a career in freelance writing can be arduous and frustrating. It takes time to launch a writing career, and even more time to become a success. The publishing world has always been a hostile environment for writers, and hasn't gotten better with time. Magazine and newspaper payment rates are often ridiculously low, and many publications haven't increased those rates in decades. Rejection is inevitable, and something a writer must learn to accept gracefully.

It's also essential to realize that, though you may be looking for an opportunity to earn money "doing what you love," freelance writing is a *business*. Unless you treat your efforts as a business—including doing market research, handling correspondence, and keeping financial records—your career is doomed to failure. Don't assume that all you need to succeed is to be creative; there's plenty of dull, mundane "administrivia" involved as well.

The good news is that a writing career is remarkably flexible. It adjusts to your hours, enabling you to invest as few or as many as you are able to spare. Most freelancers begin as moonlighters, writing in their "spare" time while handling a day job or taking care of a family. This gives you a chance to develop your skills, build a portfolio or client base, and establish a nest egg against the day that you decide to go full time. It also gives you a chance to determine, *before* taking that jump, whether this is right for you. Many writers never do go full time, but freelance as a way to supplement their incomes.

WHAT IS A FREELANCER?

According to *Entrepreneur,* nearly one-third of the US labor force engaged in some form of freelancing in 2016, and that number is expected to continue to rise. The study found that nearly 70 percent of freelancers are women, and more than half live with someone who has a full-time job. Very few freelance full time; 96 percent, in fact, freelance to supplement their regular income or their family income. Rarely does freelancing pay the rent; only 4 percent of those interviewed earned more than $50,000 a year, and most earned between $2,000 and $50,000.[1]

So . . . it's important to understand that a freelance writing career is not a shortcut to wealth. Very few freelance writers are wealthy. But it *can* bring in a decent revenue, with the advantage of very little financial outlay and the ability to work from home. This makes freelancing particularly appealing to stay-at-home parents.

Freelancing specifically means marketing your *services* to clients and customers. A freelancer is self-employed, but not all forms of self-employment are freelancing. For example, if you supplement your income by selling craft items on Etsy, this is self-employment, but not freelancing.

This can be confusing to writers, who often think of themselves as creating a "product"—such as a written article—and selling that product to a

---

1   Russ Fujioka, "We're Turning into a Freelance Nation. Here's What That Looks Like," Entrepreneur.com, March 29, 2016, https://www.entrepreneur.com/article/272707.

publication. If you think of freelancing as providing a *service* rather than just a *product*, however, you're likely to improve your chances of success. Instead of thinking of editors as customers for products that you create, think of them as clients for your writing services. When you think of yourself providing a writing service—by reviewing a market's guidelines and understanding its needs and readership—you're much more likely to generate sales. Once you have impressed an editor, you may begin receiving assignments from that publication, which means that you will indeed be providing a writing *service* rather than developing "products" on your own.

Freelance writing can include a variety of writing activities, services, markets, and clients. This book addresses the following:

- **Writing for print magazines.** Nonfiction magazines represent the largest, most accessible, and highest-paying market for freelancers. Thousands of print magazines accept freelance material in the US alone, and there are also hundreds of international markets. Though many predicted that the Internet would bring an end to print magazine publishing, many readers still prefer them—and advertisers still find magazines the best way to reach customers. The downside is that magazines work well in advance, so when you sell a piece, it may not be published for months or even a year.

- **Writing for online publications.** There are many types of online publications, including websites (which may publish material at any time); web zines, e-zines, and email newsletters, which usually publish on a periodical (e.g., weekly or monthly) basis; columns and blogs; and sites associated with commercial enterprises. Many print publications also have an expanded online presence, and may purchase additional material that is only used online. Most online markets don't pay as well as print markets. This marketplace has also shrunk in the last few years. Many publishers rushed to establish e-zines, thinking to cash in on subscriptions and advertising money, only to find that both were hard to come by; consequently many online publications established a decade ago have vanished. Paying markets can still be found, however. Some online markets publish material fairly quickly, but periodicals are likely to take nearly as long to publish a piece as a print magazine.

- **Writing for newspapers.** There are at least as many newspapers in the US as magazines, if not more, and many accept freelance contributions. As Sue Fagalde Lick explains in chapter 17, newspapers generally seek both a local angle and a news angle (e.g., what makes this article timely and useful to readers in our service area?). Most local and regional papers pay less than magazines, but it's often possible to sell the same piece to other noncompeting papers. Newspapers work on a much faster schedule than magazines, often publishing material within days of acceptance. Newspapers may also have an extended online presence, offering additional opportunities for freelancers.
- **Writing nonfiction books.** While few freelancers *start* their careers by writing nonfiction books, many find this a logical step after publishing a number of articles or columns on a particular subject, or becoming a subject-matter expert. An agent is generally not needed. Plus, with a good proposal, you may get a go-ahead and an advance before you actually complete the book.
- **Writing and editing for businesses.** Writing business and corporate materials, such as press releases, brochures, advertising flyers, and social media copy, can provide steadier work and a larger, more reliable income than writing for periodicals. The difference is that in this marketplace, you're not being asked to write creative pieces or come up with your own ideas. Instead, your material is dictated by the customer. This type of freelancing (generally called "copywriting") requires good editing skills, the ability to interact directly with your client, and sometimes some business or technical expertise. Fortunately, thanks to the Internet, it's now possible to write for businesses outside your local area.

Other freelance activities include editing (such as developmental editing, technical editing, copyediting, and proofreading); speechwriting; resume writing; teaching and speaking; writing educational and curriculum materials; writing humor and personal essays; and even illustrating and cartooning. Many of these, however, are better suited for the experienced freelancer; they're not the place to *start* your freelancing career.

You might be wondering whether writing short fiction or novels qualifies as freelance writing. The answer (as you'll often find in this book) is "it depends." The term "freelancing" implies an active attempt to earn money from your efforts. While a novel can bring you an advance and royalties once it is accepted by a publisher, it won't earn you a penny during the months or even years that you're working on it. Writing short fiction is more likely to qualify as freelancing if you can find paying markets for that fiction. However, such markets are few, low paying, and highly competitive, so this is not a good choice if your primary goal is to supplement your income. Poetry offers even fewer opportunities to make money; in fact, many poetry markets expect *you* to pay *them*.

Another type of writing that does not qualify as freelancing is any form of self-publishing that does not generate an income. Writing a blog, for example, is not freelancing. Blogging has benefits, and you may find opportunities to get paid as a blogger or guest blogger, but if you're not getting paid, it's not freelancing.

HOW MUCH CAN YOU EARN?

How much a freelancer can earn depends on a variety of factors, including skill, areas of expertise, business acumen, the amount of time available for writing, and more.

The first thing to understand is that freelancers rarely have the freedom to set their own rates. If you write for periodicals, you are expected to accept whatever pay range a market offers. If the market doesn't pay enough, don't write for that market. Some markets pay flat rates (e.g., $200 for a feature article) while others pay by the word. Many have a rate range, depending on the author's experience and the complexity of the article. New contributors are usually paid at the lower end of the range, and aren't likely to earn more until they've sold several pieces to that market.

When new writers look at market listings, they tend to make one of two mistakes. The first is to think, "Wow! I can sell an article for $1,000! I'll be rich!" I call this the *Redbook* syndrome. It affects writers who are familiar with glossy women's magazines sold at grocery checkout stands. If the first market that pops into your head when you think about where to send an article is *Cosmopolitan* or *Woman's Day*, think again. These magazines can afford to work with pros with years of experience and hefty portfolios. While new writers can *occasionally* break into these markets, the odds are against you. This is not the way to launch your career, and leads to frustration and disappointment.

A second and equally damaging mistake, however, is to assume that *because* you are a new writer, you can write only for low-paying markets. While smaller markets are more open to new and inexperienced writers (because most experienced writers won't bother with them), that doesn't mean you have no choice but to write for a penny a word. The best markets for beginners are somewhere in between, and consist primarily of special-interest magazines. The key to cracking this type of market is often your personal background and expertise rather than writing experience.

To determine how much you can realistically hope to earn as you're starting out, consider the following questions:

1. **What type of markets are you best qualified to write for?** Look for publications that match your interests and experience. If you're an animal lover, look for pet publications. If you travel, look at travel markets. Later, as you build a portfolio and gain experience in interviewing experts, you'll be able to pitch articles on topics that you don't necessarily know a lot about, but that's not the best place to start.

2. **How much do publications in this niche pay?** Check *Writer's Market* to determine the pay ranges of your chosen markets. Which magazines pay the most? Which pay the least? I recommend submitting to the *highest-paying* markets on your list first. You can always work your way down if your article doesn't sell—but if you start with the lowest market and your piece *does* sell, you've lost the opportunity to do better.

3. **How much time does it take to write an article?** Obviously you'll be able to write more articles if you can complete a piece in five hours rather than ten—but writing fast doesn't always mean creating a better product. Knowing how long it takes, however, is key to determining how much your writing can earn. For example, a two-hour article that you sell for $50 is actually worth more than a ten-hour article that you sell for $100. This is why tracking your time, particularly when you are starting out, is vitally important.

4. **How much time can you invest?** If you can invest five hours a week in your freelancing career, and it takes five hours to write a feature article that you can sell for $200, that's an earnings potential of $200 per week. However, you'll also need time for market research, queries, correspondence, research, and administration—so you may

only be able to produce an article every other week, dropping that potential to $100 per week. In addition, remember that *writing* an article per week doesn't guarantee that you will *sell* an article per week.

It's also important to remember that freelance income doesn't start arriving right away. There's a start-up period, during which you're conducting market research and sending out your first queries and submissions. Then, since many publications take weeks or even months to respond, it can still take awhile before you make your first sale or see your first check. It's wise to assume that it will be at least six months before you start to see any steady income from your efforts.

With so many variables involved, there are no hard-and-fast figures on how much a freelance writer can expect to earn at any career stage. It's not unrealistic, however, to hope for revenues of $5,000 or more in your first year, and a steady increase thereafter.

SHOULD YOU WRITE FOR FREE?

Many writers believe they have to serve some sort of "apprenticeship" by writing for nonpaying markets in the beginning. Many also believe this is a good way to build experience and clips.

I disagree. If you have a choice between offering material to a paying market or a nonpaying market, there is no reason to choose the latter. The nonpaying market will always be there if you fail to sell the piece, but it should not be your first choice, or even your second or third.

There are some good reasons to write for free. You might wish to do so for fun, when you want to write something that has no paying market. Many people write to support a cause they believe in, or to help a favorite organization—such as contributing to a church newsletter. Be cautious, however, for once an organization knows that you can write and are willing to do so for free, you'll be flooded with requests. Writing for your own website or blog can also be worthwhile, as is contributing articles to professional newsletters or writing for professional journals.

There are also bad reasons to write for free. One is the desire to "see your name in print," no matter what. Don't assume the only way to get a byline is to give your work away. Another poor reason is to find out if you're "good enough" to get published. Nonpaying markets are generally stuck with whatever they can get, which means being published by such a market is no indication that you are a good writer. Conversely, don't write for free to polish your skills. Even if a market can't pay, that doesn't mean it appreciates being a dumping ground for poor material! Finally, the worst reason to write for free is lack of self-esteem. If you don't believe in yourself, find a way to deal with this issue *before* you start freelancing.

WHAT DOES IT TAKE TO BECOME A FREELANCE WRITER?

As I said above, one of the great things about this career is its lack of prerequisites. You don't need a special degree; you don't have to major in English or journalism. You don't need a lot of equipment, and you can work from home. However, you do need a few personal qualities:

1. **Writing ability.** Most people embark on a freelance writing career because they enjoy writing, know that they have good writing skills, and would like to turn those skills and that love of writing into a source of income. If you're not sure whether you're a good writer, however, that doesn't mean you shouldn't try. One of the best ways to find out is to submit your work for publication. Keep in mind that you *will* be rejected, and that this may have nothing to do with your ability. You'll experience rejection throughout your freelance career, no matter how long you've been writing or how good you are.

    In the beginning, however, you want to find a pattern. If your first twenty or thirty submissions are rejected with form letters, chances are that your writing needs work, or that you're targeting the wrong markets or sending the wrong ideas. If you start getting rejections with feedback, you're on the right track. And, of course, getting acceptances is the best news of all.

    If you get a stream of form rejections, consider joining an online or real-world critique group, or take a writing course. Look for patterns in the feedback you receive. Do you consistently hear that your material has spelling or grammatical errors or lacks organization? The key to becoming a good writer is accepting the fact that you can always become a *better* writer. To send material out at all, you must learn to silence that little voice that says "I'm not good enough," while at the same time being honest enough to admit, "I may need to improve."

2. **Business sense.** While *writing* may be creative, *freelancing* is a business. Your goal is not to simply express yourself, but to develop materials you can sell. This means being able to make business decisions about what (and how) to write. Instead of saying, "I'd like to write about dogs," for example, you must ask, "What can I write about dogs that would interest an audience of experienced dog owners?" The business side of writing includes market research, research, and the administrative tasks of any business—including bookkeeping, billing clients, tracking hours, handling income and expense records, and so on.

3. **Professionalism.** If you appear professional, editors will assume that you *are* a professional, no matter how little experience you have. This means learning how to send a query, format a manuscript, handle email correspondence, meet deadlines, negotiate contracts, and so forth. It also means being able to manage your emotions and remain mature, courteous, and professional at all times—even when you're dealing with editors who aren't any of the above. Nothing will ruin a freelance career faster than getting a reputation for being hard to deal with. Never become known as a writer who argues over rejections, accepts an assignment and then holds out for a higher pay rate, sends flaming emails, or otherwise becomes known as a "problem" writer.

4. **Motivation.** Many people desire to write but never do. To become a freelancer, your desire to write must be stronger than your desire to do a great many other things. It means taking steps to change your life and your schedule. It can mean changing habits to squeeze in time for writing. It can mean giving up things you enjoy—including spending time with family.

Freelancing also requires the courage to face the keyboard and start translating your dream of writing into reality. I don't know of any writer who considers this an *easy* job. Freelancing means tackling challenges—projects that take you out of your comfort zone and force you to push your abilities. There are days when you can't even *pretend* that writing is fun. But we all have those days, no matter how many years we've been writing.

Motivation may also mean sticking to your decision even if no one else supports it. While some freelancers are blessed with supportive families, others aren't so lucky. If your decision to freelance means leaving a paying job, family members may resent that initial loss of income. If it means assigning household chores to other people, that can cause friction. Perhaps hardest of all, however, is when family and friends simply don't understand why you *want* to write. When your mother asks you when you're going to get a "real job," or your friends call during the day because they know you're not actually "working," just smile and keep typing.

5. **Perseverance.** Freelancing can seem like a long, uphill struggle. Your file of rejections keeps growing. You have moments when you wonder if you'll ever sell anything (or ever sell anything again). A successful freelancer isn't one who never has these doubts; it's one who perseveres in spite of them.

6. **Discipline.** One drawback of freelancing is that you don't have a boss standing over your shoulder, nagging you to get back to work, or telling you what to write and when. Often, the only deadlines you have are those you set for yourself. To be successful, you must be a self-starter—and you must also be able to finish what you start.

Many articles recommend writing for a certain number of hours every day, but this is often not practical. I recommend striving for a weekly minimum, and getting that writing in when you can. Don't stress over writing at a particular time ("two hours before breakfast"). Discipline doesn't lie in formulas; it lies in forcing oneself to ignore all the excuses we have for *not* writing.

And now for the caveat. If you're dreaming of instant fame and fortune as a writer, then I advise you to seek another career. Freelance writing is not a quick path to riches or glory. Those who embark on this path with visions of overnight success rarely last long.

That doesn't mean that you *can't* become famous, and even wealthy, as a writer. Those who have achieved this kind of success, however, didn't do so because they were looking for it. Instead, they set out to follow the dream of doing what they loved for its own sake. If you love to write, there are few things more satisfying than being able to do what you love for a living—and as a writer once said, if you do what you love, the money will follow.

CHAPTER 2

The Tools of a Freelancer

One of the benefits of a career in freelance writing is that it requires very little startup investment. You may already have many of the tools you need. However, certain tools *are* necessary as you set up your writing office—even if that office is just a corner of the kitchen.

These tools fall into two categories: absolute necessities and optional extras. The necessities are those items that you'll need to acquire before you can go very far in your writing work, even if this means laying out some expenses before you've earned any income. The optional extras may also be important, but can usually wait until you've seen some revenue.

A SPACE OF YOUR OWN

The first thing you need is a *place* to write. While writers have launched careers from the kitchen table, it helps immensely to have a space—even a very small space—that you can call your own. Many writers feel this space should include a door that can be closed against interruptions, distractions, and family members. Another advantage of an enclosed workspace is that it's more likely to qualify for a home-office deduction (see chapter 26).

So before you plop your laptop down just anywhere, give this matter careful consideration. One of the factors that often interferes with a writer's goals is lack of self-esteem. We often feel we don't have a right to "inconvenience" other family members with our writing efforts—and carving out a space of our own from a crowded household can mean doing just that. It's easy to fall into the trap of thinking that your "little hobby" of writing isn't important and you should just "make do."

Stop. You're starting a *business*. If you dismiss your writing efforts as a game or a hobby, you aren't taking yourself, or your business, seriously. If you don't take it seriously, you can't expect anyone else in your household to take it seriously either.

Don't make the mistake of thinking that you (or your family) will give your business more space and respect when it starts earning money. It takes time for any business to get off the ground. Your business deserves space and respect *now*, not when it "proves" itself at some unspecified time in the future. By giving your business (and yourself) that respect in the beginning, you give yourself a much greater chance for success. Otherwise, it's easy to give up, because you've never given yourself a fair start.

Look around your home and consider where to make a space for *your business of writing*. This space must meet certain needs. You will need room for a workspace—either a desk or a table where you can put your computer, and where you can spread out notes, books, and other research materials. You'll need room for a comfortable office chair that gives you back support. You'll need room for files. It's nice to have a shelf where you can keep reference books—a dictionary, thesaurus, and market guides—within easy reach. Your work area also needs good lighting. Make sure that your desk is positioned so that you don't get an unwanted glare on your computer screen or in your eyes.

As you consider your options, spend some time thinking about your personality, the personalities of those around you, and the traffic patterns in your home. One of the common myths about writers, for example, is that we're solitary souls. The farther away from humanity we can get, the happier we're supposed to be. This can prompt a writer to assume his office should be in some remote part of the house—the attic, the basement, or even the garage. Only in such peace and privacy, we imagine, can we get down to the business of courting the muse.

In reality, every writer is different. You may find that you don't like working in the attic or the basement. Sure, it's quiet—for the simple reason that no one *wants* to be there, including you. One of the best office spaces I've contrived has been a breakfast room off the kitchen. I have my own space, but I'm not cut off from the household (and it's easy to pop into the kitchen for a cup of coffee).

At the same time, your space needs to be absolutely, unarguably *yours*. Don't share it with your spouse's books or your children's toys. Whether it has a door or not, its boundaries must be clear. This is your *business office*, and you're going into that office to work. Noisy music, television, kids with video games, and other distractions should not be allowed to intrude.

Another factor to consider when planning your office space is clutter. I've discovered that a pleasant office layout makes a huge difference in my productivity. If awkwardly arranged furniture makes my space cramped, I don't enjoy being there. Try to keep the visible contents of your office to a minimum. Keep piles of paper out of sight, and add decorative touches, like pictures or plants.

FURNISHING YOUR WORKSPACE

Once you've decided where to set up your office, your next step will be to furnish it so that you can work effectively. It can take time to figure out just how to arrange and accomplish that, because when we're starting out, we don't always know what we'll need or what our work habits will be like. However, there are some basics that you'll need.

The first is some sort of desk or desk surface. Computer desks are OK, but they don't always offer the sort of paper-spreading room you'll need when conducting research. Good-quality computer desks can also be expensive.

If you don't want to pay for a desk, consider that old standby, a pair of boards laid across two filing cabinets. This makes an inexpensive and useful desk with loads of filing space in the bargain. A table is another option, and you can usually fit a filing cabinet beneath it. Consider looking for tables, filing cabinets, and other furnishings at thrift shops or garage sales.

Yes, you *will* need a filing cabinet. The business of writing still generates a lot of paper. While it's possible to archive a great deal electronically, the paperless office is still a myth. A filing cabinet remains the best way to organize and store files relating to current and ongoing projects, as well as correspondence, contracts, and other papers that are essential to your bookkeeping.

As you consider furnishings, be sure to consider the types of equipment you'll need. You'll need a place to put a computer and a printer at the very least, as well as a lamp (unless you have superb overhead lighting) and a phone. If you want a scanner (there are good reasons to have one), you'll need a place for that as well. You'll have different requirements depending on whether you use a desktop computer with a separate screen and keyboard, or if you plan to use a laptop.

If you use a table or boards over file cabinets, one issue you may encounter is the lack of drawer space. Basic office supplies—pens, pencils, a letter opener, paper clips, and such—can quickly clutter your desk. If you have no desk drawers, consider investing in a small drawer unit (such as an inexpensive three-drawer plastic storage cabinet) that you can set on top of your desk.

You also need a chair. Do not imagine you can just use one of the chairs from your dining-room table. Doing so is a sure recipe for an aching back. Invest in a high-quality, comfortable office chair with wheels and good back support. Otherwise, you'll be investing in the services of a chiropractor. Be sure to get a chair mat to protect your carpet or hardwood floor from the wheels.

Good lighting is essential. You're going to be using your eyes, so protect them. If you don't have good overhead lighting, invest in a desk lamp that can put light where you need it. Natural light is also helpful, if you can position your desk near windows that give good *indirect* light. You don't want to deal with the sun's glare shining into your eyes or reflecting off your computer screen.

One final consideration when arranging your workspace is pets. If you have them, you know what I mean. When you're home, they want to be with you. If they're not with you, they fuss; but if they can be near you, they will generally settle down and leave you alone. So ensure that your office includes a place where they can do just that. My cat has a basket beside my desk, which greatly reduces the amount of time she spends walking on my keyboard trying to get my attention. Besides, writing can be stressful, and it has been shown that stroking a pet can help relieve stress, so one could think of them as a helpful office accessory!

YOUR OWN COMPUTER

When I wrote the first edition of this book, many writers still had not embraced the idea of the "home computer." Today, I doubt there are very many households that do not possess at least one computer, or writers who don't know how to use one.

But is that computer *yours*? I didn't say you need to have a computer. I said you need *your own computer*.

If everyone in the family shares the same computer, this won't be sufficient for your writing business. Your writing time will always take second place to homework, games, videos, checking stocks, downloading MP3 files, and general surfing. It's difficult enough to find writing time without having to compete for computer time as well.

Fortunately, computers have become very inexpensive, so if you don't have one of your own, consider this an absolutely essential startup cost for your business. Now the question arises: desktop or laptop?

I'm a desktop fan myself. I have large hands; I prefer a full-size keyboard, and a large screen on which to display my work and the programs or files I need to access while I'm working. However, I'm also content to do my work in one place. If you prefer mobility—if you travel frequently, or want to be able to work on the deck when the weather is nice—there's no reason not to use a laptop. You might also wish to add a full-size keyboard, mouse, and display screen that you can connect to your laptop when you're using it in your home office.

Make sure your computer is equipped with Microsoft Word, as this is the program most commonly required by publishers. "Platform" is unimportant; Word can be used with both Windows and Macintosh. While it's possible to obtain free "Word" programs, such as Apache Open Office, not every publisher will accept this.

In addition to Microsoft Word, you'll need a spreadsheet program to help you manage your business finances, track submissions, and handle other business issues. An image-processing program will be helpful if you plan to sell photos; while Photoshop is the industry standard, there are many free image-processing programs available as well.

Rare is the household in America today that doesn't have Internet service. Quite probably, your service is provided by either your cable or phone company. If you use a wireless router, make sure your computer receives a clear signal. If you prefer the security of a wired connection, you may need to run some cables to connect your work computer to the household router.

Your Internet service undoubtedly offers an email account, and may offer the option of setting up several accounts. Set up a separate account for your business rather than using your personal account. Make sure that the name you use for that account is professional. "JoanSmith@mycableco.com" is fine; "CrystalPenslinger" or "LindysMom" or "CatLady" are less appropriate. Free accounts are also available through Gmail and Yahoo.

Eventually, you may decide to set up your own website and register your own domain name (see chapter 24). Then, you can use an email service associated with that site. Having your own domain in your email address ("mjones@mandyswritingservice.com") gives a more professional appearance to your correspondence than "Mandy2567@yahoo.com." Private email accounts are also less vulnerable to hacking than the generic free services.

I do *not* recommend attempting to manage your writing business with just a tablet or a smartphone, however popular these may be today. You need computing power, memory, and visual space. Having a display on your screen that approximates the size of a manuscript (or magazine) page is vital in assessing the "look" of your material. A paragraph doesn't look the same on the screen of a cell phone as it does on a full-size computer screen. You want to know exactly what your editor is going to see when he receives your submission. You'll need the ability to download files, switch between multiple programs at once, check facts on the web while you're in the midst of writing your piece, store your articles and correspondence in appropriate directories, and print what you need at the touch of a button. Tablets and cell phones won't work with external CD/DVD drives (they don't possess enough energy to power the drive), and it can be extremely difficult to print from such devices. That doesn't mean that you can't benefit from such devices, but they're no substitute for a computer.

COMPUTER PERIPHERALS

Whether you use a desktop or a laptop, you'll need some peripherals. One essential is a CD/DVD read/write drive. This will enable you to add programs to your computer and keep backup copies on disk. You may also need to create CDs to accompany submissions, particularly if you are submitting photographs or other large files. Most magazine editors will accept electronic files on CD, DVD, or flash drive—and for the beginning writer, CDs are by far the most economical option. While most desktops include a CD/DVD drive, many laptops do not, but you can obtain an inexpensive external drive that works through a USB port.

You will also need a printer. This requires careful thought about your current and anticipated needs. You will need, at the very least, the ability to print out manuscripts, queries, cover letters, and contracts—for even in this Internet age, some publications still expect paper submissions. You may also prefer to print research materials from the Internet, as it's often easier, when researching an article, to spread papers out over your desk than to keep searching through electronic files.

For this type of printing, a black-and-white printer is usually sufficient. Brother manufactures a line of inexpensive, black-and-white laser printers that are durable and have long-lasting toner cartridges. (You can also find information online on how to make your toner cartridges last even longer.) If you anticipate a need for color printing, you'll need to invest in an inkjet printer.

When choosing a printer, also consider the cost of ink or toner cartridges. If you do a lot of printing, you'll quickly find that inkjet cartridges cost more than what you paid for the printer itself! If you choose an inkjet printer, make sure you can buy individual cartridges for every color; otherwise, you'll have to replace the entire cartridge unit each time any single color runs out. With laser printers, toner cartridges are programmed to send the "out of toner" message long before they are actually empty, but again, you can find information online on how to extend their life span. And if you're feeling adventurous, there's always the option of using off-brand replacement cartridges.

Another question to consider is whether you want a device that offers more than just printing. A "three-in-one" printer will serve as a printer, copier, and scanner (and fax machine if you want one). This is useful if office space is limited. You'll often need to make copies, and it's just as easy to scan a document so that you have not only a printed copy but also an electronic copy on file. Three-in-ones are fine if you don't do a lot of scanning, but if you expect to do a lot of scanning, a stand-alone scanner is faster and more efficient. If you have a bit more space and a bit more capital, consider investing in a sheetfed scanner, which is useful for scanning receipts, clips, and even photographs. See chapter 27 for more information on using a scanner to save records electronically.

OTHER NECESSITIES

Besides office furniture and a computer, there are several other things your business needs:

A Business Phone

It's possible that you're one of the last people in America not to have a personal cell phone, but I doubt it. However, you may wish to consider obtaining a separate phone for your business, particularly if you expect to be dealing with corporate clients or if you plan to do a lot of interviews. If you purchase a separate business phone, you can claim the entire cost of that phone and phone service as a business expense. If, however, you use your personal phone or cell phone for business, you can only deduct the cost of each business call—and if you have unlimited calling, that means no deduction at all.

Another advantage of using a separate cell phone is that you can reserve it for business calls. By ensuring that no one uses this phone to contact you for personal reasons, you'll greatly reduce the number of interruptions to your work. In addition, when you know that the only incoming calls should be from clients or business contacts, you can always answer your business phone professionally.

If you get a separate cell phone for business, consider an inexpensive no-contract phone, such as a TracFone. TracFone offers a wide range of smartphones, including reconditioned phones ranging from "free" to $30.

The Writer's Market

For market research, there is still no substitute for the *Writer's Market*, the most comprehensive annual guide to markets available. Published every fall by Writer's Digest Books, it lists thousands of periodical markets, as well as book publishers, writing contests, and markets for other products such as greeting cards, screenplays and more. Listings include contact information, payment rates, rights, and what each publication seeks from writers.

The *Writer's Market* comes in a basic edition (book only) and a "deluxe edition" (book plus access to an online market database, located at www.writersmarket.com). You can also sign up for the online version only, either by monthly subscription or for an annual fee. When researching markets, however, there's nothing quite like being able to page through the book itself, marking interesting-looking publications.

Basic Writing Supplies

Every writing office needs a few basic supplies, including 20-pound white bond paper (or A4 paper if you're outside the US), business-size mailing envelopes, 9" × 12" manila mailing envelopes, blank CDs and inexpensive flash drives for backups and submissions, pens, pencils, markers, paper clips, rulers, Post-it notes, and whatever other office items you feel you might need. If you expect to submit manuscripts by mail, invest in a supply of postage in various denominations, along with a small postage scale. Get a box of file folders and hanging folders for your filing cabinet. You'll also need notepads, large and small. Large pads are great for jotting down interviews or research notes; small ones are good to keep by the computer and around the house to jot down ideas, reminders, to-do lists, and such.

Always keep a calendar in your office. If you want to track deadlines, consider a three-month calendar (available in office supply stores). You will probably find that you want some system of tracking assignments, appointments, interviews, deadlines, and such. Some writers use computerized schedulers; others prefer datebooks or day planners. There's no "right way" to do this; there's only the way that is right for you.

You can easily design a professional letterhead on your computer, then save it and use it as your template whenever you're writing a business letter. Include your name, address, phone, email, and fax if you use one. Avoid cute logos like pens or parchments, and don't use a "title" (like "author" or "freelance writer"). Here's an example of a simple letterhead design:

Moira Allen

1234 Mystreet • Mytown, VA 20151
(XXX) 555–1234
editors@writing-world.com

I like to use a decorative (but not overly fancy) font for my name, and ordinary text for contact information. This example is reduced to fit the page size of this book; for an 8.5" × 11" sheet of paper, I use a 24-point font for the name and a 12-point font for the address.

OPTIONAL EXTRAS

There are several other office supplies that can be helpful, but are not immediately essential. Some are also growing less essential over time.

For example, there's the fax machine. Some publishers do still use them. Very few writers do, however. If you want one, consider getting one that's part of a printer/copier/scanner bundle. Fax machines are still useful for transmitting contracts, but if you have a scanner, you can send a signed contract back just as quickly by scanning it, saving it as a PDF or JPG, and emailing it to your editor as an attachment.

A stand-alone copier may also be a thing of the past. I recommend having a copier, but again, a three-in-one printer solves this problem. A flatbed scanner also works perfectly well as a copier. The only difference is that the scan must be saved to your computer first and then printed if you need a copy. But this also means that you retain an electronic copy of the document, which you can print as often as you need to. This is particularly useful for saving and printing clips.

An external hard drive is a wise addition to your computer peripherals. It's a good means of transferring information from one computer to another (e.g., from desktop to laptop), and it also provides a means of backing up information so that if your computer suffers a catastrophic crash, your data won't be lost. I keep a drive connected to my desktop at all times, and back up my work at the end of each day.

If your files don't require a lot of memory, you can accomplish the same thing with a flash drive. These come in many sizes, up to 256 GB. (I'm told that even larger sizes are available, but 256 GB was the largest I was able to find on Amazon!) They're also a good way to move information between computers or to carry information with you.

Another handy tool is a label maker. Once upon a time, most writers had typewriters, but today, these are rare. Unfortunately, it's hard to address an envelope without one, unless you wish to write the address by hand, which doesn't look professional. If you expect to submit queries and manuscripts by mail, this handy tool lets you print professional-looking labels with the touch of a button.

As I mentioned before, a scanner can be a useful addition to your office. A flatbed scanner is vital if you need to scan photos, artwork, or material from books; a sheetfed scanner is an excellent way to manage receipts and other documents. While three-in-one printers *do* include a scan function, a stand-alone scanner gives more flexibility and is easier to use.

Finally, you'll want to stock your business bookshelf. In addition to the *Writer's Market,* you'll need a good dictionary. A thesaurus is also useful. If you plan to write technical, medical, or scientific articles, invest in appropriate dictionaries for those as well. Over time, you'll probably collect some basic references on writing, from style guides to marketing books to how-to manuals (like this one).

Spend a few days setting up your writing space. Take time to get it just right. Make sure it is comfortable. Make it aesthetically as well as ergonomically pleasing. If you can afford to go beyond the merely functional, pick out a desk that appeals to you visually—a desk that says, "This is the desk of a writer!" Take time to determine the best arrangement for your equipment. Make sure everything is within easy reach. Then, leave it alone. Rearranging one's workspace and reorganizing one's files are two of the most common forms of procrastination. It *feels* like you're working, but you're not. Resist the temptation to keep tinkering with your space, and start *writing*. After all, the best tools in the world aren't going to help you if you don't use them!

CHAPTER 3

Making Time to Write

Another vital element you need to start a career as a freelance writer is *time*. If you're wondering when you'll ever find enough time to start writing, I have good news and bad news. The good news is that you'll never have more time than you do right now. The bad news is . . . well, that *is* the bad news.

Time is never "found." It can only be "made." If you decide to wait until your kids are in school, or in college, or you quit your day job or retire, you could wait forever. The only way to make your writing dreams come true is to find ways to reallocate the time you have *now*.

MAKE A TIME BUDGET

People say "time is money." More accurately, time is *like* money. We have only so much available, and must make choices about how and where to spend it.

Many writers feel uncomfortable spending time *starting* their career—a period when they may need to invest a lot of time and effort without a lot of immediate results. This start-up time is essential, however. It takes time to build your skills, sell that first article, develop a client base. If you sit down today and write your first query, it could be months before you receive a response, and still longer before you see your first check. But if you don't, you'll never see that check at all.

So think about time as something that, just like money, you need to budget. The first step in doing this is to determine where you're *already* spending that time. One method is to purchase an appointment book that breaks the day into fifteen-minute segments. For two weeks, record where every block of your time goes—including eating, sleeping, even brushing your teeth. Be honest: if you spent an hour reading articles about the latest celebrity divorce, write it down. If you're not sure how much time you spend on an activity, buy a timer that includes a count-up function. Start it when you begin an activity, and pause it when you take a break to do something else.

The results may surprise you. Do you ever have days when you feel you've been running from dawn to dusk, but have no idea what you actually did? A time log will help you discover where that time went. You may be surprised by how long certain tasks take, and how many unnoticed tasks nibble away at your hours. You may also find that you spend a lot of time on tasks that don't mean as much to you as writing.

EXAMINE YOUR PRIORITIES

No matter what you're doing today—working, raising a family, going to school—you have a full schedule. Making time to write means making tradeoffs. You may need to give something up in order to reallocate that time. To figure out what that might be, look at your time log and categorize your activities. Possible categories include:

- **Tasks only you can perform.** If you're working or going to school, no one else can do that for you!
- **Tasks that are essential.** Dinner needs to be cooked, clothes need to be washed, and the dog has to be fed. One question you may need to ask, however, is whether those tasks have to be done by *you*. Often, we do things because they have become "our job"—and because we do them better than anyone else. No one else folds laundry as well as you do. But someone else could learn.
- **Tasks you enjoy.** Don't give up everything you enjoy; that's a sure way to burn out. If you feel you would lose something of value in your life by giving up an activity, include it in this category.
- **Tasks you think you "should" do.** Volunteer opportunities often fall into this category. So does being perpetually available to help out family and friends—particularly with things that family and friends could do for themselves. Certain types of housework may fall into this category; just because your grandmother ironed the sheets doesn't mean you have to.

- **Tasks someone else could perform.** We often handle tasks for other family members that they could do for themselves. Your spouse can pull shirts out of the dryer and hang them up just as easily as you can. Someone else can feed the dog. Sometimes, delegating tasks not only frees time for you but enables others to become more responsible and independent.
- **Tasks that take too much time.** Did it really take three hours to do laundry or buy groceries? Why? We often lose time through distractions and make work without realizing it.
- **Tasks that are purely recreational.** Reading, television, computer games, and, more recently, social media all fall into this category. Don't assume you have to give up all your recreations—but remember that if time is a budget, you may have to reallocate some of those resources.

ELIMINATE TIME WASTERS

We all have unrecognized habits, procrastination devices, and assumptions about things we "should" and "shouldn't" do that waste our time. Here are some of the more common ones:

- **Television.** Record shows that come on when you could be writing, and watch them at other times. Skip commercials. If you watch shows just because other family members want to, let them watch their favorites without you. Some families watch three movies in a night: one for him, one for her, one for the kids. You could save hours by sharing a his-and-hers movie and letting the kids watch theirs alone. If you watch two hours of television a day, see if you can reduce it to one—even if that means splitting a movie over two nights. This change alone would give you seven hours of additional writing time per week!
- **Mail and subscriptions.** No law says that you have to open junk mail. Make a habit of tossing anything you don't want and spend time only on mail that matters. Do you have a stack of magazines you never have time to read? Toss them and consider canceling those subscriptions. Do you need a daily paper, or could you get by with the weekend edition?

- **Errands.** Errands include travel time and "putting away" time when you get home. They also drain your energy. Try to combine as many errands as possible on a single trip. Schedule certain days of the week for errands, and devote the other days to writing.
- **Chores.** When it comes to chores, I've learned to ask, "Will this still get done if I don't do it right now?" I know that sooner or later, I *will* empty the dryer or the dishwasher—but if I leave my computer now, I may not recapture that writing time. Another option (really!) is to hire help for the housecleaning. Finally, make sure other family members are doing their fair share.
- **Social media.** Writers say that social media is addictive—they plan to use it for promotion and find they've spent hours simply reading and commenting on other people's posts. Spending two hours chatting with friends on Facebook or Snapchat is no different from spending two hours chatting on the phone. So ask yourself—if someone were to call you on the phone and ask for an hour of your time for chitchat, would you say yes?

LEARN TO MANAGE PROCRASTINATION

Notice that I didn't say "don't procrastinate." There may be writers who never suffer from procrastination, but I've never met one, and I'm not one of them. I doubt you will be either.

Procrastination seems to be a basic part of the writing life. There's a simple reason for that. Writing is a personal, often emotional process—and it is *stressful.* Those are *your* words people will be reading. You're putting yourself out there, and it's often hard not to feel that people will be judging what you write, and by extension, you. When something is stressful, we automatically try to avoid it, and we do that by finding things to do that are less stressful.

Deadlines are, of course, the best cure for procrastination, and real (external) deadlines are more effective than artificial deadlines. Any deadline, however, is better than nothing. For one thing, if you keep missing deadlines that you set for yourself, you'll begin to see a pattern that needs to be addressed. Another helpful tool is to break projects into smaller tasks and focus on completing those. Instead of thinking, "I must complete this 2,000-word article by the end of the month," think, "I need to get that interview by next week."

Procrastination can stem from causes other than stress. You may find that you are attempting to create a writing schedule that doesn't actually match your optimal work habits. Many articles tell us to spend a specific amount of time per day writing, or to always write at a certain time of day, or to always complete a certain number of words. Not every writer, however, gets up at dawn and writes 500 words before breakfast. In the morning, I am too restless to sit down at the computer; I want to handle my errands and the physical tasks of the day. After lunch, my physical energy is wearing down, but my mental energy is becoming more focused, and I'm ready to sit down. Pay attention to your work rhythms to determine whether you're procrastinating, at least partly, because you're trying to conform to a schedule that doesn't match your natural work patterns.

Boredom is another common cause of procrastination. As a freelancer, you may often end up dealing with projects that don't excite you. The longer these projects take, the less interested you're likely to be—and the more interesting other projects (*any* other projects) start to appear. This can quickly lead to project-hopping, where you abandon Project A (temporarily, you tell yourself) to work a bit on Project B, from which you move to Project C, and so on. Eventually you can end up with a trail of unfinished projects in your wake. If you do find yourself project-hopping, recognize that this can be an indication that you're bored—but hop back and forth (A to B to A again) rather than ever onward.

Another useful technique is to ask yourself which project *will* get done even if you put it off. If you have to choose between, say, emptying the dishwasher and finishing your article, remind yourself that, sooner or later, the dishwasher *will* get emptied, even if it isn't done now. If you postpone the writing, however, it may not get done in time.

It may also be important to recognize that restlessness is not necessarily the same thing as procrastination. When my husband and I write, we find that we go through an "up and down" phase, where we tend to get up from the keyboard, pace, get coffee, go back and sit down, and repeat the process two or three times. Then—we find ourselves settled, and you can't pry us loose with a crowbar.

Keep in mind that procrastination is not always a bad thing. I've found that when I absolutely can't stop procrastinating on a project, my subconscious is trying to tell me something. When I take a closer look, I'll find that I've written myself into a corner or lack vital information, or there is something wrong with my approach. Procrastination can be my mind's way of telling me, "Don't keep going down that road!"

Finally, don't beat yourself up over procrastination. We all do it. The key is to manage it, and ensure that it is only a temporary disruption rather than a permanent derailment.

KEEP A TO-DO LIST

I'm a huge fan of to-do lists. I resisted them for years, never wanting to be the sort of person driven by *lists*. But now I consider them one of the handiest tools to help you become a more organized, efficient writer.

To-do lists can help you do many things, including:

1. **Prioritize.** When you're juggling half-a-dozen tasks in your head, it's difficult to decide which comes first. The simple act of writing tasks down enables you to view them from a different perspective. On paper, it's easier to see that A is more important than C, while D should move to second place, F has been dragging on far too long, and B could certainly wait for another day.

   Prioritizing your list can involve many factors. One is deadlines. If a task is due in two weeks, it's likely to move to the top of your list. However, they aren't the only priority. If you've been meaning to research a query for a high-paying market, that task might have no specific deadline, but every week you postpone it is another week away from an important career move. To-do lists also help identify tasks you've been procrastinating over, helping you boost them to the top of the list to get done once and for all.

2. **Organize.** My list doesn't just include business tasks; it also covers the rest of my life. If I'm planning a party, knowing that part of my week will be spent running errands and cleaning will ensure that I don't load up the list with a bunch of writing tasks that simply won't get done.

   Lists also enable you to assign time values to your tasks. Once you've written your list, you'll immediately notice tasks that are going to require a lot of time, as opposed to tasks that can be done in a snap. I often find that short tasks (calls for information, follow-up emails, etc.) get postponed the longest. Moving quick-response tasks to the top of my list encourages me to get them done, adding to my week's accomplishments without significantly cutting into my schedule.

That doesn't mean you should always go for the shortest job first. Some quick tasks are important; others are trivial. Don't focus on small tasks to the exclusion of larger, more important jobs!

3. **Identify problems.** When you start maintaining a list from week to week, you'll soon notice those tasks that keep "sliding" from one week to the next. If this keeps happening, it's an indication that you need to take a closer look at why you're procrastinating on that project.

It could be that the task isn't actually that important to you. It might seem like something you *should* do, or might *like* to do, but it never reaches top priority. If that's why it keeps sliding, you might want to drop it from the list entirely, or postpone it to a later time.

Conversely, you may keep postponing a project because it *is* important. Often, the tasks we put off the longest are those most important to us—and also the most intimidating. If you feel unready or unwilling to tackle something significant, it will keep sliding until you've identified and dealt with the fears or concerns that are keeping you from tackling it.

4. **Recognize achievements.** To me, the best part of a to-do list is turning it into a "done" list. A list not only helps bring order to your schedule but also helps you identify exactly what you *have* done with your time. It helps you realize that you've achieved many, or even most, of your goals—instead of berating yourself for what you haven't done.

Some folks laugh at the idea of writing something on your list simply to cross it off. I find, however, that making a note of something I've *done*, even if it wasn't on the original list, helps me track achievements and identify where my time was spent. Then, if I'm not able to cross off all the original items on the list, seeing the new entry helps me understand why—and perhaps recognize that I achieved something even more important than I had originally planned.

Managing an Effective List

To achieve these benefits, it's important to manage a to-do list effectively. Different people will have different ideas about how to do this, but here are some tips that can be applied to nearly any type of list:

1. **It must be reasonable.** A list that reads, "write my novel, clean the garage, develop lesson plans to home-school my daughter, achieve world peace" won't help you accomplish anything. It will simply lead to frustration. Your list should include only those tasks you can genuinely hope to achieve within the time frame of the list.

   This means distinguishing between "tasks" and "projects." A "project" is the big picture. Writing a novel is a project; writing a chapter is a task. Some projects ("clean my desk") are small enough to count as stand-alone tasks. Others need to be broken into smaller chunks. For example, writing a 2,000-word article may not seem that large a project, but it may need to be broken into smaller tasks, such as interviews (each interview being a separate task), research, outlining, writing the first draft, editing the draft, and so on. Each task should go on your list as a separate item.

2. **It must be in line with your goals.** Creating a to-do list doesn't mean just jotting down a bunch of tasks for the day or week. It works best when combined with your long-term vision—the goals and achievements you wish to accomplish (see chapter 4). For example, let's say you have the goal of setting up a website. This involves a number of steps, some of which must be done sequentially, some that can be done simultaneously. By adding those tasks to your list, you remain aware of where you are in the project and what needs to be done next, which keeps you on track toward your long-term goal while keeping specific tasks manageable.

3. **It must have a defined time frame.** I prefer weekly lists, because I find it easier to aim to achieve a task by the end of a week rather than trying to assign tasks to specific days. Others prefer daily lists, while others prefer to write lists for the month. Some even make lists for the year. Studies have actually shown that keeping a more flexible to-do list with a longer time frame (e.g., weekly or monthly rather than daily) can actually improve performance. Daily lists are

too easily disrupted by unexpected events, whereas if your target is to achieve a particular task within a longer time frame, you don't feel as if you've "failed" if you need to shift tasks around to different days.[2]

Some people keep separate lists for tasks vs. projects. A monthly list might include "write travel article" and "organize photos," while the weekly list includes "conduct interviews" and "obtain photos from travel bureau." The key is identifying what you wish to achieve within a specific time frame, not simply "whenever."

4. **It must be visible.** My husband keeps his list on his computer. I keep mine on a pad of paper on my desk, where I can see it at a glance. The point is that if you can't see your list, or never remember to refer to it, it won't help you.

5. **It must be flexible.** Your list is written on paper, *not* graven in stone. No matter how well you plan, something may come up that is more important or urgent than the tasks on your list. When that happens, simply jot down the new priority, and don't be surprised when older items must be postponed. This is one reason I prefer weekly rather than daily lists; if my goal is to complete Task X by the end of the week, having to postpone it by a day or two doesn't necessarily affect my list as a whole.

It's important to remember that a list is not a schedule. A list is simply that—a list of *objectives* within a particular time frame. Many of us feel stifled by schedules, and again, studies show that attempting to impose a strict schedule on one's workflow can actually reduce creativity and productivity. A list tells you what you need to get done—but leaves the management of your time up to you, and frees you to structure your days around other requirements and unexpected events.

Tracking Achievements

What happens when to-do lists become "done" lists? My husband archives his electronically, but since mine are on paper, that's not an option. Nor do I

---

2   Tim Harford, "The Psychological Benefits of Giving Up on Cleaning and Embracing the Mess," *Quartz*, January 31, 2017, https://qz.com/898746/an-economist-explains-why-you-should-stop-tidying-up-and-embrace-the-mess/.

want a drawer full of crossed-off lists. But I also believe in tracking achievements (which are all too easy to overlook if you don't). So I also maintain a daily achievement list on my computer. This tracks what I've done each day, whether it was on my to-do list or not.

For example, I'll note whether it was an "errand" day (which can take up several hours), or whether I've had to spend time on the phone with family members. I'll note which projects I worked on and whether they were completed. I'll note anything out of the ordinary, such as a doctor's visit or a dinner party—or, perhaps, whether I've been down with the flu for a week or away on vacation.

At the end of the month I go over this list and transfer this information to an annual "achievements" list. I don't bother with the phone calls and errands and housekeeping chores, but I'll note under "personal" that we took a week-long vacation, or hosted relatives for the holidays. Then, at the end of the year, I can not only determine where my time went, but review my list to discover that, in fact, I've achieved rather a lot—and thanks to my to-do lists, most of my time has been well spent.

TEACH OTHERS TO RESPECT YOUR TIME

Finally, remember that if you don't guard your time, no one else will. It is not enough to simply ask others to respect your writing time. You must reinforce that request by refusing to drop what you're doing whenever someone interrupts you. Otherwise, people *will* interrupt—not out of malice or lack of consideration, but because you have given them no reason not to.

Many writer parents enforce the "if it's not on fire or bleeding, don't bother me" rule. This can be easier if you have an office door that you can close, but that's not essential. What is essential is convincing others that you mean what you say. When you say, "I am writing and cannot be disturbed," don't stop unless the house is on fire. When your sister calls for an hour of gossip, tell her that you'll call back after you've finished your article.

Protecting your time means cultivating the art of saying "no," "later," and "I have to go now." At first, this may seem the most difficult task of all. Eventually, however, you'll realize that your new attitude hasn't caused the rest of the world to view you as an ogre—and you're actually getting quality writing done!

CHAPTER 4

Setting Effective Writing Goals

One of the greatest challenges writers face is lack of structure in our job. There's no one to tell us what to do, when to do it, how to do it, or whether we've done it well. One way to overcome that challenge is to learn how to set goals. It's also important to recognize the difference between goals and dreams. While you may yearn to become a six-figure novelist who appears regularly on the hottest talk shows, that's a dream. The only way you'll achieve that dream is by setting well-defined goals.

To be effective, goals should meet three criteria: *measurable*, *attainable*, and *meaningful*.

1. **Measurable.** Many writers start with qualitative goals. You want to be a "better" writer, or a "successful" writer, or produce "quality" material. But how do you define better, or successful, or quality? Because these terms are difficult to measure, such goals seem to continually slip from our grasp.

   Goals are useless if you can't determine whether they've been met. It's *always* possible to become a *better* writer. Thus, *quantifiable* goals—goals that can be measured by output or results—are far more useful. For example, set a goal of writing a certain number of words per day, or sending a certain number of queries per week. If you dream of financial gain, define a specific income goal and a time in which you hope to reach it.

2. **Attainable.** The gulf between where we are and where we want to be may seem vast. Goals can help by breaking the journey into short, attainable steps. If you dream of becoming a best-selling novelist but haven't written a word, consider setting an attainable goal such as taking a writing course or studying a book on novel-writing. A second goal might be to write your first story, an outline of your novel, or the first chapter. A third might be to seek feedback, perhaps by joining a critique group or by sending a story to an editor. Each goal marks a step toward your dream, and each is attainable in its own right.

To set attainable goals, you must be honest about what you are currently able to achieve. If you've never earned a penny from writing, it would be unrealistic to set a goal of becoming self-supporting in a year. If you've never written anything longer than a holiday newsletter, it would be unrealistic to expect to complete a 500,000-word novel in six months.

Attainability also means recognizing what is feasible. One writer was frustrated at having "failed" to become self-supporting by writing science fiction stories. Unfortunately, the reality is that science fiction publications typically pay five cents per word or less. To earn even $25,000 per year, one would have to write and sell 500,000 words per year (an average of two 5,000-word stories per week). Even then, no publication would buy more than a handful of stories from a single writer in a year. Thus, even if this writer *could* produce 100 stories per year, she would be unable to find markets for them.

3. **Meaningful.** It's easy to be sidetracked by goals that appear worthwhile but don't lead in the direction you want to go. This is often the result of having competing goals. For example, you may dream of becoming a novelist, but you also need to put food on the table. Consequently, it's easy to postpone that novel for projects that will earn money *now*. In a situation like this, remember that competing goals don't have to be an either/or proposition. One possible solution is to devote 25 percent of your writing time to your novel, and the other 75 percent to articles.

Another danger is the pursuit of someone else's goals or recommendations. Writing articles are full of sure-fire secrets and formulas, but often fail to mention that these strategies don't work for everyone. I've read many articles that advise one to "get up early every morning and write before going to work." That's fine, unless you happen to be a night person. If you believe a "real" writer always gets up early, you'll either dread the sound of your alarm clock, or assume you're unable to meet an "important" goal.

The reality is that different strategies work for different writers, and part of developing your writing career means determining the strategies that work best for your own goals and lifestyle. At the same time, be careful about passing up opportunities because they don't seem immediately fulfilling. Taking a writing class may not seem exciting, but it could help toward your long-term goals.

SHORT-TERM VS. LONG-TERM GOALS

The best strategy includes a mix of short-term goals ("Today I'll locate five craft markets") and long-term goals ("By the end of this year I will have written the first three chapters of my novel").

A good way to determine long-term goals is to ask yourself where you want to be in six months, one year, five years, or ten years. By answering those questions, you define your vision and chart your course, and are better able to determine whether a project will contribute to your goal or distract from it.

Long-term goals often build upon one another. For example, your goal for your first year might be to build as many clips as possible. Once you've established a portfolio, you might devote your second year to targeting more prestigious, better-paying markets. You might decide to move from being a "generalist" to a "specialist" and establish yourself as an expert in a certain field. Conversely, you might decide to broaden your writing horizons by moving from tightly focused subjects to more diverse topics.

While long-term goals help you determine where you're going, short-term goals help you decide how to get there. If your one-year goal is to "sell ten magazine articles," your short-term goals might include conducting market research, writing queries, or submitting a certain number of articles per month.

Short-term goals are usually measured by output. Output goals are those where you have complete control over the results. For example, you might resolve to mail ten queries per week, or write three articles or stories per month. Typical output goals include:

- Number of hours spent writing per day (or week)
- Number of pages produced per day (or week)
- Number of queries submitted per week or month
- Number of projects (articles, stories, or chapters) written per month or year

Note that these goals have short time frames. A short-term goal doesn't become a long-term goal simply by expanding the quota or time frame (moving from 10 queries per week to 15, or from 10 queries per week to 520 queries per year). Instead, long-term goals are best measured by results: selling four articles per month, for example. While you can control your output, you cannot always control results. Even though you meet your weekly quota of queries, you can't control the editorial decisions and market factors that determine whether those queries will be accepted.

STEPPING IT UP

Sometimes, making the distinction between short-term goals and long-term goals isn't enough to enable you to *achieve* those goals. This is particularly true when you're not familiar with the various tasks involved in achieving a goal. You might plan to send out ten queries in a week, but if you haven't had much experience in crafting queries, this may seem hard to meet. You may find yourself falling short without fully understanding why the plan isn't working—and then it's easy to think you've "failed."

When even short-term goals seem too complex or frustrating, it's time to develop a more detailed strategy. The easiest approach is to break a goal down into a series of steps.

For example, if your goal is to send out ten queries in a week, that means more than just writing ten letters. Writing ten queries means finding ten markets. That means market research.

Now think in terms of steps. Your first step involves a decision. Are you going to base your market research on a specific topic, or are you going to base your topics on the markets you find? Either approach can work. If you know you want to write about hiking, for example, then you know that your next step will be to search for markets that might be interested in hiking articles. If, on the other hand, you like to let your market research inspire you with ideas, your next step will be to explore a market guide with the objective of developing query topics.

Your second step would be to search for possible markets. Start with a good market guide. If you've decided to search for markets for a particular topic, start by looking for publications that address that topic area. If you're looking for inspiration, start by looking at publications that sound interesting, and then ask yourself what you might be able to offer them.

Your next step is to select the markets you plan to target this week. Refine this list by looking at the publications' guidelines, pay rates, rights, and other requirements. You may decide to skip a publication because it pays too little, and another because it only accepts material from experts in the field. (It's a good idea to make annotations in your market guide alongside markets you've decided to rule out or postpone, so that you don't review the same markets over and over.) Once you've settled on the ten best choices for the week, make a list of contacts.

If you base your market research on a particular topic, your next step is to develop an appropriate pitch for each market you've chosen. If you base your market research on the "inspiration" approach, you'll need to spend some time looking at each market and brainstorming ideas (see chapter 5). Jot these ideas down as the basis for your queries.

Finally, it's time to craft the queries themselves (see chapter 7). Notice that, short of hitting "send," this is actually the very last step. When you set a goal of sending ten queries a week, it's easy to overlook the fact that *sending* a query is the final step in a more complex process. Breaking your goals into steps can make it much easier to understand the process underlying each goal, which in turn makes that goal much easier to reach.

REVIEW YOUR PROGRESS

To determine whether you're on schedule, ahead of schedule, or falling behind, it's important to review your progress regularly. Have you met your output goals, have you exceeded them, or did you set them unrealistically high? If you've met those goals, are you any closer to your long-term "result" goal, or does it seem as distant as ever?

Such assessments can help you determine whether to change your long-term goals or the short-term strategies you're using to meet them. If, for example, your one-year goal was to "get something published" and you accomplished that goal in a month, it's time to set a new long-term goal. If, on the other hand, you've sent out ten queries per week for six months without a single acceptance, it may be time to reevaluate your short-term goals. Perhaps you need to target different markets, reexamine your ideas, or learn how to write a better query. If six months of short-term output goals haven't brought you closer to your long-term result goal, don't waste another six doing the same thing!

It's also important to recognize changes in yourself—in your dreams, your abilities, your achievements, and your skills. Change is inevitable, and generally it is a good thing. What can be a bad thing is to fail to recognize change (especially growth). It's easy to get stuck in perceptions of ourselves that were formed years ago.

Today, as a beginning freelancer, you may have dreams that are not yet attainable based on your current level of skill or experience. But the worst thing you can do is assume that because your reach may exceed your grasp *today*, it will do so *for all time*. I've known many writers who assume that because they can't write a publishable novel or prize-winning poem or marketable article today, they never will. "I guess I'm just not cut out to be a novelist/poet/freelancer," they say. But today's "I can't" doesn't mean tomorrow's "I never will."

As long as you are growing and evolving as a writer—as long as you are genuinely striving to improve your abilities—your ability to reach long-term goals will evolve as well. You will always discover more and more things that once seemed impossible and that are now within your grasp.

Along the way, you may find that as your interests, dreams, and skills change, your goals can and should change as well. You may discover that a goal no longer has the same meaning it once did, or that another goal has arisen that holds more appeal. A goal that meant a lot a year ago may not seem so important now, while another goal you once considered impossible now seems attainable. Goals are not your destiny. They are simply effective tools to help you *reach* your destiny.

CHAPTER 5

From Idea to Outline

A common complaint of new writers is "I don't have anything to write about!" This isn't true. Everyone has *lots* of things to write about. The trick is to figure out how to convert one's experiences into marketable article topics. But first, you need to know what *makes* a marketable article topic! And that means knowing what editors want.

WHAT DO EDITORS WANT?

Look at the contents of almost any magazine, and (with the exception of news publications or gossip magazines) you'll find that most of the articles involve how-to information. A health magazine, for example, provides information on how to eat right, lose weight, overcome fatigue, stay fit, recognize symptoms of a serious illness, and so forth. A pet magazine discusses how to take better care of your pet. A crafts magazine gives you project tips and designs, or suggests equipment.

Women's magazines are an excellent example. They may cover a wide variety of topics, from health and beauty to home improvements and parenting, but most articles fall into the how-to category.

Another common category is information. News, celebrity gossip, profiles, and historical features fall into this category. Some magazines (such as *Discover* and *Smithsonian*) focus entirely on information. A few information-focused publications (like *National Geographic*) have a large audience, but many (such as *Military History* or *Discovering Archaeology*) have a much narrower market.

Much lower on the list are personal experience articles. Some magazines may run two or three short personal experience pieces per issue, often to highlight their theme of the month. For example, if a women's magazine is devoting an issue to heart disease, it might include several personal pieces about women who have overcome the disease. Generally, however, publications use only a small number of personal experience articles, and some don't use any. Magazines that publish essays or opinion pieces are even rarer.

The answer to "what editors want," therefore, is simple. First, editors want articles that will help readers improve their lives. Second, editors want articles with interesting information. Unless a publication focuses on information, however, you'll find a much higher ratio of how-to pieces to information pieces.

To break into the periodical market, therefore, you need to become reader-focused rather than author-focused. While this chapter will show you ways to explore personal experiences and expertise for topics, the key to sales is to find ways to share that information so that it benefits the reader.

DIGGING FOR IDEAS

The first step in coming up with article topics is looking for ideas. Here are some places to start:

- Personal life—home, family, personal history, life experiences
- Interests and hobbies
- Work experience, expertise, or professional background
- Education
- Memories—nostalgic or traumatic
- Favorite activities—vacations, family events, community activities
- Observations—people, places, and things around you
- Interests—things that intrigue you, even if you don't know much about them (yet)

Ideas also arise from the process of developing ideas. You may gain ideas from brainstorming a topic, reviewing magazines, and looking at published articles, researching market sources, and researching topics of interest. Your research for one article can often produce material for spin-off sales to other markets.

We've all heard that classic piece of writing advice, "Write about what you know." So here's the million-dollar question: "Do I *have* to write about what I know?" Can I *only* write about what I know?

First, it's important to understand that this bit of advice is intended primarily for writers of fiction. A housewife who has never left her hometown should probably not attempt to write a novel about a global jet-setter. In nonfiction, however, research is *expected* of you. Most freelancers end up writing about lots of things they didn't know about until they started.

Still, there are advantages to writing about what you know, at least in the beginning. It saves work, it's more comfortable, and it's easier to research. It also provides you with instant credentials in the form of your own experience. But there are disadvantages as well. It's often easy to overlook what you know, because it's so familiar that you don't realize you may know something that other people don't. Subjects that are too close to home may not excite you, so you may not feel motivated to explore them. It's also easy to start relying on the "safe zone" of what you know, and fail to expand your knowledge or market opportunities.

One way to move beyond what you know is to write about what *interests* you. Think about things you'd like to learn more about. Write about things you don't know about, but wish you did! As a writer, you're going to do lots of research, so it might as well be on a topic that you find fascinating. If it interests you, chances are it will interest someone else as well.

BRAINSTORMING IDEAS

As you begin to develop ideas, imagine your mind working like a camera lens. Sometimes you want to "zoom out" to get the big picture—to see the perspective, the surroundings. Sometimes you need to "zoom in" to sharpen your focus and concentrate on the details. This process goes back and forth as you work your way from "idea" to "article topic."

Start with a wide-angle focus. Take another look at the list of idea sources above. Jot down areas you'd like to explore for article ideas. Let's start with "personal life."

If I were brainstorming, I'd write this topic at the top of a piece of paper or file. (By the way, sometimes ideas flow better when you use old-fashioned approaches. If you're not getting anywhere by staring at the computer screen, try working with paper and pencil.)

Anyway—you've put "personal life" at the top of your "idea" page. Now, shut down that inner voice that is whispering, "No one wants to know about my personal life!" This is true, but it's not what we're here for. We're here to find out what aspects of your personal life might lead to articles people *will* want to read. So let's jot down a few things about "personal life."

- **Family**. Do you have a spouse? Children? In-laws? Parents? Grandparents? Siblings? Extended family? Family members who don't speak to each other? Family members in or from other countries or cultures? Are you (or is anyone in your family) adopted? What about experiences like marriage, divorce, childbirth, or death?
- **Holidays**. Jot down a list of the holidays you celebrate. Does your family have special ways of celebrating those holidays? Do they avoid certain holidays? Do you celebrate holidays that are less familiar to the general public? Are holidays joyful or stressful? What holiday activities or traditions do you share with your children? (If you don't have children, what traditions would you want to share if you did?)
- **Pets**. Do you have a pet? An unusual pet? How about past or childhood pets? How do you take care of it? What activities do you pursue with your pets? What problems do you experience? What challenges have you faced and overcome? What tragedies have you endured? How do your children interact with your pets?

This is part of the "zooming out" process. We started with a single idea—personal life—and expanded it into at least three subtopics (family, holidays, pets). We then expanded each of *those* topics into several additional areas. If you try this exercise with all eight of the subject areas proposed above, you could find yourself with dozens of potential topics.

This is a good exercise to do with a spouse, friend, or writing buddy who can help you come up with ideas you might otherwise miss. Someone who knows you is likely to think of things you might overlook simply because they're too familiar.

FOCUS AND EXPAND

So far, none of the subjects above are sufficiently focused to serve as article topics. The next step, therefore, is to zoom in even more closely, and then to expand once again.

On another sheet of paper or file, select one of the topics you generated. For example, consider "holiday activities." Zoom in further. What holiday? What activities?

The obvious temptation is to tackle Christmas because it offers so many topics. On the other hand, this holiday also gets the most "ink," which means you're competing against a lot of other writers. So let's focus on a holiday that gets a little less press: Easter. Now brainstorm again, jotting down everything you associate with Easter. Here's my list:

- Eggs
- Bunnies
- Easter baskets
- Easter egg hunts
- Onion skin Easter eggs
- Rabbits or chicks—good for pets?
- Easter history/folklore
- Easter in other countries—Greek Easter candles
- Easter trees

Now we're getting somewhere. Some of these are still a bit vague (what about Easter eggs, exactly?), but others are ripe for the plucking. Let's see what articles we might generate from this list.

- **Easter baskets**. Does someone in your town make fancy Easter baskets? Check the classifieds for a "gift basket" store. That might make a profile for a local paper.
- **Onion skin Easter eggs**. Few people know how to create this beautiful holiday tradition.
- **Rabbits and chicks: Good for pets?** Your local paper might be interested in an article on the perils of giving bunnies or chicks to the kids. Interview a representative of your local humane society, and check online for statistics on how many bunnies end up at humane societies after Easter.

- **Easter history and folklore.** This is a perennial favorite. I know, because it was one of the very first articles I ever sold, and I've sold articles on this topic many times since. No reason why you can't do a bit of research and sell something on this topic too!
- **Easter in other countries.** We visited Greece on our honeymoon, and I was struck by the sight of families returning to the islands carrying elaborately decorated Easter candles. This might be an interesting feature for a travel magazine or newspaper travel section.
- **Easter trees.** These are popular in Germany, and are catching on in America. Consider a how-to article on how to make your own that you could sell to a local paper, or to a crafts or home-decorating magazine. Or slant this as a children's activity—how kids can make an Easter tree—and aim for a family publication such as *Family Fun*.

I've just identified five articles I could write, with little effort, from this one subject. Easter, however, was a subtopic of the larger category of holiday activities. Imagine how many more ideas you could generate by exploring the entire range of holidays! Follow other branches—holiday foods, holiday safety, holiday reminiscences, nontraditional holidays—and you'll develop even more possibilities.

Keep in mind, too, that categories can overlap. If you have children, expand your market potential by looking for topics that combine holidays and children—crafts, safety tips, inspirational stories. For a less obvious approach, combine "holidays" and "grandparents" for a nostalgia piece or a how-to article for a senior living magazine. Try taking a general topic, such as food or decorating or travel, and see if you can combine it with one of the topics on your list—for example, Easter treats, the five best restaurants in your area for Thanksgiving, ten snow-filled places to go for Christmas.

DON'T ELIMINATE THE NEGATIVE

When you begin brainstorming, the topics that will appeal to you the most are probably going to be positive. Your first instinct will be to look at things readers might like to do, share, and enjoy. But you may have also triggered some negative memories that made you shudder and move on.

Don't overlook the value of negative experiences! Perhaps you hate Christmas because that's when the family gets together and picks up old fights. By the time the holiday is over, you're so stressed that you wish Christmas could be banned forever. Not a happy picture, right? Besides, who wants to hear about your troubles? But stop and think for a moment. Do you suppose you're the only family with this problem? Might there not be hundreds of families who go through something similar every year? Can you write something that speaks to those families?

Here's where "writing what you know" meets "writing what you don't know." What you *know* is that Christmas can be a huge, stressful family gathering. What you *don't* know is how to change that. If you could find out, you could write an article that might change many lives!

One approach is to write a story that portrays your family in such a way that others see *their* families in your experience—and laugh about it even if they can't change it. Or, you could interview a therapist who *does* know how to address this issue. Try a search on "holiday stress" and "family gathering" and see what comes up. Chances are, you'll find not only information but also experts to interview for more tips.

When you're brainstorming, there are no wrong answers. Your inner editor may start whispering, "Oh, that's a waste of time," or "No one would have any interest in *that*." And you're bound to run into some dead ends. But it's important not to block your progress by assuming a path has no merit before you've explored it a bit. Let yourself play; let your imagination wander; let your memories spill forth. Right now, you're simply mining for ore; the process of refining those ideas and potential topics comes later. The current goal is to come up with *possibilities*.

CATEGORIES, SUBJECTS, TOPICS, AND SLANTS

By now you should have several ideas for articles. Some are nearly ready to go. Some aren't. This next step will help you bring at least one idea to the starting gate by choosing the right market, audience, and slant for that audience.

To begin this process, you need to know the difference between a *category* of ideas, a *subject*, a *topic*, and a *slant*. Each of these is a stage in the refinement process, bringing you closer to a final article.

Category

A category is not an idea for an article; it may not even be a subject. Often, it's a catchall bin of potential ideas. For example, if I say, "I want to write historical articles," that's a category. I haven't defined a subject; I haven't even defined a period or type of history. However, I *have* defined an area in which to proceed, both in developing topics and locating markets. The same applies if I wanted to write about "health" or "pets" or "families" or "cooking."

Choosing a category is an important step. It tells you where to start your process. You might now start researching markets in this category. If your category was "pets," how many pet magazines or related markets (such as online pet stores or blogs) are there? What do they want? Do they accept freelance material? Gathering the answers helps you move on to the next step.

Subject

Once you have a category of interest, pick a general subject out of that category. If your category is "holidays," your subject might be "Christmas." From my category of "history," I might choose a subject like "Mary, Queen of Scots." However, these are still not topics. You can't simply write an article about "Christmas," because an editor is going to ask, "Well, what about it?" Similarly, many books have been written about Mary, Queen of Scots. If I want to write an article, I must choose something more specific.

Topic

Now you're ready to begin developing the seed of your actual article. Let's suppose I know lots about Mary, and I've decided to focus on her imprisonment under Queen Elizabeth. That's a good beginning, but what am I going to say? I could still spin this off into several articles. That's where it's helpful to do some market research, to determine what type of article might actually *sell*.

So off I go to the bookstore, to see what magazines might accept my article. I pick up copies of *BBC History Magazine*, *Renaissance*, *Realm*, *British Heritage*, and *Scottish Life*. Flipping through my treasures, I discover that *BBC History Magazine* is written primarily by experts, and focuses on topics covered by BBC programs. *Renaissance* is produced by the Society for Creative Anachronism, and might be a place for a general historical piece. *Realm* focuses on travel. *Scottish Life* focuses more on modern life than on history. *British Heritage*, however, focuses on visiting interesting historical places. It looks like a good market.

By studying the publication, I find that it focuses as much on *location* as *history*, so a general article about Mary's imprisonment probably wouldn't sell here. But a guide to the various *castles* in which Mary was imprisoned sounds ideal. It also would provide great photo opportunities. I've now refined my topic to something specific: "The castles in which Mary was imprisoned."

Slant

I have a topic, but what am I going to say about it? I can't just say, "Mary, Queen of Scots, was imprisoned in this castle, which is located *here*, and looks like *this*." I look at that magazine again to determine what slant will attract the editor. Since *British Heritage* focuses on places people might like to visit, I decide my slant will be: "How you can visit the castles that imprisoned a queen." My article will take the reader on a guided tour of the castles where Mary was imprisoned. Where are they? What are they like? Can you still visit Mary's accommodations? I'll provide a bit of history of each castle, details about Mary's stay, and what you'd find if you visit today. The article will have a sidebar on how to get there, tour details, hours. . . . If I've read my market correctly, this should get the editor's attention. (And if you're wondering whether I can pull this off, yes, I *have* sold an article to *British Heritage*.)

The point is you can't sell an article based on category ("history") or subject. You *might* be able to sell an article based on topic, but it's difficult. Your best bet is to include market research in your process, choose something that seems appropriate, and *slant* your article directly toward that market.

As you work on developing a slant, consider two vital factors. First, take yourself *out* of the picture, and figure out ways to bring the reader *in*. In your slant, find ways to express how this article will help "you-the-reader." Why should *you* visit this location? How can *you* get the most out of this trip? What are ten ways that *you* can overcome this problem? Why will *you* love or benefit from this product? This is the most important step you can take toward winning over you-the-editor.

Second, think in terms of a phrase or sentence while developing your slant. Try to avoid a slant that is just a subject ("haunted castles," "Christmas decorations"). Express your slant in an active phrase that includes a verb: "Tour the haunted castles of Scotland," or "Decorate your home Victorian-style." Such a slant may even become the title of your article.

Once you have a slant, you are ready for next step: developing your *core concept*. This is the central theme or idea of your article. You should be able to sum up your slant and core concept in a single sentence: "My article is about how you can. . . ." Everything within it must relate to this core concept.

REFINING YOUR CORE CONCEPT—OR, THE OUTLINE DEMYSTIFIED

I don't know anyone who likes creating an outline. That's probably because we all remember being taught that "1,2,3–A,B,C" format in high school. So . . . forget about that!

An outline is simply a way to construct a road map of where you want to go with your article. Think of it as a filing cabinet. When you research your article, you're going to gather a lot of information. How will you know what to put in and what to leave out? An outline is like placing labels on the folders in your cabinet. It makes it easier to determine where a bit of information belongs, or whether perhaps it doesn't belong in your article at all.

When I first went full time as a freelancer, one of the first articles I pitched was on cancer in cats. When I got the assignment, I roughed out the areas I planned to cover:

- Types of cancer
- Breed-specific cancers
- How to detect cancer
- My experience with a cat with cancer
- Preventing cancer
- Treatments
- Hope for the future
- High-tech treatments
- Diagnostic techniques

A quick look at this list showed me that some ideas were subcategories of others. "Breed-specific cancers" fit under "types of cancer," while "diagnostic techniques" fit under "how to detect." "Hope for the future" fit under "treatments." One category stood out as *not* fitting with the rest: "My experience." I ended up with four "folder headings" to work with:

- Types of Cancer
- Detecting Cancer
- Treating Cancer
- Preventing Cancer

This is an outline. It can be as simple as that. Besides serving as a framework for my article, it provided a framework for my research. I researched the article on the web and interviewed experts, asking questions based on my topic areas and "filing" that information in the appropriate place. If I found information that didn't fit into one of these four areas, I knew it probably didn't belong in my article.

I also had a slant or core concept: "What you need to know about cancer in cats." (Again, a slant can make a great title: "Is your cat at risk of cancer?" or "How you can reduce your cat's risk of cancer.") Having that core concept is vital. It tells you what is essential to your article and what isn't. If you have information that doesn't relate directly to your core concept, it doesn't belong in the article.

Five Ways to Approach the Outline

Again, I'm no fan of the "1,2,3–A,B,C" approach to outlines. This tends to get one bogged down in mechanics. Is this idea a subset of number 2? Should I move this section *here*? There are easier ways to organize your ideas and information.

1. **Ask yourself what questions a reader would ask.** What would a reader want to know about this subject? Make a list of those questions. For example, a reader interested in feline cancer might want to know:
   - How common is cancer in cats?
   - What kinds of cancer affect cats?
   - What cats or breeds are at greatest risk?
   - How can I tell if my cat has cancer?
   - What kinds of treatments are available?
   - What are their success rates?
   - What are their risks?
   - How long will my cat live if it has cancer?

- Can I prevent my cat from getting cancer?
- Where do I go for help?

Sometimes, jotting down a list of questions is all you need to define the areas your article will cover, and even the order in which you should cover them.

2. **Think in subheads.** Most articles are divided into sections with subheads. This is a good way to organize your information, and adding subheads always pleases an editor. The four "file folders" I developed for my feline cancer piece served very nicely as subheads:

- Is your cat at risk?
- Protecting your cat from cancer
- Detecting the signs of cancer
- Choosing a treatment plan

Subheads help you organize information logically. You'll also be able to determine whether the subsections of your article are in balance. If, for example, you have 250 words under one subhead and 1,000 under another, you may need to reorganize the article.

3. **List events or concepts chronologically.** What happened first? What happened next? What happened last? This works well for an article that focuses on events that occurred over time, such as a historical piece or a personal account or profile.

4. **List points in logical order.** Many how-to articles have an obvious order: do this first, do this next, do this last. This type of outline might consist simply of a list of things to do and the order in which one should do them. A travel article might also have a logical order. If, for example, you begin at Point A and travel to Point X, present your information in the order in which a traveler would encounter it. This works even for a single location, such as a castle or museum.

5. **Make a list.** List all the pieces of information you'd like to include in the article. Then, assign numbers to each item based on its importance. For example, if you're writing a piece on ways to improve communication between spouses, jot down a list of tips to cover. Which are most important? Which are less important?

Which could be omitted? Your list might become the actual structure of your finished article ("Five ways to improve communication with your spouse"), or it might become the framework underlying your piece even if you don't number the points in your article.

Managing a Word Budget

A final consideration as you outline an article is your word budget. Every magazine has length requirements. A common amateur mistake is to propose an article that tries to address more topics than can be covered within that word count.

For example, I reviewed a query letter from a woman who wanted to write about a controversial treatment for breast cancer. In 2,000 words or less, she wanted to cover traditional treatments, alternative treatments, a profile of a woman who chose an alternative treatment, interviews with her doctor and other patients, and a discussion of why women aren't told about alternative treatments. I'd reject this query as unfocused and impossible to cover in 2,000 words. In addition, since the woman had just begun treatment, the writer couldn't tell us the most important detail of all: did it work?

When you do all that research, it's *hard* to throw any of it out. But don't despair. Chances are, you can use extra information to write a different article for another publication. You might also be able to include additional information in a sidebar.

Think about your word budget as you develop your outline. Keep in mind that the more subtopics you include, the fewer words you can allocate to each. If you have four subtopics in a 2,000-word article, you can devote approximately 500 words to each of them. If you have ten, each gets no more than 200 words. Keep in mind that you'll also need to save some words for an introduction, a conclusion, and transitions between subtopics.

This brings up the difference between an in-depth article and an overview. An in-depth article will have only a few subtopics (three to five). If you have a lengthy list of subtopics, your article is more likely to be an overview. For example, an article titled "Ten Tips on Beating Holiday Stress" is an overview. It will include ten ideas, but won't be able to provide in-depth information on any them. An article titled "Put an End to Holiday Stress" that includes an interview with a therapist and four or five suggestions will be more in-depth.

Which should you write? This gets back to your market research. What type of piece does your target market prefer? Choose the type that seems most likely to appeal to the editor, and audience, of your chosen market. Simply be aware that the more subtopics you have, the less information you can provide about any of them.

By now, I hope you're getting the idea that "ideas" aren't difficult to get. In fact, if you follow this approach, chances are that your next problem will be having more ideas than you know what to do with!

CHAPTER 6

Exploring the Markets

I have to smile at market listings advising contributors to read five or six back issues. Yeah, right! At an average of $5 per issue, the cost of ordering more than one per publication would be prohibitive.

At the same time, if you don't know anything about a publication beyond a *Writer's Market* listing, you'll find it difficult to develop appropriate article ideas. How will you understand the needs and interests of the audience? How can you be sure you're matching the tone and style of the publication? How can you avoid submitting an article on a topic that was covered two months ago?

RESEARCHING DOMESTIC MARKETS

Fortunately, the Internet makes it much easier to find the information we need. Many publications post sample articles, indexes of previous articles, information on what's coming up, guidelines, and contact information. In fact, one way to discover a host of publications you've probably never heard of is to simply search on "submission guidelines" and see what comes up. Then try searching on "writer," "author," or "contributor guidelines."

However, online information gives you only part of the story. Nothing compares to seeing the *actual* publication, as it is laid out. Here are some ways to explore publications without breaking the bank:

1. **Start with magazines you know.** What magazines do you read or subscribe to? Chances are, these reflect your areas of interest. Look carefully at special-interest publications on your list, such as hobby,

craft, sport, or recreation magazines. It's much easier to break in to these than the big, general-interest magazines.

2. **Visit newsstands.** The magazine sections at bookstores like like Barnes & Noble offer publications you won't find in your grocery store, including many international magazines. A newsstand has an even greater selection.

3. **Send for free samples.** Many publications listed in *Writer's Market* offer free sample copies, or ask only for the cost of shipping. Send for any that interest you, and some that don't! You never know what will spark an article idea.

4. **Research writers' guidelines.** Start online. If you don't see an obvious link, check "About Us" or "Contact Us." Explore guideline databases, which can often be searched by subject area or pay rates. (Find links to guideline databases at www.writing-world.com/links/guidelines.shtml.) If you can't find guidelines online, check *Writer's Market* to see if the publication will mail them to you for a self-addressed, stamped envelope (SASE). (Don't request guidelines by mail unless you're sure they're available; otherwise, you simply waste stamps.)

5. **Research back issues online.** Many publications post article archives, or selections from previous issues. Review these to get an idea of the publication's tone, style, content, and coverage. Are articles aimed at a specialized audience or the average person? Do they offer overviews or in-depth research? Do the authors have special credentials or degrees? Even if a publication doesn't post full articles, it may publish lists of the contents of back issues, which will help you avoid submitting a query on a topic that has already been covered.

6. **Look for other publications from the same company.** Often, not every magazine issued by a publisher is listed in *Writer's Market*. For example, while *Writer's Market* lists about a dozen pet magazines published by BowTie Inc. (formerly Fancy Publications), BowTie actually has more than thirty publications. Besides their print publications, some publishers also offer webzines, newsletters, or blogs.

7. **Subscribe to a marketing newsletter.** Several excellent email newsletters offer market information, including WriteMarketsReport

(www.writersweekly.com/books/677.html) and WorldWide Free-lance Writer (www.worldwidefreelance.com).

8. **Look for trial offers**. You can subscribe to many magazines for a free trial period (usually ninety days). All Free Magazines (www.all-freemagazines.com) offers trials of consumer magazines, while FreeTradeMagazines.com offers trials of trade-related magazines.

Another way to get information about upcoming issues is to request photographers' guidelines. Many publications publish separate guidelines for photographers. These list topics coming up in future months so that photographers can set up photo shoots. This gives you a chance to pitch an article related to topics you *know* the publication will be covering. Don't assume that because a publication is planning a special issue on, say, traveling with dogs, it already has all the articles it needs on file!

Another way to find information on upcoming topics is to search for a publication's media kit. This information is provided to advertisers, and often includes a list of topics to be covered in future months. Try searching on a publication's name plus terms like "advertising rates," "media kit," or even "editorial calendar." You can also send for a media kit, but these often take a long time to arrive.

EXPANDING TO INTERNATIONAL MARKETS

International publications are an excellent way to expand your markets. If you live in the US, consider targeting English-language publications in Canada, Great Britain and Ireland, Australia, New Zealand, India, South Africa, Singapore, and other regions. If you live outside the US, consider expanding to *American* markets. If you write fluently in another language, your options expand even further, as there is a great demand for good translations of materials that have been previously published in English.

Unfortunately, international markets aren't as easy to research. Non-US publications are less likely to post back issues, guidelines or even contact information; many simply offer a subscription page. Sadly, too, several international market guides (including *Canadian Writer's Market* and the *Australian Writer's Marketplace*) have folded in the last few years. British markets can be found in *Writer's and Artist's Yearbook* and *Children's Writer's and Artist's Yearbook*. The best online source of international market information is Worldwide Freelance Writer (www.worldwidefreelance.com), which offers a marketing newsletter and an extensive market database.

Since email contacts may be hard to find, you may need to connect the old-fashioned way, by mail. (Don't bother with a SASE; simply ask the editor to *respond* by email.) Keep in mind that what passes for casual in the US may seem discourteous abroad, so err on the side of caution and prepare a formal query, as described in chapter 7.

It's also important to know what types of articles are best suited to international interest. Obviously, topics of local or regional interest are out. (However, a local "color" piece can be converted into a useful travel article aimed at tourists visiting the US). Even more general articles, such as pieces on health or how-to articles, should be examined with care. A health-care article, for example, won't be useful if the methods or medications aren't available in the publication's country (and keep in mind as well that over-the-counter medications often have different names abroad). Articles that rely on the reader's understanding of American culture, society, idioms, humor, or jargon will also be difficult to sell.

When pitching or submitting to international markets, avoid American slang, idiomatic phrases, or humor that might not translate well, even if targeting an English-language publication. It's less important to be aware of international spelling differences, punctuation, or usages like dates, times, numbers, and currencies; editors can generally resolve those differences.

International publications are often less concerned about lengthy, formal contracts. Don't be surprised if all you receive is an acceptance letter or email. You may also find that editors don't keep in touch, so follow up politely to find out when your piece is scheduled.

Payment can also be an issue. Many international publishers prefer to issue a check in their own currency. Before accepting such a check, find out whether your bank will accept it, whether there is a fee for depositing an international check, and how long it will take for the check to clear. Fortunately, more and more publications are turning to PayPal as a means of paying writers in other countries. While this, too, involves fees, they are far lower than international check deposit charges. Some larger publications may also have accounts with US-based banks and can issue checks in US currency.

While dealing with international publications can be complicated, the benefits are extensive. They are often open to topics that you can't sell at home, and can be excellent reprint markets. And if you write fluently in a language other than English, your potential markets expand dramatically —both for original pieces and for translations of articles you've already published in English.

SHOULD YOU SPECIALIZE OR GENERALIZE?

As you begin searching for markets, one question to consider is whether you wish to focus your writing on a single general subject, or whether you wish to tackle a wide range of subjects and markets. Each option has advantages and disadvantages.

Specialization

Specialization can help you build a reputation as a subject expert. It also makes it easier to build on previous work as you climb from lower-paying markets to more prestigious publications in the same field. As long as you work within your specialty, your clips will always be relevant, and editors may be familiar with your reputation even before you pitch to them. It can also be easier to focus on developing your writing skills if you can focus on a subject you already know quite a bit about.

It is only useful, however, if you are specializing in a field that offers a wide range of markets. For example, a writer choosing to specialize in dogs and dog care would find market opportunities very limited. There are only two major national dog publications (*Dogster* and *AKC Gazette*), and a handful of smaller general-interest pet magazines such as *The Bark*, *Animal Fair*, and *Dog and Kennel*. Beyond that, the market grows more specialized, with publications like *Gun Dog* (for hunting dog owners) and *Mushing* (for sled dog enthusiasts). Each publication has specific requirements, and because the market is so limited, most won't accept reprints of pieces that have appeared in any of the others. Even if one expanded that specialty to pets in general, the market doesn't offer many options for freelancers.

On the other hand, a writer choosing to specialize in, say, nutrition and natural health would find a considerably larger market. Besides the many high-paying health and nutrition magazines, the market includes dozens of general-interest publications that regularly feature articles on these topics. Special-interest magazines on other subjects—such as sports, recreation, parenting, fitness, and even religious publications—also offer market opportunities.

The question, therefore, is whether your area of specialization offers sufficient market opportunities. If you choose the right topic, becoming a subject-matter expert can open many doors. If you choose too narrow a topic, however, you're likely to find yourself stuck.

Generalization

Generalization—choosing to write about all sorts of topics for all types of markets—can help ensure that you never run out of markets to write for. It's also helpful if you don't want your name associated exclusively with one type of writing or subject area. You might also want to build a more diverse portfolio of clips.

This approach requires not only good writing skills but also good research skills. When you generalize, you won't be able to rely exclusively on your own expertise, or contacts you may already have in your field. You'll need to learn how to ask the right questions about subjects you may know little about. You'll also have to be able to find good interview sources, and learn how to conduct effective interviews (see chapter 11). Most of all, you'll need to be willing to take chances, and say "yes" to assignments that take you out of your comfort zone.

While this can mean more work, it also means that once editors know you can be relied upon to turn in a well-researched, well-written article on nearly any topic, your range of assignments is likely to increase. Nor do you have to worry about the limitations of a narrow niche. The market is wide open. You may write for a dog magazine today, a health magazine tomorrow, and a religious publication next week.

There is a downside, however. When you generalize, you lose the advantage of being recognized as an expert in a particular area. Some editors do prefer writers with subject-specific credentials, or with a history of being published in the field.

There is no single answer to this question. Either decision will open some doors and close others (or at least make them more difficult to enter). As with so many writing decisions, the only real answer is "it depends." You must make this decision based upon your interests and goals.

WHAT MARKETS WANT

Another key question that should be on your mind as you begin researching markets is "what do they want?" It's not enough to look at a dog magazine and assume that it wants articles about dogs. What about dogs? What kind of dogs? Does every dog magazine want the same type of articles? (No.) It's important to evaluate the specific focus of a publication. *Dogster* (formerly *Dog Fancy*), for example, focuses on pet owners; the *AKC Gazette*, being the official publication of the American Kennel Club, addresses the needs of breeders and exhibitors. Examine a publication's articles from the perspective of its audience. Does it target beginners, experts, or both?

Again, special-interest publications are a good place to start. They usually have lower budgets, and are therefore more open to newer writers. They're often more interested in a writer's experience than in clips. You might think you're not an expert, but you have something to offer that experts don't:

- You know what interests you about this topic, so you can develop ideas that will interest readers like yourself.
- You know what questions someone like yourself would ask.
- You know the basics, and can therefore help beginners.
- You know the "lingo" of your specialty.
- You are interested in learning more about the subject, and can share what you learn with others.
- You have experience in the subject area.

Writers who can interview experts and turn in a readable piece are often of more value to editors than the experts themselves. Experts often have difficulty communicating with a lay audience. Plus, a single expert may present only one side of an issue, whereas a writer can interview several experts for a more balanced view. So don't let a lack of initials after your name deter you.

Though the subjects covered by special-interest publications are unimaginably diverse, their basic needs tend to be very similar. As you begin to evaluate your sample publications, start looking for their "must-have" article categories.

Magazine "Must-Haves"

"Must-have" articles are those that appear in nearly every issue. To determine what these are, you'll need to review the contents of several back issues, or search for an index online. You'll find that most special interest publications publish a mix of articles from the following areas:

- **How-to.** Most special interest publications tell you how to do something—how to repair a car, plant a garden, raise a puppy, catch a fish, knit a sweater. Within that general subject context, how-to articles focus on such questions as how to do something new or unusual, solve a common problem, develop a new skill, or increase one's enjoyment in the subject.

- **Health and safety.** Many special interest areas involve health and safety issues, such as how to avoid hazards, handle emergencies, or improve one's health by participating in an activity. A hiking magazine, for example, will have regular pieces on trail safety, proper nutrition, first aid, how to avoid certain hazards, hot- and cold-weather tips, and so forth. This type of article may require interviews with experts, but editors often prefer that they be written from the perspective of a typical enthusiast.

- **Equipment.** What are the tools of your trade? Consider an article on how to choose the right equipment, how to determine the tools needed for a specific project, how to take care of your equipment, how to build equipment (e.g., how to build a birdhouse), or how to use equipment safely. This type of information can often be combined with other how-to topics.

- **Seasonal.** Some activities are seasonal by nature; others have seasonal concerns. If you love gardening, for example, think about the "off" seasons, such as how to add fall color to your garden or winterize your fruit trees. Pet magazines look for articles on summer travel and winter safety, as well as seasonal issues such as flea control. Seasonal articles should be submitted four to six months in advance.

- **Destination.** With a little imagination, you can incorporate a destination slant into many types of articles. For a fishing publication, you might cover the "Top Ten Trout Streams of Northern Idaho." For a dog magazine, you might cover "The Ten Most Dog-Friendly Parks in the US." For a quilt magazine, consider covering an event like "Pennsylvania's Annual Amish Quilt Spectacular."

- **Historical background.** A background piece can be a good way to break in to some publications. Consider combining your information with how-to tips. For example, a look at the history of English pewter could include tips on collecting or care.

- **Personal profiles.** Profiles usually highlight someone whose work has achieved recognition, who has made a significant contribution to the field, or who is doing something unique or unusual. For example, a woodcarving magazine might be interested in an artist whose work has just been featured in a major gallery or museum, or an immigrant who has "carved out" a new life with a rare old-country skill. Some magazines prefer to combine "who" with "how." For example, I found an article on a lace maker in an embroidery magazine that profiled the artist and gave tips on how readers could apply those same traditional skills.
- **Current issues and controversies.** If your interest area is affected by controversy or legislation, a magazine may be interested in such coverage. A pet magazine, for example, might be interested in antibreed legislation or laws restricting pets. Be sure the issue has more than regional appeal, however. Also, be aware that controversies may be time sensitive; will this issue still be "hot" if the article won't be published for several months? (Keep in mind that online publications can publish this type of article more quickly than print magazines.)
- **Personal experiences.** These are generally lowest on a magazine's needs list, yet editors are flooded with this type of article. While it's not impossible to sell such a piece (as I'll explain in chapter 9), it takes a truly unique (and well-written) piece to rise out of the slush pile.

To improve your chances of a sale, look for categories that overlap. Editors love articles that fill two "must-have" slots at once—such as a piece on seasonal health hazards, or a how-to article that includes a discussion of equipment safety.

So take a look at your favorite activity, sport, or hobby. Ask what you could say about that topic that fits into one or more of these categories. Don't limit yourself to the things you already know; consider questions you might ask, subjects you'd like to learn more about. If you have questions, chances are that readers will have them as well—and by answering them, you could turn your curiosity into a sale.

IS A MARKET RIGHT FOR YOU?

Knowing what publications want is only half the battle. Don't get so focused on whether you have something to offer a publication that you forget to determine whether that publication is actually a good market for *you*. When I review a market, I consider four issues: demographic, technical, personal, and business.

Demographic Issues

"Demographics" simply means "audience." What type of person will read your article? The answers can be found not only in a magazine's editorial pages but also in its advertisements and illustrations. For example, are the photos of glamorous models, or does the magazine include "real" people as well? Do the ads depict young people, families, seniors, or a mix? This is another example of the need to see the actual publication, as much of this information can't be gleaned from guidelines or even sample articles. Here are some things you'll need to know:

- **Gender.** Is the magazine aimed at men, women, or both?
- **Age.** Many magazines target specific age brackets, such as "youth," "twenty-something," "adult" (twenty to fifty), or "senior." Sometimes that target audience is obvious from the magazine's title or content (*Seventeen*); sometimes it can be determined from the advertising (*Reader's Digest*). Don't pitch an article on "planning for early retirement" to a magazine that targets recent college graduates!
- **Ethnicity.** Does a publication target a specific ethnic group? Do the pictures and advertising feature primarily white models? Or does it appear to be seeking diverse, multicultural material?
- **Economic Bracket.** How much is a reader prepared to spend? This makes a big difference when writing about, say, collecting antiques or taking a dream vacation. Advertising is a good way to determine the audience's economic bracket. I recently reviewed two lifestyle magazines that looked similar; one, however, contained ads for expensive antique reproductions, while the other advertised cheap collectible figurines.
- **Religion.** In some markets, religion is unimportant; in others, it is. Religion may be implied rather than overtly stated. For example, while *Reader's Digest* is not a "religious" publication, it clearly assumes that its readers prefer material with a conservative Christian slant. Other publications may assume just the opposite, and reject material that even hints of a traditional religious viewpoint. Within

the religious marketplace itself, one must also be aware of the differences between (and even within) denominations.

- **Geography.** Does a magazine focus on city pleasures or country delights? Does it focus on active recreational activities, or more intellectual pursuits? Even a national magazine may have a larger readership in certain parts of the country, and will be more interested in articles that appeal to readers from that region.

- **Lifestyle.** Lifestyle issues (including interests, activities, and values) cut across all other demographic groups. Two magazines that target young women, for example, may have very different audiences. Does a woman's magazine assume its readers spend most of their time in the office, the kitchen, or the bedroom? Values are also important. You won't find an article on "how to cheat without getting caught" in *Woman's Day*, and you don't find many pieces on "fidelity" in *Cosmopolitan*.

These demographics can give you a picture of your target audience. But is that all you need to know? Just because a magazine targets young, upwardly mobile professional women doesn't mean you necessarily want to write for it. You may also wish to consider:

Technical Issues

The technical aspects of a magazine include:

- **Physical presentation.** What is the quality of the publication? Is it printed on glossy paper or newsprint? Are articles laid out effectively, or pasted up sloppily? Are photos clear, or do they look like outdated Polaroids? A magazine that is poorly produced usually has a low budget, and that means it probably doesn't pay well.

- **Writing style.** Magazines that appear to address similar audiences may, in fact, have very different editorial styles. Read several articles carefully. Do you like the way they are written? Can you imagine writing in a similar style? If the style seems jarring to you, or violates your personal taste, you may not be able to write for that magazine simply because your style won't match the tastes of the editor.

- **Depth.** How much research, investigation, or analysis is involved in a magazine's content? Some magazines may expect more than you can provide. If you don't have the connections to get the right interviews, or the experience to provide the level of analysis required, or the budget to visit five different locations to get the story, don't worry. That doesn't mean you'll never penetrate that market; it simply means you won't break in today.

Personal Issues

I want to know not only what a publication says to a reader, but also what it says to me. For example:

- **Does the magazine interest me?** Often, I find myself skipping and scanning rather than reading. The material doesn't hook me, and I may reach the end of the magazine without finishing a single article. Can I write for a publication that doesn't keep my attention? Probably not. The editor's tastes and mine do not mesh, and I doubt I could change my style sufficiently to match the editor's preferences.

- **Does the magazine share my values?** A writer is also an individual, with his own values, ethics, background, and so on. The question of ethics is no different in the business of writing than in any other business. Are you willing to compromise what you believe just to earn a paycheck? If the answer is no, don't struggle to write for markets you don't agree with, or produce articles that violate your values or viewpoint.

- **How will my material be presented?** If a magazine suffers from poor presentation—bad editing, poor design, or inappropriate illustrations—your work comes out worse than it goes in. No one stops to ask whether an article's bad grammar was the result of poor editing; most people (and editors) assume it was the fault of the writer. And while no one will blame you for a bad layout, a shoddy-looking article won't present you in the best light. If clips from this publication would do me more harm than good, I'll try elsewhere.

- **Would I be proud to be featured in this publication?** I recently examined a woman's magazine that looked like a good market for a health article. A closer look, however, gave me second thoughts. Most of the advertisements seemed to be for sexual aids. While I might have sold the article, did I really want to show off clips of my work displayed next to a half-page ad for vibrators? If a magazine makes you uncomfortable, angry, or disgusted, move on; you'll feel happier about your checks.

Obviously, these decisions are highly individual. Your decisions will be different from mine. It's important to remember, however, that your tastes and values are as important as those of the markets you're trying to penetrate. If those tastes and values don't mesh, you can waste a lot of time trying to break into markets that will never be right for you. Even if you do break in, success may not taste so sweet, particularly if you feel you've compromised your values or writing skills just to get a byline. By learning to evaluate markets across a broad spectrum of issues, you'll find plenty of publications you cannot only work with but also thrive with.

Business Issues

Perhaps the most important information you need to ascertain about a market is how it does business with its writers. There's no excuse for getting an acceptance and then asking, "Oh, by way, what do you pay?"—or worse, withdrawing an accepted article because the pay rate isn't high enough. And there's nothing more painful than having to decide to withdraw an article because you've only just discovered that the publication demands all rights. It's also unprofessional. So before you even approach a market, be sure you know:

1. **What's the pay rate?** Some publications pay a flat rate per feature, others pay by the word, and a few still pay by the printed column or page. Most have a payment range (e.g., "from $200 to $500 for a feature article").

   Keep in mind that rates quoted in a publication's guidelines usually represent the low end of the available range. Rates are often based on the difficulty of the article (including the amount of research or number of interviews required), as well as the skill of the writer. Many publications offer higher rates to regular contributors, particularly if the writer is easy to work with and his material needs little editing. It's never a good idea to ask for a higher fee on your first submission, but after you've sold two or three articles to an editor, it doesn't hurt to ask how you might get into a higher pay bracket. If there *is* no higher bracket, the editor will tell you.

Publications that pay by the word may pay for the number of words you submit, or the number they actually publish. Be sure to ask which basis is used! If an editor asks you to submit an invoice, submit it for the number of words in your original article. Magazines that pay by the column or page won't be able to give you an exact quote until the article is laid out, but they should be able to give you a rough estimate based on the length of the article (or the amount of space they expect to need to fill).

What if you can't find out what a publication pays? Some publications *don't* share that information or provide it in their guidelines. Some editors will ask *you* what you wish to charge for the piece. If so, don't assume the sky's the limit; what the editor is really hoping is that you'll name a figure that's lower than their regular rates.

If this happens, check comparable publications to determine what they pay. If a similar publication pays $500 per feature, ask for $750 and expect a counteroffer. Or ask for help in the writing community. Check the magazine for names of contributors, and send a polite email to one or two of those writers, explaining that you are negotiating an article with the publication and would be grateful for some insight into its pay ranges. When an editor asked me "what I wanted" for a piece, I remembered that I knew a writer who had been published in that magazine, and asked him what they paid—and thus got several hundred dollars more than I might otherwise have asked.

2. **Will you be paid extra for sidebars or illustrations?** Editors often try to pay a flat rate for text and photos. However, they'd have to pay extra for photos if you don't provide them, so there's no reason that compensation shouldn't go to you. If you submit photos, find out what the publication pays for artwork alone. Cover photos are worth more than interior images, and full-page or two-page images pay more than partial page images. Once you know what is typically offered for photos and text, you can discuss a package deal that would probably be less than the publication would pay if it had to purchase artwork separately, but more than it would pay for an article alone.

Some publications pay extra for sidebars; others don't. If a publication pays by the word, adding a sidebar is a great way to increase your word count without going over the limit for the main article. The editor can choose to accept or reject the sidebar, without affecting your pay for the main piece.

3. **When does the publication pay?** Publications pay on acceptance or on publication. "On acceptance" means you're paid once an article is accepted and you've signed and returned the contract. More accurately, it means you'll probably be paid within thirty days of sending back the contract or your invoice. Sometimes it takes longer. If you haven't seen payment in forty-five days, ask politely when to expect it. Don't be surprised if, at this point, you're told (for the first time!) that you need to submit an invoice. Publishers have many ways of delaying payments; this is one of them.

   Once a publisher pays for an article, that doesn't actually obligate them to *use* it. They have fulfilled their part of the bargain by purchasing a set of rights to the article. Though most editors try to publish what they buy (no one wants to waste money on material they can't use), sometimes an article never makes it onto the schedule. If this happens, you have little recourse, but you may be able to request a reversion of unused rights, or even first rights if the editor really has no intention of using the piece.

   Publishers that pay on publication won't issue a check until the material is actually used—even if that doesn't happen for a year or two. Once the piece *is* published, you may still wait another thirty or sixty days for payment. However, in this case, if a publisher is holding your piece for an unreasonable length of time, it's easier to ask for it to be withdrawn and the rights returned to you, because those rights haven't actually been purchased yet.

4. **What rights does the publication require?** This is even more important than the question of payment, because it determines what you can do with your material in the future. Print publications tend to demand more rights than electronic publications. If, after all, the publication does not yet have a website (though this is becoming increasingly rare), it could easily launch one in the future. However, an electronic publication isn't likely to launch a print edition, so it is unlikely to ask for print rights. See chapter 13 for details about the types of rights a publication is likely to ask you for, and what they mean.

Don't make the mistake of thinking these issues don't matter when you're starting out—or that, in the beginning, all that matters is getting published at any cost. Don't assume you won't care if your article looks bad just as long as it's published, because that could cost you the ability to use it as a clip to break into other markets. Don't assume you'll never use a piece again and can afford to give away all rights for virtually nothing. Naturally, you want to see your name in print. But you're in this for the long term, not just for the immediate high of getting that first byline. Don't fall into the trap of being willing to do anything a publisher asks just to get it. You may not think of yourself as a "pro" today, but professionalism is a skill you need to practice from your very first submission. Remember, the only person who can protect you in this shark-infested marketplace is *you*.

CHAPTER 7

How to Write a Successful Query

Many writers don't like queries. When you're excited about an article, you want to write that article—not wait weeks for an editor to give you the go-ahead, by which time your interest may have waned. Worse, querying means making an effort to sell yourself and your work. When you submit an article, you can hope that it will sell itself—but when you write a query, you must pitch and persuade. This isn't always an enjoyable task—but as more and more publications close their doors to unsolicited manuscripts, it has become an essential one.

Actually, queries benefit both editors *and* writers. Even if an editor does accept unsolicited submissions, it's easier to review a one-page proposal than a ten-page article, so responses are often faster. Queries also enable an editor to determine whether you write effectively, have a well-thought-out idea, have a grasp of grammar and punctuation, understand the publication, and have any necessary credentials.

Queries benefit *you* by ensuring that you don't waste time and energy writing an article that won't be accepted. Articles are often rejected for reasons that have nothing to do with quality. A query will save you time if an editor already has a similar piece on file or ran something on the same topic in the past year. It also gives an editor the chance to make suggestions or changes to your article idea before you write it. The editor might prefer a different length, or a different approach. He might suggest that one of your subtopics be pulled out as a sidebar, or request artwork. By finding out exactly what an editor wants *before* you write an article, you'll spend less time revising later.

Queries can be submitted by surface mail, email, a publication's online submission form, or (less commonly) by fax if the guidelines request this. It's rarely acceptable to call an editor with your query. Since print publications and many electronic publications work months in advance, no idea is so "hot" that it needs an instant response. (Even newspaper editors, who do work on a much shorter schedule, don't appreciate phone queries.)

A good query can result in assignments you didn't expect even if it doesn't sell your original article. If an editor can't use your proposal but is impressed by your writing style, she may offer you the chance to write a different article. This can be the beginning of a rewarding relationship!

THE ELEMENTS OF A QUERY

A successful query generally includes five basic components: the hook, the pitch, the body, the credentials, and the close.

The Hook

Your very first line must grab an editor's attention. It must demonstrate that you can write effectively, and that you understand your market. There are several ways to approach the hook:

1. **The problem/solution hook** defines a problem or situation facing the reader:

   For anyone who enjoys decorating with antique or delicate quilts, care is a vital concern. Most of us realize that we can't just pop Granny's handmade quilt into the washing machine or douse it with bleach, but what are the alternatives? How can we protect fine fabrics from further dirt and damage? ("Caring for Quilts: How to Preserve a Perishable Heirloom," sold to Traditional Quiltworks.*)*

2. **The informative hook** presents two or three lines of information (such as facts or statistics), followed by an explanation of how this applies to the reader:

   Thanks to a translation glitch, Microsoft was forced to pull its entire Chinese edition of Windows 95 from the marketplace. Microsoft recovered—but that's the sort of mistake few small businesses can afford! ("How to Localize Your Website," sold to Entrepreneur's Home Office.*)*

3. **The question** is often is a problem/solution or informative hook phrased interrogatively:

   Did you know . . . ?
   What would you do if . . . ?
   Have you ever wondered . . . ?

4. **The personal experience/anecdote hook** is useful for a publication that uses personal stories, or to establish a writer's credentials:

   Last summer, our beloved fifteen-year-old cat succumbed to cancer. Along the way, we learned a great deal about this disease and how it affects cats. ("Answers to Cancer," sold to Cats Magazine.*)*

5. **The attention-grabber** is designed to make the reader sit up and take notice—hopefully long enough to read the rest of the story. This might be a good hook for a query about parachuting in Yosemite:

   As I fell from the top of Yosemite's El Capitan, I wondered if my life would truly flash before my eyes—or if I would stop screaming long enough to notice.

Conversely, certain hooks are guaranteed to speed a query to the rejection pile, including:

- **The personal introduction.** Never start with a line like "Hi, my name is John, and I'd like to send you an article about. . . ." Don't offer irrelevant information, such as "I'm a housewife and mother of three lovely children."
- **The "suck-up" hook.** Don't tell editors you've been reading their publication for twenty years; prove it by offering an appropriate proposal.
- **The "bid for sympathy."** Don't tell an editor how much it would mean to you to be published in his publication, or that your children will starve if you don't sell an article.
- **The "I'm perfect for you" hook.** Don't inform the editor that your article is brilliant, wonderful, or perfect for his readers. Prove it.

- **The "I'm an amateur" hook.** Never announce that you haven't been published before, or that your article has been rejected by twenty other magazines, or that your friends/writing teacher/mother suggested that you send your article to this magazine. You may be an amateur, but you can still act like a professional.

The Pitch

Once you have an editor's attention, move on to the pitch. Usually this is your second paragraph, and its purpose is to explain exactly what you're offering. If possible, your pitch should include a working title for your article, a word count (based on the preferences expressed in the publication's guidelines), and a brief summary. Here's the pitch that followed the "Microsoft" hook:

> *I'd like to offer you a 1,500-word article titled "Internationalizing Your Online Market." The article would discuss how small businesses can take advantage of "localizing" agents to tailor their products and market strategies to the international marketplace.*

The Body

The body of your query should present the details of your article in two to four paragraphs. Be sure you can explain *exactly* what the article will cover. If you don't know yet, go back to the outline and research stages! A good way to present your topic is to break it into logical subtopics, as described in chapter 5. Here's how I described the article on quilt care:

> *The article covers techniques of hand cleaning delicate quilts to avoid damaging fragile fabrics and prevent fading and staining. It discusses ways to remove spot stains (including blood spots and rust stains from needles and other metal contact). It also discusses ways to mend damaged quilts without destroying the integrity of an heirloom piece. Finally, it discusses the best ways to store or display quilts in order to preserve and protect them.*

The body of your query can be written in block paragraphs, or as a bullet list, as in my "Cancer in Cats" proposal:

My article will cover:

- *The types of cancers most common in cats (including mammary tumors and cancers of the mouth, lips, and gums—some of which are preventable!).*
- *How to recognize the signs of cancer early (what is that lump?).*
- *The symptoms and progression of various types of cancer (weight loss, diminished appetite, coughing, and wheezing can all be signs of cancer).*
- *The types of treatments available, pros and cons of different treatments, how treatments can affect a cat's life expectancy and quality of life, and how to find treatment (not every city has an animal cancer clinic).*

Either style is effective; there are no "rules." Choose the style that gets your information across quickly; don't ask the editor to wade through extremely long paragraphs of text.

The Credentials

Editors want to know why you feel qualified to write the article you're proposing. One type of credential is a list of relevant publications. Note that I said "relevant." If you're proposing an article on gardening, articles on computer maintenance may not help. If you don't have relevant publications, cite your most prestigious publications, or list the publications rather than the titles of the articles. (For example, you could write, "My work has appeared in *Good Housekeeping, Maine Parenting*, and *USA Today*," avoiding the question of just *what* you wrote.) List four or five publications, not your entire resume. Never list unpublished credits, except for forthcoming articles. Never list nonprofessional credits, such as articles published in a church or office newsletter, letters to the editor, or self-published materials, including materials posted on your website or blog.

If you don't have publication credits, don't despair. Other useful credentials include:

- **Education.** A relevant degree or educational background can help establish you as an "expert."
- **Work experience.** One of my writing students was planning an article for a trade magazine on how to avoid safety hazards in

landscaping. His selling point was that, as a lawyer, he knew what advice to offer landscapers.

- **Personal expertise.** Your skills or hobbies may impress an editor. Another student sold her first article—a lovely piece on forget-me-nots—based on her gardening experience.
- **Personal experience.** Sometimes, having "been there, done that" makes you an expert. Just make sure your experience sets you apart from the crowd. Offering a parenting article on the basis that you're a parent won't impress an editor. Offering an article on how to cook for a child with food allergies on the basis of having personally dealt with that issue for years will.
- **Interviews.** You can often sell an article by mentioning the experts you've chosen to interview. Just be sure you can get the interviews if you get the assignment!

List your credentials in your next-to-last or last paragraph:

My husband and I spent fifteen months in England, and became adept at photographing inside dimly lit cathedrals and similar buildings. I have been a freelance writer for more than thirty years, and am the host/editor of the popular writing site Writing-World.com (which attracts over one million visitors per year) and the British travel site TimeTravel-Britain.com. ("The Chichester Cathedral Flower Festival," sold to British Heritage).

The Close

Use the final paragraph to thank the editor for reviewing your proposal— and nudge the editor to respond. I usually include the amount of time in which I can deliver the article if it's accepted:

I hope this topic interests you, and look forward to your response. If you would like to see the article, I can have it on your desk within two weeks of receiving your go-ahead. Thank you for your time!

FORMATTING YOUR QUERY

The presentation of your letter can be as important as your content. A traditional paper query should include the following elements:

- **A professional letterhead** that includes your name, address, and other contact information at the top. (See chapter 2 for tips on designing your letterhead.)
- **A business-style body.** If you aren't familiar with terms like "block" or "modified block," see the sample query at the end of this chapter. Always include a blank line between paragraphs, and don't indent more than five spaces.
- **A formal salutation.** Don't address the editor by first name unless you know him personally.
- **Clean, proofread copy.** Don't rely on your spell-checker; review your query yourself.
- **Quality paper.** Use at least 20-pound bond paper for queries. Neutral-toned parchment or linen bond is fine as well. Don't use colors, however; pink or blue paper scream for rejection. If you're querying from another country, use the paper size available in your country.
- **A SASE** (self-addressed, stamped envelope). This should be a business-size envelope, folded in thirds. Be sure it includes adequate return postage. Don't use a return address label for your SASE; print out a larger mailing label or type your address on the envelope.

When you're sending a query to another country, your best option is to use email if possible. In the old days, one could obtain IRCs (International Reply Coupons) to include with a SASE; the recipient could exchange them for their country's postage. IRCs seem to have gone the way of the dinosaur, and even when they were available, recipients hardly ever bothered to use them. If your target publication won't accept an email query, send one by post but request a response by email.

Needless to say, email queries break nearly all of the format rules listed above. I'll explain how to compose and format an email query in the following pages.

MULTIPLE-PITCH QUERIES

A multiple-pitch query proposes several articles at once, usually with a brief paragraph describing each. Though an editor is unlikely to accept all the proposed topics, such a query can often result in more than one assignment. However, as you won't be able to provide much detail about any one topic, the editor already needs to know that you're capable of delivering on your proposals, so this isn't a good approach for a first-time contributor. Save multiple-pitch queries for editors you've already worked with.

Here's a multiple-pitch query I submitted to an online publication, which resulted in two assignments:

> Dear Debbie,
>
> We've talked about several articles recently, and I wanted to find out whether you're interested in any/all of these:
>
> 1. Author chats—are they useful? I've talked to several authors who have given "chats" online. This article would discuss whether an author chat is worthwhile and how to make the best of one.
> 2. Teaching writing classes offline. This piece would discuss how to teach a writing class in a "real world" environment.
> 3. Teaching writing classes online. The follow-up to the previous article would discuss how to teach a successful online writing class.
> 4. Giving a talk—this would fall under the category of "promotion." I'd like to include information on how to prepare for a talk, and also information on the technical side—how do you give a good presentation? What will your listeners want to hear? What about handouts, outlines, charts, and other visual aids?

An editor may respond to a multiple-pitch query with a request to describe one or more ideas in more detail. In this case, don't worry about a hook or credentials, because you're already past that point. Instead, concentrate on explaining exactly what will be covered and how the article will be organized.

EMAIL QUERIES

Email is the preferred method of correspondence for most editors, and usually the only way to approach online publications. Email saves time and money, and often results in a faster response.

Don't assume, however, that because email makes nearly instantaneous communication possible, responses will *be* instantaneous! Editors often complain that writers now follow up within hours of sending a query, rather than weeks. The response times specified in a publication's guidelines still apply, regardless of the mechanism.

Another complaint is that the instantaneous nature of email queries seems to encourage writers to dash them off with little attention to style, presentation, or content. Many are poorly proofread, and tend to be less formal, more chatty, even "cutesy"—qualities editors rarely find endearing. Just because a query can be transmitted quickly doesn't mean you should treat it as a quick note rather than a formal proposal.

While email queries contain many of the elements described above, the hard-copy format rules no longer apply. Email has its own format issues, which you ignore at your peril. They also contain unique elements that require special attention.

The Header

With email, you can't impress an editor with nice paper and a snappy letterhead. Your header is your first impression, so make sure it's a good one. Pay attention to these sections:

- **To:** Address your query to the right person. Some publications ask you to contact a specific editor; others ask you to send queries to an address like "submissions@—."
- **From:** You wouldn't sign a traditional query as "Rafe Moondragon," so don't let that type of nickname appear in your professional correspondence. Set up an email profile that includes your real name. Similarly, if your personal address is "2hot2trot@wowser.com," set up a more professional account for editorial correspondence. And remember that editors have already seen every variation on "WriterLady" or "CatswithPens."
- **Subject:** Include the word "Query" in your subject line, along with a brief (two- to three-word) description of your topic (e.g., "Query: Cancer in Cats" or "Query: Writing for Pet Magazines"). Never leave this line blank. Conversely, if you're querying from your cell phone, don't cram your entire message into the subject line! Avoid excessive informality. Watch out for phrases that could sound like

spam, like "Could I have a moment of your time?" or words like "urgent" or "important."

The Text

One way to handle an email query is to treat it just like a traditional query, with all the essentials described above. This will rarely go wrong.

However, the advantage of email is its ability to save time, and many editors prefer email queries to be shorter and more concise than postal queries. Editors often like to be able to read the entire query without having to scroll down the screen. Consequently, many writers send queries of one to three paragraphs. The hook may be eliminated entirely; the writer may lead with the pitch, followed by a paragraph of description, and closing with credentials. So think about ways you can condense your information without losing anything vital to your proposal.

Here's an example of a short but successful query to the UK women's magazine *My Weekly*. The author, Abby Williams, notes that this was her first successful pitch:

Dear (editor name),

I am currently researching the growing environmental nuisance of plastic bags. I wondered whether you might be interested in an article about this, firstly advising readers of the global problem, its effect on our natural world, what alternatives readers can use (including photos) plus useful contacts, and if governments/supermarkets are actually doing anything about this problem. I was interested to learn that turtles often mistake upturned plastic bags in the ocean for jellyfish, which they eat, causing either a blocked digestive tract, or worse!

I look forward to hearing from you if you feel an article of this type might be of interest to your readers.

Credentials, Contacts, and Clips

List your credentials and a list of writing credits in an email query just as you would in hard copy. Many writers also add a link to a website or blog where an editor can learn more about their qualifications or view writing samples.

In a traditional query, your name and address and other contact information would appear at the top of the page or in your letterhead. In an email query, include this information at the bottom, below your signature. Be sure you *do* include that information; I've received queries in which the writers don't even include their last names! (Be sure to include it on your submission as well—too many submissions these days lack contact information or even a byline.)

If you use a signature block, make sure it's appropriate. This is a good place to include your website, or the title of a book you've published. Don't use cute signature blocks or graphic elements. If necessary, set up a separate profile with a signature block designed for professional correspondence.

Formatting for Email

The best way to create an email query is to type it *directly* into your email program. Single-space text, and insert an extra line between paragraphs. Do not indent paragraphs. Avoid long blocks of text; try to limit paragraphs to three or four sentences. Don't use bullets. Don't use special formatting, such as italics or boldface. If you're listing the names of publications, it's perfectly acceptable to put these in quotes. Use plain text, not HTML. You can never be sure that HTML styles will show up as planned at the receiving end; my email program, for example, displays italics as boldface.

If you compose your query (or submission) in a program like Microsoft Word and copy and paste it into an email, you can run into formatting issues. Special characters and formatting characters in Word, including smart quotes, apostrophes, and dashes, may turn into something very different when translated into email text. Your query could end up looking something like this:

> Yet I,m not alone˜every writer I know struggles with „writer,s anxiety‰. „First you,re anxious if you don,t have work, but then when you do, you,re anxious about making it the best you can,‰ says fulltime St. Louis freelancer Kris Rattini, who,s written for Family Money, Family Circle, and Boy,s Life. „If it,s a new editor, it,s just intensified because you want to make a good impression and get more assignments.‰

To avoid this, go into the "AutoFormat" menu and turn off all special characters, such as smart quotes, dashes, ordinals, and so forth.[3] If your text already includes these characters, you can then do a search-and-replace by typing a quote mark or apostrophe into both the "find" and "replace" boxes and doing a "replace all." Replace em dashes with two hyphens. Don't use special characters such as accents or tildes. Again, don't use italics or bold.

If you paste a document into an email from Word, mail it to yourself first to check for errors. The extra line between paragraphs often disappears and may need to be reinserted.

Finally, avoid using special characters or abbreviations in your emails, such as emoticons, smileys, LOL, and so forth. Don't use colors or graphics. Finally, never send an attachment of any kind—including your article, photos, or clips—until the editor asks for it. Nothing gets an email routed to the spam box faster than an unsolicited message with attachments!

WHY QUERIES FAIL

While there are many reasons why a query may not result in an assignment that aren't related to the quality of that query, sometimes—let's face it—the problem lies with the writer. Here are some common query problems:

- **You're trying to squeeze too much into an article.** An editor will notice if you have too many ideas or subtopics for the type and length of article you're proposing. I often receive queries promising to explain "how to write a novel" in 700 words or less! Determine and focus upon the central core of your article, and save any additional information for other pieces.
- **You have too little to say.** The topic may be interesting, but you're not offering enough information to justify a 2,000-word feature. Try offering a shorter piece.
- **You have questions without answers.** Beware of phrases like "I'd like to explore whether" or "I'll find out if. . . ." If you don't know

---

3   For users of Microsoft Word 2007 and later, check the "Help" index to find out how to add the AutoFormat icon to your Quick Access toolbar, as this function may no longer be included in the regular drop-down menus.

the answers to the questions your article is going to address, find out before you query.

Sending an inappropriate idea won't make a bad impression unless you're so far off the mark that it shows you're completely clueless about the publication. (For example, a writer once kept pestering me to buy his travel articles, on the basis that my website for writers, Writing-World.com, had the word "travel" in its navigation menu!) Sending a poorly written, badly organized, misspelled query, however, will convince an editor he doesn't want to work with you—ever. Such a query sends the message that no matter how interesting your ideas are, you don't have the skill to express them effectively. Think of your query as a letter of introduction, your first and perhaps only opportunity to get your foot through that particular door. If you make a good impression, you still have a chance of getting in even if your original pitch is rejected. If you make a bad impression, that door may close to you forever.[4]

---

4   An expanded version of this chapter, along with a variety of sample queries, can be found in my book *The Writer's Guide to Queries, Pitches and Proposals* (Allworth Press, 2010).

Figure 7–1: Sample Postal Query

Moira Allen

1234 Mystreet • Mytown, VA 20151
(XXX) 555–1234
editors@writing-world.com

(Date)

(Editor's name)
Entrepreneur Magazine
(address)

Dear Ms. (Editor):

Thanks to a translation glitch, Microsoft was forced to pull its entire Chinese edition of Windows 95 from the marketplace. Microsoft recovered—but that's the sort of mistake few small businesses can afford! Yet thanks to the Internet, international markets are suddenly only a few keystrokes away. Just about any home office entrepreneur with a computer and a modem can create a web page that may be accessed around the world. If those keystrokes are wrong, however, that same page can drive international business away.

I'd like to offer you a 1,500-word article titled "Internationalizing Your Online Market." The article would discuss how small businesses can take advantage of "localizing" or "internationalizing" agents to tailor both their products and their marketing strategies to the international marketplace. Localizing includes not only translation assistance but also advice on "cultural correctness" in both one's product and marketing approach. For example:

- When is a mailbox not a mailbox? "Standard" computer icons often reflect images that are incomprehensible or offensive to other cultures—including images of American-style mailboxes that may have no counterpart in the market you're trying to reach.

- When are pictures of babies offensive? In Muslim countries, the display of bare body parts (even diaper-clad babies) is unacceptable, even when considered modest by Western standards.
- Is it really black and white? In the West, black is the color of funerals and white is the color of weddings. But in Asia, white symbolizes mourning and death, while red symbolizes marriage.
- Does anybody know what time it is? Depending on your market, it could be 3:30 p.m., 1530, 15h.30, 15.30, or 15:30. Times, dates, and currency expressions vary widely throughout the world!

My article would describe the types of services available from a localizer, the costs involved, and how to find such services. It will highlight "internationalizing" a web page to make it more effective, "culturally correct," and user friendly in the international market. The article will include an interview with Sol Squires, president of Twin Dragons, who will share some of the blunders that can be avoided with localization help.

When even the smallest of businesses are capable of offering products and services via computer to the international marketplace, business owners need to know how to avoid the pitfalls of this type of marketing. I believe this article would be timely and useful to your audience; if you agree, I can provide the piece within thirty days of your go-ahead. Thanks for your time; I look forward to hearing from you.

Sincerely,
Moira Allen

Figure 7–2: Sample E-Mail Query, submitted to Writing-World.com

Dear Ms. Allen,

Are you looking for a tasty take on success with selling books at a booth for Writing World? Having sold books at dozens of events over the past five years, I've put together a "recipe" for connecting with readers and making sales. Since so many authors try to market their books this way, I thought it would be a good fit for your site, which is so clearly focused on working writers. And working a booth is work!

This how-to article covers ten ingredients for successful events: making that first connection, standing up to convey energy, offering prospects the book, resisting the urge to loom, giving away a sample or take away to nonbuyers, steering prospects to other authors, making friends with fellow vendors, eating out of sight and being ready to be "on stage", taking notes about book buyers, and enjoying oneself.

Under my pseudonym, I've sold over thirty short stories to various anthologies since 2004, and Lethe Press published Rough Cut, my short story collection, last year. I've sold books at library events, book festivals, Pride events, and other venues, and honed my skills on making those one-on-one connections with readers and book buyers. Currently, I freelance edit for Torquere Press, Samhain Publishing, and Publication Services, and my recent story sales include Lycanthrope: The Beast Within from Graveside Tales and Gay City Health, Volume Two.

Thank you for your time; I look forward to hearing from you about the article.

Sincerely,
B. T.

CHAPTER 8

Creating Your First Draft

Few things are more intimidating than the blank page (or screen) when you have a deadline. You may have known what you wanted to say when you wrote your query, but now you have a stack of research notes and no idea how to get started. Or, perhaps you're stuck on the first sentence. This doesn't just happen to new writers; it happens to us all. Here are some ways to get that article going.

IDENTIFY YOUR SUBJECT

The first step is to ask yourself whether you know exactly what your article is supposed to be about. Now that you've done your research, your brain may be stuffed with all sorts of information, and you're having trouble sorting it out into a workable structure. It's time to go back to the basics.

Start by making sure you can state the central concept (or "thesis") of your article in a *single sentence*. This sentence should contain no more than one "and" (or commas inserted in place of the word "and"). For example:

TITLE: "Your Child's First Hike"
Market: Family-oriented travel or hiking publication
Good Topic Sentence: "How to introduce your child to hiking safely and enjoyably."
Bad Topic Sentence: "How to introduce your child to hiking, and what to pack, and where to go, and a look at my own experiences taking the kids on hikes, plus a look back at my first hike when I was a child. . . ."

TITLE: "Discover the New Olympic Sport of Skeleton!"
Market: Winter sports publications
Good Topic Sentence: "What 'skeleton' is and how to get involved."
Bad Topic Sentence: "What 'skeleton' is, how to get involved, profiles of some notable 'skeleton' athletes, a history of skeleton and the Olympics, and places where you can learn how to do it, plus some of the risks. . . ."

The purpose of a topic sentence is not only to help you focus on the central point of your article, but also to *limit* you. Everything in your article should relate to that topic sentence. If it doesn't, it doesn't belong in this article, no matter how interesting it may be. A tightly focused topic sentence will keep you on track; a rambling topic sentence will get you lost.

Another way to define your topic sentence is to turn it into a question that would be asked by the reader. Then, you know exactly the answer or answers your article must provide. Here are some sample questions that would make good core concepts for articles:

- How can I introduce my child to the sport of hiking?
- What is "skeleton" and how can I get started in this sport?
- Should I refinance my home?
- How can I learn to crochet?
- How do you cook chestnuts?
- How can I communicate more effectively with my spouse?
- What do I need to know about "natural" vitamins?
- What are some romantic things I can do for less than $20?
- How can I keep the kids entertained on a rainy day?

Not every article idea can be expressed as a question, but you'd be surprised how easy it is to turn *most* ideas into questions. From there, your goal is simple: *answer* the question.

When you do so, make sure you're answering the *right* question. One common flaw I've seen in submissions is the tendency to explain *why* something is important but not explain *how* to do it. For example, a writer might describe why it's important to create believable characters in fiction, but fail to explain exactly how you do that. Make sure the "why" part of your article is limited to the introduction, and use the rest of the article to show the reader exactly how to accomplish what he needs to do to resolve the problem you've identified.

Besides establishing the question your article will be answering, you also need to know who will be *asking* that question. If, for example, you're writing about "how to plan for retirement," you need to know who will be reading the piece. The questions asked by a twenty-year-old single woman will be very different from those asked by a forty-year-old married man whose children will soon enter college, or a divorced mother, or someone who is self-employed.

Returning to our article on hiking with children, you'll need to know whether you're writing for experienced hikers, or readers new to the sport. A more experienced audience might be interested in the latest high-tech equipment suitable for kids, or the best hiking trails for kids in the region; they don't have to be told *how* to hike. A less experienced audience will need more explanation of basic concepts.

IDENTIFY YOUR SUBTOPICS

Once you've defined your topic statement, identify subtopics that support the original thesis. For example, your article on a child's first hike might cover such topics as how to make a trip enjoyable or safe. An article on whether to refinance one's home might address when this is a good idea and when it is not, or steps you can take to find the best deal. Each of these subtopics may lead to additional subtopics. For example:

- **Child's hiking trip → Safety → Risks:** Common trail hazards, including sunburn, dehydration, toxic plants, insect bites, animals/snakes, injuries such as cuts, bruises, sprains.
- **Child's hiking trip → Safety → Precautions:** Warning your child about hazards, things to pack in case of hazards, how to protect against sunburn, and so on.
- **Child's hiking trip → Safety→ Remedies:** What to do if any of the hazards are encountered (how to treat poison ivy, snake bite, etc.)

The key is to make sure that everything you're trying to cover relates *directly* to your core topic. If it doesn't, save it for another piece. If you have too many subtopics, you can always use one as a sidebar.

Be sure you know how long your article is supposed to be. As I discussed in chapter 5, you can allocate only so many words to each point in your article. If you're covering many points, your article will be more of an overview, with only a small number of words to be allocated to each topic. If you have only a few points, you can provide more in-depth coverage of each.

While there is no hard-and-fast rule, I find that for an in-depth article, you need a budget of at least 300 to 500 words per subtopic. Thus, a 2,000-word article might include four major subtopics. An article that needs to cover a large number of subtopics often works well as a list, such as "ten tips to keep your kids safe on a hike."

DETERMINE YOUR STRUCTURE

Next, determine the best order in which to present your information. Often, once you know the question that you're answering, a logical order may become obvious. You may also have defined this order in your outline. Here are some common structures:

- **Logical Order.** What comes first, what comes next, what comes after that? What's the first question a reader would ask, the second, the third, and so on?
- **Chronological Order.** What happened first? What happened next? What happened after that?
- **Instructional Order.** What should the reader do first? What will he do next? What is step one, step two, step three?
- **List Order.** Lists work well for articles like "Ten Ways to Entertain Your Children on a Road Trip" or "Twenty Ways to Clean Up Stains and Spills." Shorter lists work fine without numbers; longer lists often benefit from numbering. Your number can also become your title.

If all else fails, try what I call "sculpting." Write down paragraphs, at random, based on your research. Don't worry about putting them together in sequence or polishing them; the goal is to get something on the page. This process is like throwing wads of clay into a pile that will eventually become a sculpture. The first step is simply to get all the clay in the right place. *Then* you can worry about shaping and smoothing.

Whatever method you choose, keep in mind that order and organization are vital. A common reason for rejection is lack of organization—and I've received many articles that appear to have been jotted down as ideas came to the author, without any effort to put them in any sort of order. Even if such an article contains good information, no editor wants to revise a piece paragraph by paragraph.

CHOOSE YOUR STYLE

Structure is only half the battle. You also need to decide *how* you will write your article—its tone, style, language, and other issues of presentation. While most of us develop a distinctive writing style over time, you'll also need to pay attention to the style and tone of your target market. Always be sure to consider:

- **The level of the audience.** Know your audience's reading level and degree of knowledge/expertise on your subject. Do your readers expect technical terminology, or simple writing with lots of explanations? Do they expect the author to be a friendly, handholding guide or a more authoritative "expert"?
- **The appropriate narrative voice.** Should you write in first person ("I/we"), second person ("you"), or third person ("he/she/they/one")? Again, this depends on the publication. Some publications never use first-person narratives; some prefer them. Some types of articles (such as how-tos) are best written in second person ("Do this, then do this; you can also do this."). Some prefer third: "One can achieve this effect by...."
- **Personal vs. impersonal.** Some publications prefer personal, conversational articles; some prefer articles to present information without a sense of the author being part of the article. As a general rule, I believe it's better to stay out of the way of the reader as much as possible; let your information speak for itself, without rambling on about what *you* think about it.

Another type of style to consider is your "narrative style." Often, an article that is written as a straight narration of facts from beginning to end can be boring. Consider ways you can add variety and interest to your piece, including:

- **Anecdotes**. Used sparingly, anecdotes can spice up a piece, providing personal examples to illustrate your information. Your entire article can be based around an anecdotal example, or you could open with an anecdote that introduces your subject, and then close with a concluding anecdote that shows how your introductory story turned out.

- **Interviews and quotes.** These should also be used sparingly. Instead of quoting everything a person says, paraphrase most of your interview information and use direct quotes that serve as interesting highlights or provide special insights into the character of the interviewee.

- **Statistics**. Some people love numbers; some don't. Statistics can be a useful way to back up your point, but they can also cause some readers to nod off. Watch out for sentences like "In 2015, 50 percent of the 1,750 hotels in the 55-mile radius of Metropolis experienced a 92 percent increase in their revenue, for a total of $72 million. . . ."

- **"Made-up" anecdotes.** Some publications like to illustrate a point with artificial anecdotes: "Because John backed up his computer data, his business didn't fail when his computer crashed. Unfortunately, Mary didn't. . . ." I've never been a fan of this approach, but some editors like it!

- **Personal experiences.** Even in a more factual how-to piece, you can use personal experiences to illustrate your topic. For example, if you were writing about caring for a pet with diabetes, you might use your own experience to help put the reader at ease (if you can do it, he can do it!), and provide a logical way to "walk through" the information. Keep in mind that in such article, the experience is the vehicle for your information, not the point of your article.

BEGINNINGS, MIDDLES, AND ENDS

Every article needs a great beginning, an introduction that hooks the reader and draws her into the article. Generally, your introduction should be no longer than one paragraph. Use it to establish what the article is about and why it will be relevant or interesting to the reader. (You may find that your query hook works well as an article hook!)

Avoid rambling introductions. If your introduction goes on for two or three paragraphs, it's too long. Worse, the editor will probably cut most of it, costing you precious words. Here are some introductions to avoid:

- **The personal introduction,** in which the writer introduces herself, her background, her credentials, or a personal experience that "sets the scene" for the article itself.
- **The analogy,** in which the writer compares what she is about to discuss to something else—for example, comparing writing to gardening ("learning to prune") or cooking ("choosing the right ingredients").
- **The "setting-the-stage" introduction,** in which the writer wastes several paragraphs on background information before getting to the point.

The middle of your article—everything that falls between your introduction and conclusion—should fulfill the promise made by your introduction. Don't promise anything you can't deliver! Also, make sure the tone of your introduction matches the tone of the rest of the article. Don't open with a joke and move on into an article that is morbid and depressing.

Every article needs a conclusion. Don't just stop when you run out of information. Provide a final paragraph that wraps things up and provides a sense of closure to the article. The reader should feel that everything that needed to be said has been said. He shouldn't be flipping the page wondering if there is more to the article. Try to mirror your introduction in your conclusion. For example, if you opened with an anecdote, close with an anecdote, or with the conclusion to the story you started with. If you open with a quote, close with a quote. Bring the reader full circle.

One common approach to is to set up your article in the "problem/solution/call to action" format. Here, the introduction establishes a problem to be solved or question to be answered. It may explain *why* this issue is a problem, *why* the reader needs to know more, *why* the reader needs to take action. For example, a common type of health article covers "symptoms you can't afford to ignore." The introduction explains that certain symptoms can be signs of serious illness, establishing the problem that needs to be solved. The middle goes over the symptoms and what they could mean. The ending is a "call to action"—if *you* see these symptoms, go to a doctor!

Articles that cover a personal experience should conclude with the end of the story. If you don't know how the story ends, don't try to write an experiential article! For example, if you've just gotten divorced, don't try to write an article on "how to survive divorce" until you've actually gone through the process and are in a position to look back upon it.

SIDEBARS

Editors love sidebars. Some publications require them; for example, travel magazines generally ask for sidebars that explain basic "how to get there, where to stay" information. In other cases, sidebars add extra information or interest to a feature. Sidebars are also a great way to use up information that didn't fit in your main article. Here are some basic types of sidebars:

- **Lists.** Lists are useful if you have a number of short pieces of information. For example, on that article about hiking and children, consider a list of trail hazards, first aid supplies, or equipment. If it's for a regional publication, consider listing local trails that are appropriate for children.
- **Personal experiences.** Sometimes a short personal account makes a good sidebar to a longer, more factual piece. When I edited *Dog Fancy*, I always liked to balance a technical medical article with a personal article about the same topic.
- **Factual information.** The reverse is also effective: try balancing a personal article with a brief overview of factual information.
- **Quizzes.** Editors love quizzes. For example, I converted the checklist in chapter 29 to a quiz and sold it to *The Writer* as a sidebar to an article on how to survive as a full-time freelance writer.
- **Where to find it.** A sidebar on where to find more information, buy products mentioned in the article, or find organizations related to the topic, and so on, is always useful. Be sure to cover online resources as well.

Remember that you don't need to format a sidebar when submitting it; just add it to the end of your article with its own heading and word count.

Finally, remember that your first draft *is* a first draft. It's not your final article. It doesn't have to be perfect; it doesn't even have to be very good!

Your goal is not to get everything right the first time; it is to simply get the basics on paper in a reasonably coherent form. Only then can you move on to fix problems, reorganize your thoughts, and refine your material.

No editor will ever know what you went through to complete your piece. But in its own way, this is perhaps the most important piece of writing you can create—because this is where far too many would-be writers stumble and fall. For many, the first draft seems an insurmountable obstacle, and their writing dreams remain unfulfilled. Don't let that happen to you!

CHAPTER 9

Personal Experience Articles

When I was editor of a national pet magazine, my desk was swamped with personal experience articles—accounts of funny, moving, or tragic events in the author's life. And every day, the majority went straight to the rejection pile.

It wasn't because they were poorly written. Many were quite good. We simply couldn't use them because they didn't match our editorial focus.

Personal experience articles make up a huge portion of a publication's unsolicited submissions, yet they are the least likely to be accepted. The problem is that personal experience pieces are typically about the *writer*. Editors are looking for articles about the *reader*. This makes the odds of acceptance extremely low.

You can beat those odds, however, by offering an editor the best of both worlds: a personalized service article. To do this, you must determine how your experience relates to the reader. For example,

- Is this an experience the reader might wish to share or enjoy?
- Is this an experience from which the reader can learn or benefit?
- Is this an experience the reader might wish to avoid?
- Is this an experience that will help the reader cope with difficulty?

EXPERIENCES TO SHARE

Have you had an experience others might like to share? Perhaps you've achieved a success or a goal, or simply had a good time. Would others want to do the same? If the answer is yes, you're in the ideal position to tell them how.

For example, perhaps you've just come back from a great vacation. Tell us about it! Most travel articles are personal experience pieces at heart. But they are written in such a way that they become the reader's experience as well—either vicariously, or by enabling the reader to duplicate the experience.

If your vacation involved a fascinating destination, tell us how to get there, what to see, where to find the best food and lodgings, or what to expect from the culture or environment. Tailor your account to your audience. Will your readers want to know about the most challenging hiking trails, the best restaurants, or how to get a bargain in the shops or bazaars? Should your article focus on the little-known details of an exotic culture, or the nuts and bolts of travel and hotel arrangements?

Focusing on the service aspects of your article broadens your market options dramatically. That story of your "best camping trip ever" can discuss equipment and supplies for one magazine, the ten best campgrounds in a particular region for another, and how to get the kids unplugged from their smartphones and into the great outdoors for a third. In short, ask yourself not only how a reader can benefit from your experience but also how *different* types of readers might benefit.

Your experience should be one a reader would *like* to share, not one he has already had. One of the most commonly rejected articles at the pet magazine was the "my first pet" article. Authors were enthralled by this delightful new experience, so full of surprises—forgetting that most readers of the magazine had already been through that experience themselves. For the readers, it was old news. Focus on experiences that will be new to the reader, not just new to you.

EXPERIENCES THAT ENRICH

Self-improvement themes fill periodicals of every description. You'll find endless variations on how to improve your health, well-being, relationships, careers, skills, homes, and hobbies. Nothing attracts a reader like the promise that an article will make life *better*.

To tap into this market, explore areas in your life that *you* have made better. Topics might range from the deeply personal (overcoming a fear, meeting a challenge) to the seemingly trivial (brightening your work area with potted plants). Any improvement you've made in your life could make a difference to someone else.

Suppose, for example, that you quit the corporate rat race to start your own business. Presumably, your goal was to improve your life. (I've yet to read an article about *joining* the rat race to improve quality of life!) Your article could explain not only why you did it, but how, including the pros and cons of your decision.

Has your decision led to more quality time with family members, more freedom to control your destiny, more opportunities to enjoy the "little things" like gardens and sunsets, more time to linger over the morning coffee? Those are all points on the plus side. On the minus side, have you had to deal with developing good work habits, the lack of social interaction, and no steady paycheck or benefits? While these may seem like "cons," they can be "pros" when it comes to marketing your article, if you can offer tips for others facing similar issues.

Self-improvement articles don't necessarily have to be based on life-changing experiences. In many cases, an area of your life that *hasn't* changed can also be the basis of an excellent article. For example, is your relationship with your spouse running smoothly? Are your children well behaved, getting good grades, and staying off drugs? If your life is going well, keep in mind that thousands of readers would love to know your secrets for a successful relationship or how to raise happy and well-adjusted children!

EXPERIENCES TO AVOID

Sometimes the experiences from which we learn the most are the negative ones. Writers don't simply learn from their mistakes; they write about them. At least, they should!

Experiences you wish you could have avoided often make wonderful service articles. What would you have done differently if you had known then what you know now? What would you do differently today? It may be too late to avoid a problem, but it's never too late to help another person facing a similar situation.

Unpleasant experiences don't have to lead to unpleasant articles. Someone once said that comedy equals tragedy plus time. Sometimes, the best time to write about your experience is when you're finally able to look back on it and laugh. The resulting article could not only be useful, but entertaining as well.

For example, what about that disastrous family hiking trip in the MegaBugga Woods? The trip during which your dog broke its leash and tangled with a skunk, you got the worst sunburn of your life, and your child became a hands-on expert at identifying poison ivy? By the time your sunburn faded, you knew you had an article! Throw in a sidebar on how to identify toxic plants, or what type of protective clothing to wear, or what first-aid supplies to carry along, and you'll have an article for any number of markets.

Of course, not every unpleasant experience lends itself to lighthearted treatment. Many should be handled with sensitivity and care. Yet even potentially devastating experiences can often be avoided with the proper precautions. If you've suffered through such an event, you will be providing a valuable service to others by putting those precautions on paper.

EXPERIENCES TO ENDURE

Some experiences cannot be avoided; they can only be endured. When someone faces a tragedy or loss, they often want to hear from a writer who has been through a similar experience. They want to read a piece by someone who understands and knows how it feels, whose advice and comfort comes from the heart.

This is the big difference (and the big selling point) between a "coping" article written by an expert, and one written by an ordinary person who has been through it, endured, and somehow managed to pull his life together again. Experts have good advice that you may be able to incorporate into your article. But it is your personal experience that humanizes this advice and makes it meaningful to the reader.

Writers will never run out of markets for articles on how to cope with grief, trauma, or loss, because people will never cease to experience these things. And because traumatic events affect different people in different ways, an effective article can reach many different markets.

For example, suppose you're writing about losing a job. You might focus on how you coped with feelings of anger, loss, helplessness, and frustration. You might write about how you found a new job. You might deal with issues of financial adjustments, or how to find support during your job hunt.

Your options don't end there, however. Unless you're single, with no one to support but your cat, the loss of your job will affect others as well. How did it affect your spouse? How did it affect your children? How could a reader help his family members cope? Strategies that can help different family members can be sold to a wider range of markets.

Any type of loss, large or small, raises issues and emotions that must be dealt with, either as an individual or as a family. By using your own experience as the basis for a service article, you send the message that resolution and recovery are possible.

FIRST EXPERIENCES

As I mentioned above, magazines are flooded with "first experience" pieces, such as articles about the writer's first pet. Most of them are rejected, because the magazine's readers have already had that "first experience" and aren't particularly interested in hearing about yours.

However, first experience articles can still find a home if you look for ways to match your experience with the appropriate market:

1. **Look for readers who haven't shared your experience.** Don't send the story of your first dog to a dog magazine. Instead, look for an audience that will find your experience new and different. An article about the difference a new pet made in a single parent's relationship with her child, for example, might sell to a family or parenting magazine.
2. **Look for an uncommon element.** A "my first dog" story *will* sell to a pet magazine if there's something unique about the dog, its owner, or their relationship. I once accepted an article about a canine escape artist who chewed through a chain link fence. Readers appreciated the conflict faced by the writer. Could she confine the dog without harming it, or would she have to give up this problem pet? Your resolution must be appropriate to the audience; had the author sent the dog to the pound, we wouldn't have bought the article.
3. **Look for an unusual perspective.** A story about "my first trip to the supermarket" would be as exciting as Valium—unless the supermarket is in a foreign country and you can't speak the language,

read the labels, or guess the prices. The "outsider looking in" approach can often lead to a sale. But there's a catch. You must know enough about the "inside" to understand what makes your perspective unique and different. I once sold an article about my first visit to the strange world of dog shows to the *AKC Gazette* (the official magazine of the American Kennel Club). To do so, however, I had to know enough about the sport to understand what would come across as humor rather than ignorance.

4. **Look for smaller "first experiences."** Instead of writing about your first dog, write about a specific event. How about the first time your dog became ill, or your first obedience class or dog show, or the first time you took your dog camping? Such stories can focus on areas where others may not have shared your experience, or where they may be able to learn from it.

EXPERIENCE AS EXPERTISE

Many publications prefer writers with the kind of expertise that comes only through personal experience. While an expert can provide useful information on a topic, it is the writer like you—someone who has lived it—who brings that information to life. Your experience provides you with special credentials, including:

- **Understanding.** You understand the needs and interests of the reader. You know what a reader needs to learn about the topic, and how to get that information across. For example, while a veterinarian might write about the pathology of a particular disease, you can share what it means to take care of a pet with that disease.
- **Communication.** Writers serve as translators between technical experts and readers. A veterinarian might tell you about histolytes and platelets, but it's up to you to convert this information into terms the reader understands, and make it meaningful.
- **Balance.** An article written by a leading authority may be brilliant but one sided. Writers, however, can examine controversies from all sides, exploring various angles by interviewing experts with differing opinions or in different fields.

- **Tact.** Some experts simply aren't good at communicating with a "lay" audience, yet don't take kindly to having their work edited or "dumbed down." While "communication" may not be part of their toolkit, it's definitely part of yours! If you can bridge the gap between expert jargon and the reader, editors will find you a joy to work with, and will come back to you again and again. They'll also be happy to let *you* handle the difficulties of talking to experts!
- **Flexibility.** Experts, by definition, are specialists. An editor won't be able to ask an expert on dermatology for an article on obedience training. You, on the other hand, can cover both subjects, and find experts to interview for the information you lack. This makes you the more appealing contributor, because editors know they can count on you to handle many different needs.

USING EXPERIENCES WISELY

Once you've decided what experiences to write about, you must decide how to incorporate them into your article. While there are many ways to use experiences effectively, these four are perhaps the most common:

- **As a framework to support factual information.** Use your experience as a vehicle to convey the information you've gathered from interviews or research. Show how that information affected, or is reflected in, your experience. Use phrases like "we learned" or "we discovered" instead of "experts say."
- **As anecdotal material to illustrate factual information.** Use the information as your framework, and highlight each point with a personal example or illustration.
- **As an anecdotal lead and conclusion.** Some articles begin and end with a personal anecdote (e.g., "When Mary's house burned down, she had no idea her troubles were just beginning. . . ."). The body of the article, however, may be purely factual, with few personal details.
- **As a sidebar.** You may prefer to restrict your article to the facts, and use the personal experience as a sidebar to illustrate those facts. Another approach is to use the factual material as a sidebar to a personal story. This works particularly well when the information can be presented as a list.

STAY OUT OF THE PICTURE

Some years ago, I read an article about canoeing in the Alaska wilderness. Here's a paraphrased sample of the author's account:

> After a long day of paddling my canoe through the twisting waterways of the Someplaceorother Delta, I was glad to see the sandbar on which we would camp that night. The sun was setting, and the colors on the river reminded me of a blurred watercolor painting. I watched as a skein of geese descended toward some marsh I could not see, their wild cries reminding me just how far I had traveled from the land of cell phones and car alarms. As I steered my canoe to the shore, I marveled yet again at the magnificence of this wilderness. . . .

What's wrong with this picture? Nothing, if it is intended as a self-portrait. If it is intended as a portrait of a location, however, it fails miserably. Why? Because instead of seeing what the author sees, I am forced to watch the author "seeing" it. Instead of being allowed to react to the description, I am forced to share the author's reactions. The author can't get out of the way.

First-person narration isn't necessarily a bad thing. For some types of articles, it is desirable and appropriate. For others, however, it is out of place. One of the things an author needs to know is when to be part of the scene, and when to remain invisible, painting the picture without entering it.

When transcribing an interview, for example, watch out for references to self (I sat, I asked, I listened, I turned on my tape recorder, etc.). If you want to describe a location, don't write, "I settled myself in one of Mary's overstuffed chairs" when you could just as easily write that *Mary* settled herself in one of those chairs. Another way to remove yourself from the scene is to choose verbs that don't require an indirect object. For example, instead of saying "Mary proudly showed me her award," try "Mary proudly displayed her award."

When writing about exotic destinations, you want to convince the reader that you actually climbed that mountain, slept in that hotel, ate in that bistro. One way to sharpen your focus is to remove interpretive or reactive statements from your article. If you liked the food in a restaurant, don't say you *thought* it was good; just say that it *was* good. If the hotel bed was lumpy, don't say it *felt* lumpy, say it had lumps. Watch out, as well, for "me" phrases such as "they told me," "it seemed to me," or "he showed me." Whenever possible, use verbs that act alone. For example, instead of writing, "The locals told me that a ghost walks those halls at night," try "Locals say" or "Locals claim."

Because self-help and how-to articles often result from personal experience, it is tempting to include hefty doses of your experience in the article. Again, the best and most marketable type of article really isn't about you, but about the reader. Thus, the easiest way to stay out of it is to consciously shift from a "me" perspective to a "you" perspective. Whenever you find yourself writing in the first person, consider whether you could express the same information in another way, such as second person ("you can do this"), third person ("many people do this"), or directive ("do this!"). Each approach shifts the article's viewpoint away from the narrator and toward the reader.

Writing, by its nature, is an invisible occupation. Consequently, it can be tempting to try to stand for a moment in the spotlight of our own creations. The bottom line is simple, however: the less editors see of you, the more they'll want to see of your work.

SOME FINAL TIPS

Before you attempt to share a personal experience with your readers, it's important to examine where you yourself stand with respect to that experience. For example:

- **You must be over the experience.** If you don't know how the story ends, you're not in a position to write about it. If an event is painful, you need to have gained some closure before you write about it for others.
- **You must offer a solution.** Readers want to know how to change things, fix things, make things better. If you see no hope for improvement, write about something else.
- **You must offer the reader an attainable goal.** If your idea of the perfect vacation is to climb Mount Everest, that's fine, but your experience may find a rather limited readership. Offer readers an experience they can attain, and offer specific steps to help them attain it.

- **You must be able to demonstrate that your suggestions work.** If, for example, you're describing "Ten Ways to Get Your Novel Published," you'd better have published a novel!

Editors hunger for articles that combine useful, factual information with the warm, human touch of experience. Turning your story of "what I did" into an article on "how you can do it" is one of the best ways to save your material from the slush pile.

CHAPTER 10

Conducting Research on the Web

Now that you've selected an idea, developed it into a topic, and perhaps even outlined your article, the next step is to fill in the gaps. While you may have chosen a topic that draws upon your own experience and expertise, chances are that you're also going to have to do some research.

Once, this was a writer's most time-consuming task. Thanks to the Internet, however, research that once took weeks can often be handled in hours. No longer do you have to drive to the library, comb through catalogs to find a likely reference, search for the reference only to find that it's been checked out, ask for another book through interlibrary loan that will take weeks to arrive, and so forth. While libraries are still rich sources of information, a lot of the searching we once did in the stacks can now be accomplished with the keyboard.

DEFINING EFFECTIVE SEARCH TERMS

Search engines enable you to research general subject areas—for example, everything you wanted to know about seventeenth-century costumes—or look up the answers to specific questions ("What is the planetary mass of Jupiter?"). The key is defining an effective search term (or set of terms). Your goal is to choose terms that will bring up the most relevant sites, while excluding those that are irrelevant.

To accomplish this, your terms should be as specific as possible. Often, a good way to accomplish this is to specify two, three, or more precise words

that you want to find within the same document. For example, if you wanted to research "cat care," simply searching on "cats" would bring up a host
of inappropriate sites. However, by entering terms such as "cats" and "care,"
you'll get more focused results. An even better approach is to ask yourself
what type of phrase an article on "caring for cats" would be most likely to
contain, such as "how to care for your cat" or "how to take care of your cat."

Another approach is to determine what terminology an expert would
use. If you're researching "cancer in cats," for example, using a combination
of terms like "cats" and "cancer" will certainly produce good results. However, searching on "feline oncology" may be even more productive, as this is
the terminology that would be used by veterinarians.

To search for more than one word in the same document (e.g., "cats"
and "cancer"), simply type both words into the search engine. If you wish to
search for a specific phrase (for example, a person's name, a book title, or a
quotation), enter it in quotes. If you wish to *exclude* irrelevant results from
a search, try putting a minus sign in front of the word you'd like to exclude.
For example, if you want to search for information on limericks, but wish
to exclude search results relating to Limerick, Ireland, try entering the word
"limerick," followed by "-Ireland."

Keep in mind that search engines are specific. They can't "guess" or
provide information that is close. They can only find *exactly* what you enter.
(Google now does a decent job of coming up with alternate spellings if your
search term does provide any results—or, less helpfully, if it doesn't believe
you meant what you entered.) Most engines rank the results based on how
many times your search term appears in a document, or how close to the
beginning of the document it appears, along with a number of other variables. That doesn't mean, however, that you should look only at the first few
results provided. You may find that the perfect site is number thirty on the
list, or even number fifty. If you scan three pages of results without finding
a likely site, however, you probably need to refine your search.

Another thing to keep in mind is that different countries use different
spellings. If you're using American spellings, your search results may exclude non-US sites that could offer valuable information. If a word has both
an American and a British spelling, try both (e.g., "catalog" vs. "catalogue").
Similarly, if you're searching for information about a specific date, remember that while the US format would be "May 4, 2017," the European format
would be "4 May 2017."

IS IT ACCURATE?

There's a flip side to the ease with which we can now search for information online: the question of whether what we find is accurate! In the old days of checking out library books, you could be reasonably certain that most of those books had gone through some sort of review process; sadly, that's not true of most of what you'll find online.

The Internet offers just as much misinformation as information. One classic example is an article that appeared in the *Boston Globe* in July 2000, touching on the grim fates of the men who signed the Declaration of Independence. This article was based on an email that has been circulated since about 1995—and was passed along as "fact" by Ann Landers. As *American Journalism Review* columnist Carl Cannon pointed out, this email (and the *Globe* article) was, in fact, almost entirely false. According to the oft-quoted account, five signers of the Declaration were captured by the British and tortured to death as traitors, while nine fought and died in the Revolutionary War. In reality, no signers of the declaration were tortured by the British, while two were merely injured in the war (none died). One signer who supposedly "died in poverty" actually became governor of Pennsylvania.

The Internet is also a hotbed of urban legends, hoaxes, and scares. You've probably gotten plenty of "virus threats" characterized by the telltale phrase, "Please pass this on to everyone you know." Perhaps you've heard that the government is about to start charging everyone for using email to help subsidize the Post Office (it isn't). Even accurate information (such as the news that certain cold medicines were to be withdrawn from the market) gets circulated until it becomes misinformation simply because it is out of date.

How can you determine whether information is accurate? It's impossible to be 100 percent sure—but by asking the following questions about everything you read, you'll improve your chances.

- **Does the author, site, or information appear to exist primarily to support a particular point of view?** Does the material contain an obvious bias toward a particular point of view, agenda, or belief? If so, chances are that the material will be slanted toward that bias—even if it is factual—and there's also a good chance that information that does *not* support the author's views will be omitted.

- **Does the site seem overly emotional?** It's often easy to spot "emotional" sites—they're full of boldface phrases and LOTS OF CAPS. They look as if the author is "shouting" at you. If a site uses phrases like "Don't believe what those Commie bastards in government are trying to pull off!!!" I'm inclined to believe that the author has an axe to grind, and that accuracy may not be his highest priority.

- **Is the author trying to sell something?** I'm always wary of sites that purport to offer "valuable medical information" that "doctors won't tell you"—but just happens to be available in the author's book, or that supports a line of supplements or exercise equipment. That doesn't mean that an author is necessarily providing misinformation. But if the information seems primarily offered as a sales pitch, beware!

- **Who is the author?** Does the author have any credentials? The Internet is a place where anyone can post anything. Keep in mind, however, that a *lack* of credentials does not necessarily mean information is inaccurate. The Internet is also a place where thousands of ordinary folks post accurate information, based on their personal research. If the author doesn't have credentials, look for references, such as a bibliography, that can help confirm the information.

- **Is the site up to date?** Many sites post a copyright notice, usually at the bottom of the page. If the copyright notice has not been updated in the last five years, that's a good indication that the site hasn't been either. Some sites also post a "last updated" notice. Another way to determine if a site is current is to test a few of its links. If you find that most of the links are dead, you can assume the author hasn't updated the site recently.

- **Does the information agree with other sites on the same topic?** When I see ten sites that list Shackleton's death on January 5, and only one that lists it on January 4, I'm inclined to believe in the voice of the majority. By reviewing several sites on a topic, you'll get an idea for what the accepted facts are and be able to spot a site that seems out of line.

What About Wikipedia?

These days, one of the sources that is most likely to turn up in a search on almost any topic is Wikipedia. Wikipedia is a marvelous resource, packed with information on nearly any imaginable subject. And much of that information is excellent. But . . . is it a good resource for articles?

Wikipedia itself has a statement on this very question. This statement is aimed primarily at students conducting research for academic papers, but it applies equally to writers conducting research for articles. Wikipedia points out:

> Wikipedia is not considered a credible source. Wikipedia is increasingly used by people in the academic community, from freshman students to professors, as an easily accessible tertiary source for information about anything and everything. However, citation of Wikipedia in research papers may be considered unacceptable, because Wikipedia is not considered a credible or authoritative source.
>
> This is especially true considering anyone can edit the information given at any time, and although most errors are immediately fixed, some errors maintain unnoticed. However, it can be noted that Wikipedia's Good Articles and Featured Articles are some degree more advanced, professional, and generally more credible than an article not labeled Good or Featured. It is because these articles are reviewed heavily and edited many many times, passing a lot of "tests" before being confirmed Good or Featured, that they can be used for some deeper research than usual. It is Wikipedia's Featured Articles that are especially trustworthy in contrast to normal or even good articles, as they have to pass even harder "tests" to become featured, as they are to be "the best of Wikipedia," "a model for other articles," and thus, a much more reliable source than average articles.[5]

This short article goes on to compare Wikipedia to an encyclopedia, and points out that an encyclopedia should be a starting point for research rather than the sum total of that research. The same is true for an article. You wouldn't really want to create an article that was drawn entirely from an encyclopedia (we did this in grade school but, hopefully, have outgrown it). By all means use Wikipedia as a starting point. Then take a look at an

---

5   "Wikipedia: Academic use," last modified March 25, 2016, https://en.wikipedia.org/wiki/Wikipedia:Academic_use.

article's references and external links as a means of locating more information on your topic. But don't rely upon it as your sole or primary source.

USING PUBLISHED SOURCES

While it's appropriate (and often necessary) to conduct research online and in other published sources when writing an article, how you *use* that research in your article is another issue. Editors aren't fond of articles filled with quotes drawn from other published materials. They much prefer "live quotes" from interviews.

If you use quotes from published sources, be sure you don't cross the subtle line between research and plagiarism. It isn't always easy to determine where that line is. A certain amount of quoting, for example, is usually considered "fair use" under copyright law. Here are some do's and don'ts to consider when quoting published sources.

- **Use the information to *support* your article, not to actually *write* the article.** I once reviewed a piece on pet training that was based entirely on quotes drawn from various authors' published books. If the quotes had been removed, there would have been no article, which indicated that the writer really didn't have an original article of her own.
- **Use quotes sparingly.** The question of whether something is "fair use" often depends on the amount of material being quoted. You aren't likely to get in trouble if you quote a few lines or even a paragraph from a published work, but be cautious of using anything more extensive.
- **Make sure your quotes don't contain the "essence" of the previously published work.** If you quote an author so much that reading your article is like reading a condensed version of the author's own work, step back and rewrite.
- **If possible, go to the authors and get "live" quotes** instead of using material from their published works.
- **Attribute the information.** You don't need to footnote your information. Simply provide a reference within the text, such as "Dr. Gordon Chalmers of the American Institute for Research notes in his book, *Good Stuff by Chalmers*, that. . . ." Make sure that the

reader will not draw the conclusion that the information originates with *you* rather than with your *source.*

- **Provide a list of references for the editor.** Some publications insist that all facts be supported with references and documentation, so be sure you can show where your material came from.

Let me add one final reminder that shouldn't be needed, but is such a common problem that I feel I must mention it. Information that you find online is not "free" or "in the public domain."

Many people assume the term "public domain" means "freely available to the public." Since most information on the Internet is exactly that, many believe this means it's "in the public domain." Nothing could be further from the truth. Online information is protected by copyright just like information in a book, magazine, or newspaper. It's not "free to use." It's not free to copy. Misuse of that information can result in a suit for copyright infringement. It can also ruin your reputation as a writer—because when editors encounter a writer who borrows too heavily from online sources, word *does* get around.

CITING ONLINE REFERENCES

Many writers struggle with the question of how to cite Internet sources in a bibliography or within one's text. It doesn't fit into the typical bibliographical style we were taught in school. Often, online information offers no copyright or publication date. To confuse the matter further, different style guides have different requirements for Internet citations.

The basic approach, however, is to treat a web page much the way you'd treat any other citation. Start with the author, if you can find one. Then put the title of the material in quotes. Follow it with the name of the website or online publication, if there is one, and italicize that as you would the title of a book. Follow that with the URL, without the http:// prefix. After that, you can either add the date that the material was published and/or last modified, or, if this is absent, the date on which you accessed the material. (Some publications and style guides prefer that you include both dates.)

Hence, a citation of an article from my Writing-World.com website might look like this:

> Allen, Moira, "Rules vs. Tools," *Writing-World.com,*
> www.writing-world.com/coffee/coffee104.shtml, 2015 (accessed
> January 15, 2018).

This citation would be appropriate for a footnote or a bibliography entry. If you need to provide a citation within your text, you might refer to this as "Moira Allen's 2015 article, 'Rules vs. Tools,' from Writing-World.com (www.writing-world.com/coffee/coffee104.shtml)."

Again, different style guides have different requirements, so find out from your publisher which style guide they prefer before creating your citations! Here are some links to the Internet citation standards for various style guides:

- American Psychological Association (APA): *EasyBib,* www.easybib.com/reference/guide/apa/website
- American Psychological Association (APA): "Reference List: Electronic Sources (Web Publications)," *Owl: Purdue Online Writing Lab,* owl.english.purdue.edu/owl/resource/560/10/
- Modern Language Association (MLA): "MLA Works Cited: Electronic Sources (Web Publications)," *Owl: Purdue Online Writing Lab,* owl.english.purdue.edu/owl/resource/747/08/
- Chicago Manual of Style: "Chicago-Style Citation Quick Guide," *Chicago Manual of Style Online,* www.chicagomanualofstyle.org/tools_citationguide.html

The Purdue site makes the valuable point that web pages come and go. URLs change with depressing frequency, and a site that you found today may no longer be available, or accessible at the same address, by the time your article is published. Therefore, it's a good idea to make your own copy of web pages or articles that you use in your research. Purdue recommends "printing" the page in PDF format, so that you can retain an electronic file. This function will usually include the date of the printing, giving you a reference of when you accessed the information.

Today, the Internet offers writers instant access to a range of information that would have taken us days, weeks, or even months to seek out before. This means we can now tackle topics that once would have been nearly impossible to research effectively. However, it also means we have access to a realm of information that is unedited, unreviewed, and unauthenticated. So it is still up to us to be vigilant. The Internet puts an infinite array of data at our fingertips, but we must be more careful than ever to *check* that data, or we can spread misinformation that could damage our readers—and our careers.

As Wikipedia points out, the Internet is a great place to start your research. Your task as a writer, however, is to take it further, and give the reader information he can't find by doing, basically, the same search you did. Get interviews; dig deeper. This is the extra value that you, and only you, can bring to your material.

CHAPTER 11

Conducting Interviews

While you can get loads of wonderful information from the Internet (or from books or magazines), it's important to remember that an article is not a research paper. While some publications do accept material that is "pure research" (such as historical topics), most editors don't want articles that draw heavily on published sources. What they want is live quotes.

Interviews frequently scare new writers. We feel we don't have the credentials to ask for an interview, or that we may insult an expert by approaching them. I'll share a little secret: if you're not the outgoing, go-get-'em type, you may *never* enjoy doing interviews. I've been doing this for more than thirty years, and I still don't like making that call! But this can be your little secret (and mine). You can hate interviews and still present a professional "face" to your interviewee.

MAKING CONTACT

Your first step is to find appropriate experts to interview. If you're doing a profile, obviously the subject of that profile is your primary interviewee. However, you may also want to interview people who know that person (a boss, a spouse, a friend). If you're covering a specific topic, you'll want to interview experts on that topic. For an article on "cancer in cats," for example, you'd interview someone who specializes in animal cancer treatments. Often, the easiest way to find experts is to search on your topic online.

Many writers wonder whether to contact prospective interviewees before or after they have an assignment. It works both ways. Having a list of interviewees can help you *get* an assignment—and having an assignment is more likely to encourage interviewees to talk to you. I generally contact interviewees after I have an assignment in hand. However, if I believe my query will be strengthened by the promise of a valuable interview, I will contact that person in advance and ask if he would be willing to talk to me *if* I obtain the assignment. So far, no one has ever said no!

I don't recommend *conducting* interviews before you have an assignment. This could be a waste of your time and theirs. There is no point in conducting an interview if you don't know whether you can sell the article. You might also find that you need to gather information you didn't anticipate, if an editor suggests changes to your article idea after you've submitted a query. There are exceptions, of course. If you're traveling and come across someone who's perfect for a profile, don't miss the opportunity!

The next question is whether to interview by phone, email, or in person. If you're profiling someone local, an in-person interview is usually best, as you'll be able to pick up visual details such as the person's appearance, environment, mannerisms, and so on. Telephone interviews are the next most personal way to talk to someone, and are the best choice if you need to ask lots of questions and get clarification on the answers. They're also useful if you want to let the interviewee take more control of the interview and "follow their lead," rather than keeping the discussion to a predefined list of questions.

When setting up a telephone interview, be sure you know what time zone your interviewee is in and that you know exactly when the interview is supposed to occur in *both* time zones. There's nothing as embarrassing as discovering that the call you thought you were supposed to make at 9 a.m. your time is actually being received at 6 a.m. by your interviewee.

Email interviews can also be very effective. They are less intrusive than telephone interviews, and can be more comfortable for you if you're nervous about actually talking to someone. Many interviewees also prefer the option of responding in writing. An email interview gives them more time to consider the questions and compose thoughtful answers rather than having to answer "on the fly." Others, however, don't like writing, and may give much less useful responses in writing than by phone or in person. (I'll discuss email interviews in more detail below.)

Once you find a potential interviewee and decide how you'd like to conduct the interview, the next step is asking for the interview. Remember, *the interviewee doesn't need to know you're nervous.* You may be shaking in your boots; she'll never know. If you're going to interview someone by phone or in person, the first contact should usually be made by telephone. Simply call the person and explain who you are and what you are writing about. For example:

> "Hi, my name is Moira Allen, and I'm working on an article for *Cats Magazine* about cancer in cats. Would you be willing to talk to me about some of the treatments your clinic provides for feline cancer patients?"

If you don't have an assignment yet, just say, "I'm working on an article about. . . ." Nine times out of ten, they'll never ask what publication it's for. If they do, just say "I'll be pitching this to . . ." and fill in the publication name.

If the person agrees to do an interview, ask when would be a good time. Frequently, the person may say, "Now would be a good time," so *be prepared to do the interview on the spot.* Have your interview questions ready and make sure you've called when *you* have time to do the interview. It's embarrassing to have to tell your interviewee, "Oh, sorry, I don't have time to talk to you right now; can we schedule an appointment?" If the person *does* want to do the interview at another time, he may want to know how long the interview will take, so you should have a time estimate. Generally, you should call the person for the interview. The exception is when a person can't guarantee being available at a certain time and would prefer to control the timing of the interview by calling you. (Business folks, for example, often need to figure out when to work an interview into their schedule, and will often arrange to call you; in this case, expect the call to come in from the interviewee's secretary, and prepare to wait until you're transferred to the person you want to talk to.)

If you aren't comfortable cold-calling a person, or can't find a phone number, try to make contact by email. The same approach works just fine (leaving out the "Hi" part). Close your email with something like "Could I call you next week to discuss this?" Include your phone number; some people will be happy to call you back.

BEFORE THE INTERVIEW

By taking the right steps to set up your interview, you can ensure that you make a good impression, get the information you want, and perhaps gain a long-term contact you can use for future articles.

- **Prepare your questions in advance.** By having a list of questions handy when you set up the interview, you'll be able to answer an interviewee who asks, "What do you want to talk about?" Create open-ended questions rather than questions that can be answered yes or no. For example, if you're interviewing a children's author, don't ask, "Do you enjoy writing children's books?" If the author just says "yes," you have to come up with another question, like "why?" Instead, ask something like "What do you enjoy most about writing children's books?" or "What is the most fulfilling part of writing children's books?"

- **Ask for a specific amount of time.** Do you want half an hour? An hour? This will help your interviewee schedule the appointment (and is especially important if you're scheduling through a secretary).

- **Be honest about your purpose.** If you don't have a firm assignment, don't pretend that you do. You can, however, explain that you're pitching the article to a specific market. Don't claim credentials you don't have. Unless you're trying to interview a celebrity, you'll find that most people are willing to talk to "ordinary" writers.

- **Don't confuse time zones.** Always refer to the interviewee's time zone when making appointments—for example, "I'll call you at 2 p.m. your time." Don't even mention your own time zone; if you say something like "I'll call you at 2 p.m. your time, which is 4 p.m. my time," you may confuse the interviewee (and yourself!).

- **Let the interviewee schedule the interview.** Often, you'll be asked what time is convenient. Instead of setting a time, suggest a range of times, such as "any afternoon next week," or "any time on Wednesday or Thursday." This gives the interviewee flexibility to work you into the schedule. Try not to leave interviews to the last minute. While many interviewees try to respect deadlines, you never know when someone will be out of town, too busy, or otherwise unavailable.

- **Ask how the interviewee would prefer to be interviewed.** Many people prefer email interviews, as this allows them to respond on their own time, and gives them the leisure to provide more in-depth answers. However, if you feel you may need to follow up on questions, or need more control over the interview, you may prefer to push for a telephone interview. Another option is to send your initial questions by email, and then follow up on additional questions or clarifications by phone.

- **Be prepared to email your questions to the interviewee in advance.** Business executives often prefer this, as it enables them to prepare for the specific types of information you're looking for. This won't always work if you're conducting a sensitive, personal, or controversial interview, but it does work if you're gathering basic facts.

DURING THE INTERVIEW

Keep your interviewee happy with the interview process by remaining courteous and professional—no matter what! As long as you remain polite, your interviewee is unlikely to be offended, even if your questions are sensitive or controversial.

- **Be prepared.** Again, having a list of questions in advance can help you guide the interview in the direction you want it to go. It can also help you double-check to make sure you've gotten all the information you need. Note that you may not actually ask every one of your questions. Often, an interviewee's response to one question will give you the answers to other questions.
- **Remember that the interview is about the interviewee, *not* about you.** You're there to gather information, not to judge the person or the material. It doesn't matter how you feel about the person, whether you agree or disagree with her perspective, or whether you like what you hear. If you remain calm and nonjudgmental, you're likely to get far more material than if you react negatively to the responses.
- **Interact with the interviewee.** Don't just fire off questions and jot down the answers. Respond. Make "uh-huh" and "I see" and "Oh, really?" noises. Let the interviewee know you're listening and interested in the information. Volunteer an occasional comment that shows you understand what you are being told.
- **Let the interviewee set the tone.** Don't assume familiarity; let the interviewee determine whether the discussion proceeds formally or informally. Don't volunteer personal information or "chat" unless the interviewee has indicated this seems appropriate.

- **Pay attention to nonverbal parts of the interview.** If you're writing a profile and interview someone in person, jot down details about the person's surroundings, appearance, tone of voice—anything will give the reader a clearer picture. Did the person's clothing clash with the "personality" you expected? (For example, a rich CEO wearing torn cutoffs.) What did you notice about the person's environment? Was it filled with mementos, or barren and austere? Did it seem to reflect the interviewee's interests and personality, or clash with them? What did you notice about the person's body language and facial expressions? What questions make your interviewee tense? Does the person's expression or body language match his words? For example, if someone says, "I have a wonderful marriage," but sits back with crossed arms and a frown, you might have doubts about the statement.

- **Keep the interview on track.** Interviewees often go off on tangents. In some cases, a tangent can bring up more interesting information, but if you have only a short period of time for the interview, you'll need to bring the conversation back on track. One way to do this is to use the interviewee's earlier responses to redirect the interview. For example, you might refocus the conversation by saying something like, "Getting back to what you were saying earlier about. . . ."

- **Don't be afraid of silences.** Silences are wonderful tools. They make people uncomfortable, so people tend to try to *fill* a silence. If you're not getting a response to a question, or if the response seemed too short or insufficient, just wait a moment without saying anything. Often this will cause the person to say more. Don't rush to fill silences yourself!

- **Always thank the interviewee.** If you think you might have follow-up questions, ask if you can contact the interviewee later (briefly) with further questions or clarifications as needed.

A common question is whether to record interviews or transcribe them by hand. I prefer both. I hate transcribing recorded notes, so I try to write everything down, but a recording provides backup if I can't read my handwriting, or if the interviewer talks so fast or gives so much information that I can't get it all down. It's also a good way to support your article later, in case an interviewee claims you've misquoted him. Always save your recordings for a couple of years after the article is published.

When I interview by phone, I usually type responses directly into the computer. Some devices will enable you to make a recording of a conversation. If you do so, be sure to inform the interviewee that you're recording the call. Different states have different laws about the legality of recording a telephone call without the knowledge of the other party; for more information on recording interviews, see the *Reporter's Recording Guide* at www .rcfp.org/reporters-recording-guide/introduction.

AFTER THE INTERVIEW

An interview isn't necessarily over just because you've hung up the phone. You may need to come back for more information or clarification. You may also want to call upon that person's expertise for other articles. The following courtesies can help keep you in the interviewee's good will.

- **Send a thank-you note by email or snail mail.** Let the interviewee know when and where the article will be published, or provide that information once you have it.
- **Ask your editor to send complimentary copies of the issue to each interviewee.** Be sure to include a list of interviewees (with their addresses) when you send in your article. I like to contact interviewees once an article comes out to make sure they received their complimentary copy. If they didn't, send a copy yourself; it will be appreciated. (In some cases, the editor may send you a PDF file of your article, which makes it very easy to forward a copy on to your interviewees.)

Many interviewees will try to pressure you into letting them review (and in some cases, approve) an article before it goes to the editor. The consensus among authors and editors on this point is to say *no*. Never promise to let an interviewee see your article before it goes to press. Never give an interviewee approval power over your article. If an interviewee puts pressure on you to do this, simply say you're sorry, but your editor won't permit it.

One reason many interviewees want to see an interview before it is published is because they've had bad experiences with writers who want to put their own, biased spin or slant on an interview. In such a case, be understanding but firm. (If you have done previous interviews that demonstrate your balanced and professional reporting style, share those with the interviewee; they may put his mind at ease about your approach.)

The only exception to this rule is when you're interviewing someone about a highly technical subject and want to be absolutely sure you've gotten all the information right. In such a case, the only interest the interviewee is likely to have in reviewing the article is the same as yours: accuracy. If I have any doubts about how I've transcribed and presented the interview information, I may pass it back to the interviewee for a check, but *not* for preapproval.

EMAIL INTERVIEWS

Email can be an effective and convenient way to conduct an interview, and is often appreciated by busy experts who don't have time for a face-to-face or telephone interview. It enables you to compose questions carefully rather than on the fly, and gives your interviewee time to respond carefully as well. Another plus is that the interviewee gets to do all the typing! Email also offers a good way to follow up on a traditional interview when seeking clarification or additional information.

Email interviews are less effective when you're trying to develop a profile that includes not only the individual's words but also your observations of his appearance, actions, skills, emotions, tone of voice, and other nonverbal cues. They are also less effective if you're more likely to get information from a natural exchange of questions and answers than from a predefined script. In an email interview, you can't change direction if a more promising tangent emerges from the conversation, you can't nudge the interviewee back on track if the conversation strays, you can't ask follow-on questions if your first questions don't elicit enough information, and you can't ask for immediate explanations or clarification.

The following strategies can help you develop and refine an email interview:

- **Determine your goals before writing your questions.** Decide exactly what you need to know; then develop concise questions that will best elicit that information.

- Ask open-ended questions rather than questions that can be answered "yes" or "no."
- Explain why you're asking a particular question, so the interviewee knows what type of response you're looking for.
- Let the interviewee know what audience you're writing for, so the interviewee will know how detailed or technical the information should be.
- Keep your questions as clear, uncomplicated, and short as possible.
- Keep your list of questions short. Ten is good; twenty is likely to tax an interviewee's patience.
- List your questions numerically, and leave space between each question for the interviewee to insert the answer.
- Include a final "open" question, such as, "Is there anything else you'd like to say on this subject that hasn't been covered above?"
- Let the interviewee know when you need the answers. Remember that the interviewee is doing you a favor, and is under no obligation to meet your deadline.
- Don't be afraid to ask for clarification, or to follow up on questions or answers that beg for additional information. And always thank your interviewee!

Email Surveys

Another way to gather information via email is to conduct a survey. Email enables you to send a list of questions to hundreds of potential respondents, at no cost.

At the same time, caution is in order. Some respondents may regard a survey as a form of spam. Your email should state the nature and purpose of the survey as quickly, succinctly, and courteously as possible. Assure respondents of privacy, and guarantee that you won't cite anyone by name or organization without permission. If you're soliciting comments as well as statistics, ask respondents to indicate whether or not they may be quoted, and how they should be cited.

Like interview questions, survey questions should be short, clear, and well organized. Unlike interview questions, however, survey questions should encourage "yes/no" answers, or answers to a multiple-choice selection. Respondents are more likely to answer a short questionnaire than a long one.

An easy format is to follow each question with the answer options (e.g., "Yes" or "No") on separate lines. Place a set of parentheses in front of each option, with space for a response. Here's an example from an email survey I sent to a number of magazine editors:

1. Do you accept email queries?
   ( ) Yes
   ( ) No

2. How do you prefer to receive manuscripts?
   ( ) Hardcopy (printed)
   ( ) On disk
   ( ) By email, in the body of the message
   ( ) As an email attachment

This enables the respondent to insert an "x" in the appropriate space and mail the form back as a reply. If you're offering a multiple-choice question that could have more than one answer, indicate whether you want the respondent to "check only one" or "check all that apply."

To ensure your respondents' privacy, place all your survey addresses in the "bcc" (blind copy) field of your header. Leave the "to" field blank. If you have a large number of addressees, send the survey in several batches rather than all at once.

When you mail your survey, several may bounce back as undeliverable. Keep track of these bounces so you know exactly how many surveys reached their destination. This will enable you to calculate the correct percentage of responses. For example, if you send out one hundred surveys, get ten back as undeliverable, and receive fifty responses, you have a 55 percent response rate.

The bulk of your responses will typically arrive in a flood within the first two or three days of your mailing. After that, the flood will taper to a trickle. At some point, you'll have to decide when it's time to cut off the survey and tally the results, even if you're still getting an occasional response. I recommend setting up a separate folder in your email program to store responses until you're ready to use them.

Once you've completed the survey, make a list of the respondents and send them a thank-you note for participating. If respondents are interested in the results of your survey, let them know when and where the article will appear.

Sites like SurveyMonkey.com and SurveyPlanet.com make it possible to set up an online survey. Then, all you need to do is send the link to your respondents. Some respondents may feel more comfortable dealing with a legitimate survey site than an email from an unknown writer. Plus, survey sites add the advantage of collating your responses for you. However, you may have to pay a fee to get the level of response you need, as free surveys are limited both in terms of how many respondents you can have and how many questions you can ask.

USING INTERVIEW MATERIAL

Once the interview is finished, write up your notes as soon as possible, while they are still fresh in your mind. You'll often find you have too much information to fit in your article, but that's fine. Some of what you've gathered might be the basis of another article, or you might find that a personal experience makes a great sidebar. Interview material is like raw ore; your task now is to refine it, and find the precious metal hidden inside. (By the way, by granting an interview, the interviewee is considered to have granted you the right to use those responses, not only in the original article but also in other articles you might choose to write.)

I compared interview material to ore, and that's exactly what it is. You don't want to dump everything the person said into your article. Instead, you want to mine it for quotes that add *spice* to the article (assuming it is not a straight Q&A piece). You may find your article works best if you paraphrase most of the interview and add direct quotes that bring home the point you're trying to make.

Here's the text of an email interview I conducted with author Kate Elliott:

> *The American Heritage Dictionary* defines culture as "the totality of socially transmitted behavior patterns, arts, beliefs, institutions, and all other products of human work and thought characteristic of a community or population." According to the *Oxford English Dictionary*, the word "culture' is related to 'cultivate" in the sense of tending crops.
>
> Words grow from specific roots for a reason. Definitions of "cultivate" include "To improve or prepare (land), as by plowing or fertil-

izing, for raising crops . . . To grow or tend . . . To promote the growth of . . . To nurture . . . To form and refine." (*The American Heritage Dictionary*)

I think that these definitions and that relationship between culture and cultivation can give writers clues as to how to approach writing, and creating, a "believable" culture in fantasy or science fiction novel.

For that purpose, one can draw out the metaphor of tillage, however labored it might become in time: When the writer creates a culture in the science fiction/fantasy field, she starts with untilled ground, a kind of blank slate. That ground has to be prepared, tended, formed, and refined. A culture, likewise, must show arts, beliefs, institutions (to whatever extent), technologies, and roles. In the role of "cultivator," the writer can, in addition, not merely impose her own notions onto that developing culture but see what comes of giving it a little room to evolve naturally in the course of planning and writing the novel.

Here's what I wrote in the final article:

Elliott likes to draw an analogy between "culture" and "cultivate," two words that spring from the same root. "When a writer creates a culture, she starts with untilled ground, a kind of blank slate. The ground has to be prepared, tended, formed, refined. Likewise, a culture must show arts, beliefs, institutions, technologies, and roles. In the role of 'cultivator,' a writer doesn't simply impose her own notions onto that developing culture, but gives it a little room to evolve naturally in the course of planning and writing the novel."

The one absolute rule of interviews is this: *never twist a person's words to imply something other than what the person meant.* Do not use quotes out of context, or partial quotes, to make it seem someone said (or intended) something they did not.

Other issues are less clear. For example, there are two schools of thought on "cleaning up" quotes. Let's say you have interviewed someone who does not express himself clearly or in an educated way. Maybe his quote sounds something like "Well, uh, y'know, really, that's tough, but I'd have to say,

I think, probably, I'd want to see the guy fry, y'know?" Some writers and editors suggest using the entire quote. Others would use only the last eight words (or even cut the final "y'know"). The "use it like it is no matter what" school says that if a quote is grammatically incorrect, you still use it just "as is." Others feel this can cause unnecessary embarrassment for the interviewee, and that minor corrections to grammar are acceptable as long as they don't change the meaning and tone of the quote.

This can get a bit sticky when you're doing email interviews. When you interview someone on the phone, you don't know whether the person knows how to spell. Nor does it matter, because you're writing it down yourself and are responsible for the spelling. But what if a person has sent you an email full of misspellings? Should you use it verbatim (or riddle it with "sics" to indicate that he, not you, was the source)? My view is that, unless you have a *profound* reason to keep those errors, it's better to clean it up. Not everyone has a perfect grasp of spelling, and I believe an interviewee should not be made to look stupid—especially when that person has done me the favor of giving me the information I asked for. My goal is to present the interviewee's ideas, not his education level.

Finally, remember that an interview is *not* about the *interviewer*. I've read too many interviews in which the writer keeps intruding with her own thoughts, reactions, interpretations, and personal observations. Don't write something like "I really felt a connection with what Mary was saying about her marriage, because of my own bad experiences. . . ." If the article is about *Mary*, what are you doing in this picture?

This can be not only intrusive, but also unethical if the interviewer attempts to "interpret" the interviewee's comments for the audience—especially if the interviewer is trying to cast the interviewee in a bad light. If you feel that an interviewee is a horrible person, let that person's words speak for themselves and let readers draw their own conclusions.

CHAPTER 12

The Submission Process

Developing a marketable article is only half the battle. The other half is getting that article *to* the market. Here, the appearance of professionalism can count as much or more as your actual credentials. Even if you've never published a single article, you can impress editors by providing a professional-looking submission package.

Your first step is to review the guidelines. These will tell you what type of material a publication is looking for, the preferred word count, whether to send queries or complete manuscripts, the payment rates and rights required, and whom to contact. The guidelines may also specify response time—how long you should wait before following up on a submission. Demonstrate your professionalism by following these guidelines to the letter!

WHOM TO CONTACT

Contact information in *Writer's Market* listings is often out of date. Before you submit, therefore, check the publication's website. The "contact us" section may list the current editors, and even provide their emails.

Generally, guidelines will specify where to send submissions. If you can't find any guidelines, check the publication's masthead (either in print or online). Usually the best contact is the *Managing Editor*, who makes most acceptance decisions. If there is no managing editor, send material to the *Editor*, unless the guidelines say otherwise.

For a publication with several departments, you'll generally send submissions to a *Features Editor* or *Articles Editor*. Or, you may have to send a piece to a specific *Department Editor*, such as a health editor, food editor, fitness editor, or some other department head. If you can't determine where to submit from a publication's guidelines or masthead, don't hesitate to contact the publication and ask!

Don't send material to an assistant editor, editor-in-chief, or contributing editor, unless the guidelines say to do so. Assistant editors usually don't make acceptance decisions, while an editor-in-chief generally supervises a group of publications but doesn't handle the management of any one publication. A contributing editor isn't even on staff; this is a title given to a freelance contributor or columnist.

WHAT TO SEND

A publication's guidelines should tell you what to submit and what *not* to submit (e.g., query or manuscript). You may also be asked to send the following:

Clips

Many publications ask writers to "query with clips." Clips are copies (print or electronic) of published articles. Note that "published" doesn't have to mean "paid"—clips from reputable nonpaying publications are acceptable. (This does not include high school newspapers, company newsletters, church bulletins, or self-published materials.) Try to match your clips to the subject matter of the market. If you don't have relevant clips, use those from your most prestigious publications.

If you've been published online, a printout of the article is acceptable. If you're sending a query by email, you can also reference the URLs of your online publications. Never send a clip as an attachment unless requested.

Unless a publication states it won't work with unpublished writers, don't let a lack of clips discourage you. Unpublished writers often fear they can't get published without clips, but even publications that ask for clips will often accept other credentials in their stead.

Resume

Some publications ask writers to "query with resume." Generally, this means the publication is looking for writers with relevant credentials who can handle assignments. Such a market is usually not open to beginning freelancers.

Publications List

Sooner or later, you'll need to develop a publications list to send with queries. This is a list of the articles you've published, where they appeared, and when. You can prepare it on your regular letterhead, or create a separate sheet with your name and address and other contact information centered at the top. I recommend starting your list as soon as you publish your first article. It's easier to keep track as you go along than to try to recall or look up that information later.

List publications chronologically, with the most recent first. Include the article title, the publication in which it appeared, and the publication date. If an article appeared online, you can also include the URL. Your list will look something like this:

"My Current Article," *TravelDigestDaily.com*, forthcoming, June 2019
"My Latest Article," *Dog Fancy Magazine*, June 2017
"My Next Article," *Entrepreneur*, February 2017
"My First Article," *Newport News Gazette*, December 2016

Eventually (yes, really!) your list will grow too long to fit on a single page. At that point, it's a good idea to break it into smaller lists focusing on subject areas (garden publications, pet publications, etc.). It's still advisable to keep a master list for your own records. You may also wish to subdivide your list by *type* of publication—books, magazines, newspapers, online publications. You might also include a section for awards and prizes.

SASE or Return Postcard

Publications that ask for submissions by mail generally expect a writer to include a self-addressed, stamped return envelope with submissions.[6] Some, however, prefer a return postcard with "check-off" options. The postcard is used for rejections; a publisher will usually send an acceptance letter on their own stationery. A return postcard should look something like this:

---

[6] Many people wonder how to *pronounce* this term: Is it "sayse" or "S-A-S-E"? The answer is pronounce it whichever way you want. In writing the term, however, it's generally considered correct to refer to "a SASE" rather than "an S-A-S-E."

Date: _____
RE: Article Title

_____ We have received the article [or query] listed above and will give you a decision by (date) _____.
_____ We have decided to accept the article/query listed above, and will send you a formal letter of acceptance/contract shortly.
_____Sorry, we can't use this material.

Editor's Name: _____

You can obtain postage-paid postcards at the post office. If you expect to use only a few, it's easy to type each one individually. If you plan to send lots, however, have them printed at a copy shop.

Bio

Usually, you won't be asked for a bio until an article has been accepted, but if you're sending a complete article, save the editor time by including one at the end of the piece. You don't need writing credentials to produce a bio. Instead, consider what you could say about your experience or expertise that relates to your article. For example, if you've written about hiking with dogs, your bio might read:

LilyAnne Rizzetta has hiked with her dogs in nearly twenty-four state and national parks, including Yosemite, Yellowstone, and the Grand Canyon. Rizzetta is also an accomplished backpacker and "family camper." She lives (and writes) in Alpharetta, Georgia, where she shares her home with a husband, two cats, and four Samoyeds.

Most publications want a bio of between 50 and 100 words. You can include a web address in your bio, if your site is either a basic writer's site about you, or relevant to the article. If your site is on a completely different topic, however—your article is about hiking and your blog is about parenting—don't bother to list it. Don't include your email or any other contact information.

Publicity Photo

Some publications like to include a photo of each contributor. It's wise to prepare for this in advance. While you can use a snapshot in a pinch, I recommend having a professional photo taken. You're trying to create a professional image, and a professional photo is part of your business package. A publicity photo can be a formal head shot or candid (a shot of you at your desk, for example). Since color photos can always be reproduced in black and white, get your shot in color. Make sure the photographer has experience with publicity photos; don't go to a department store photo salon. You may need to provide the photographer's name for copyright purposes.[7]

FORMATTING YOUR MANUSCRIPT

Manuscript format is a fairly simple issue. Yet some people like to make it complicated—from editors who prefer a particular style and therefore declare that *all* editors want the same style, to writers' groups who believe one must use a particular font and layout and so forth. If conflicting advice on format has left you confused, the following tips should help.

Print Manuscripts: The Basics

Most editors in any genre (articles, fiction, etc.) want a manuscript to conform to certain basic requirements. It should be printed on good paper (20-pound bond minimum, never erasable), of the standard size in your country. If you're in America, use 8.5" × 11" paper. If you're in Europe, use A4 paper. Don't worry about using the paper size of your target market. Editors *do* understand that international submissions will arrive on the paper that is available in the sender's country and not their own.[8]

Your manuscript should be double-spaced, with one-inch margins on all sides. Use a clear, readable font (more on this later). Don't put an extra line between paragraphs; indicate paragraphs with a five-space indent or tab. (If you will be submitting the same manuscript electronically once it is

---

7   For more information on publicity photos, see "Your Publicity Photo," by Patricia Fry, at www.writing-world.com/promotion/prphoto.shtml.

8   There is one exception to this. If you are submitting a manuscript electronically, be sure to set the page settings for the country of destination rather than your own. If, for example, you have set your page layout to A4, and you send that manuscript to a US publication, it won't print properly.

accepted, I recommend using tabs, as setting an indent can create problems when the editor is trying to reformat the piece for publication.)

Articles should begin about halfway down the page. Your name, address, and other contact information (phone, email, etc.) should be placed in the upper left corner of the manuscript, in a single-spaced block. The word count of the article (rounded to the nearest ten or fifty) should go in the upper right corner. Your title should be centered on the page at the halfway point, in a larger font than the text (boldfacing is fine). Skip two lines, and center your byline (either your real name or your pen name) in a slightly smaller font. Skip another two lines and begin your article.

Running headers are expected on articles, short stories, novels, and nonfiction books. A running header should appear at the top of every page (except the first), and include your last name, the title of the article or story (or a keyword or two if the title is too long), and the page number. For example, a running header for an article titled "A History of Feline Chiropractic Care" might look like this:

Allen/Feline Chiropractic/ . . . 2

Contest submissions are formatted much like regular submissions, with one exception: your contact information should be included on a cover sheet. Do not put your name or any identifying information on the first page of the piece itself, and do not include your name in the running header. The cover sheet will be removed from your submission, so that judges won't know anything about the author of the piece. If you see a listing that asks for work to be submitted in "contest format," this is what it means.

Fonts and Format

People get into heated discussions over what fonts editors prefer. Some claim that all editors want manuscripts in Courier (which looks like a typewriter font). Lately, some editors and writers have come to prefer Arial. So what do editors really want?

The truth is, most editors don't care, as long as the font is readable. (In a survey I conducted of over five hundred editors, 90 percent expressed "no preference" with regard to font.) Very few editors will reject your manuscript because it happens to be in Palatino instead of Arial. Generally, it's best to use a 12-point font size, and to choose a font that doesn't squish letters together too closely.

The rationale for Courier dates to the days when editors did an eyeball "guesstimate" of line lengths to determine how much space a piece would fill in on the printed page. Courier is a fixed-width or no-proportional font, meaning that each letter takes up the same amount of space. This made it easier to estimate how an article would appear when typeset. Today, however, few editors need to do this.

Arial is a nice, readable font, but it is also a sans serif font, which many editors don't like. (To see the difference between a serif and sans serif font, compare Arial to Times.) Don't use this font unless the guidelines request it.

The bottom line is simple. If an editor expresses a preference, or if you've heard through the grapevine that an editor is obsessive over fonts (some are), use the font the editor prefers. If your editor has expressed no preference, don't assume he has one, and don't agonize over it.

Electronic Submissions

Electronic submissions, of course, break nearly all the rules listed above. Many editors do accept electronic submissions, and some have complex guidelines as to exactly how these must be formatted. Some accept attachments (usually in Microsoft Word); others prefer that the submission be embedded within the text of the email. It's also becoming increasingly common for publications to have an online submissions form, where you will copy and paste your article or story or even your query.

If you're sending a submission as an attachment, format it just as you would a print submission. If you are asked to include it within your email, you'll need to follow the email format guidelines described in chapter 7. Don't double-space your text. However, you *will* need to add an extra line between paragraphs, rather than adding tabs. Include your contact information and word count at the beginning of the email, before the title.

It's also a good idea to email a copy of your submission to yourself *before* you send it to the editor, just to make sure that it came through correctly.

Don't submit a piece in HTML format, even if your email program allows you to do so. Yes, HTML is prettier than text—but text is safer. If your piece includes a considerable amount of formatting, such as bold and italics, try to arrange to send it as an attachment.

Finally, never send attachments, such as clips or photos, until you have confirmed that it's OK to do so. If you're going to send a large number of photos, the editor may prefer you to submit them on a CD or flash drive.

Counting the Words and Other Format Issues

Another issue that confuses writers is how to estimate the word count of a manuscript. You will still occasionally read some complex formula ("count the number of lines on each page, divide by X, then multiply by . . .").

These formulas are left over from the days when we had no way to count words other than ticking them off with a pencil, and editors estimated the printed length of a manuscript based on such formulas. Today, the word count feature of your word processing program is perfectly acceptable. You also don't have to be precise. If your article is 1,562 words, call it 1,550. If it's 1,975 words, call it 2,000.

One space or two? Those of us who are old enough to have taken typing classes remember the rule: put two spaces after periods and colons. Today, we are told to leave only one space, as modern typesetting programs don't need this extra space.

While many editors prefer that you leave only one space after all punctuation, it doesn't really matter. If you're "old school" and automatically hit that second space, it's not going to result in a rejection. It's also perfectly easy, after you've finished your manuscript, to do a global search and replace and replace every double space with a single.

Should tabs be five spaces or fewer? Again, in the old days of typing, we were taught that tabs should be a standard five spaces. Most word processing programs have default tab settings at every half inch. To many writers (and editors), however, such tabs look far too large. There's no longer a hard-and-fast rule on tabs; just make sure that the editor can tell that it *is* a tab.

Should you underline or italicize? The practice of underlining words to indicate italics also dates from the age of the typewriter. Word processors enable one to indicate italics and boldface type directly. However, many editors still prefer underscoring (it often makes text easier to read). Check the publication's guidelines to see if they express a preference, and if they do, then follow it. If they don't, I use italics and bold as needed.

One area that often confuses writers when it comes to italics is how to indicate a character's thoughts. Although this is primarily an issue in fiction, it deserves a mention. Thoughts are typically italicized in the print version of a story or article rather than placed in quotes like dialogue. In your manuscript, therefore, you can indicate a person's thoughts with either italics or underlining.

For more information on manuscript format, I recommend *The Writer's Digest Guide to Manuscript Format*, which covers a variety of manuscript types, including poetry, essays, books, and scripts.

DO YOU NEED A COVER LETTER?

When you submit a hard-copy manuscript to an editor, should you include a cover letter? On the one hand, a manuscript stuffed into an envelope all by itself seems so—well, raw! On the other hand, stating the obvious ("enclosed is a manuscript . . .") seems an insult to an editor's intelligence.

Under certain circumstances, a cover letter can be an important addition to your manuscript:

- **When material has been requested.** It doesn't hurt, especially if you're new to a publication, to remind the editor that the manuscript is requested rather than unsolicited. Simply state, "Enclosed is the manuscript you requested in your letter of (date)," or "that we discussed in our conversation/email/whatever of (date), titled (title)."
- **To provide supplementary information.** You may wish to note that you can provide photos, illustrations, contacts, sidebars, or sources of additional information. If a publication needs to fact-check your article, a cover letter is a good place to list your sources.
- **To provide information about yourself.** If the article is unsolicited, use your cover letter to list your credentials, expertise, or other qualifications for authoring the piece. You can also use it to list the credentials of experts you've interviewed for the article.
- **When you write under a pseudonym.** In your cover letter, provide your real name and address, along with the pseudonym you wish to use as your byline.
- **To provide a record of your article and contact information.** Your manuscript may be passed from one editor to another, so a cover

letter gives an editor an easy way to find your name and address even when the manuscript isn't on her desk.

- **When you have been referred to the editor.** If you have been referred to an editor by someone the editor knows, such as another contributor, mention this in your cover letter. For example, you might say, "Sue Jones, your nutrition columnist, suggested that I send this piece to you."

Your cover letter should be prepared in a standard business format, as follows:

Moira Allen

1234 Mystreet • Mytown, VA 20151
(XXX) 555–1234
editors@writing-world.com

March 15, 20XX

Editor's Name
Publication
Address
City/State/Zip

Dear Mr./Ms. Jones:

Enclosed is a manuscript of XXXX words, titled "Xxxx," for your consideration. A SASE is enclosed for your response; the manuscript itself need not be returned. Thank you for your time and consideration; I look forward to hearing from you.

Sincerely,
Moira Allen

Encs. (optional)

Nine Things to Leave Out of Your Letter

While a professional cover letter can't hurt you, an unprofessional letter can. Don't send a letter that might prejudice an editor against you, or convey the impression that you're not a professional writer. That means avoiding the following topics:

1. **Irrelevant personal information.** One of the cover letters that has stuck in my memory for years began, "Dear Editor, I am an unpublished mother of three. . . ." Don't offer information about your age, gender, family status, or anything else unrelated to your article.

2. **Announcements of your unpublished status.** Don't try to play on an editor's sympathies by explaining this is your first article.

3. **Hype.** Don't tell the editor that your article is brilliant, thoughtful, exciting, inspiring, or sure to please. Editors prefer to make these decisions for themselves.

4. **Apologies about your article (or yourself).** Some writers apologize for flaws they perceive in their articles or themselves. If your article is flawed, don't send it, fix it! If you have doubts about your abilities, keep them to yourself.

5. **Explanations of why your material doesn't match the publication's guidelines.** If your article is twice as long as the word limit, or written from the viewpoint of your dog, or typed on pink paper, don't explain. Rewrite.

6. **An explanation of why the article differs from your assignment or proposal.** Sometimes a change is appropriate (you found new information, or couldn't contact an expert you hoped to speak with). However, if you must change the focus of an article after it has been assigned, discuss this with the editor in advance.

7. **Demands.** Don't tell an editor what you expect to be paid, or what terms you offer, especially if these differ from the terms specified in the guidelines. If you wish to negotiate payment or contract terms, do so before you submit the article or after you become an established contributor.

8. **Opinions of your work from family, friends, or writing teachers.** Editors don't care what your loved ones think of your writing!

9. **A list of prior rejections.** Never tell an editor that a submission has already been rejected five times. Editors are likely to assume there was a good reason for this!

When submitting a manuscript by email, always include a cover email that provides a basic introduction to yourself and the subject of the manuscript. Never send a submission as an attachment to a blank email, or try to put all this information into your subject line. (This seems especially common among writers who submit from cell phones.) Be sure to include your contact information in the email *and* on the manuscript itself. I have received many electronic submissions with no identification—even a byline!—on the manuscript.

WAITING FOR AN ANSWER

The next step is to wait. Typical response times range from four to eight weeks. At one end of the scale, some online publications respond almost immediately—and at the other, I know one print magazine that may take a full year to respond! Response times apply no matter how you send your submission; sending a query by email does *not* guarantee an "instant" reply! (I was once contacted by a writer who was concerned because an editor hadn't replied to her in over four hours!)

Response times are not a promise that the editor *will* reply within that time. It is simply the minimum time you are expected to wait before following up. Today, sadly, many editors don't bother sending rejections, which has prompted many writers to dispense with SASEs; however, I do recommend including at least a postcard in a surface-mail submission.

Once you've waited the allotted time, follow up. Use the same mechanism—postal mail or email—that was used for your original submission. Be polite:

Dear Editor,

I am writing to inquire whether you received my query for an article on [TOPIC/TITLE], dated July 27. In case you did not receive it, I have enclosed another copy of the query. If you did receive it, could you let me know when you might be able to make a decision on the piece?

Sincerely,
Moira Allen

If you're following up on a query, include the original with your follow-up. If you're following up on an article, however, don't resend the manuscript unless the editor asks you to.

If you don't receive a response after another two weeks, follow up again. In this case, a polite phone call is acceptable. If you still don't get a response, or don't want to wait any longer, you can withdraw your submission from consideration. Just send a short letter to the editor:

Dear Editor,

On July 27, I sent you a query/submission regarding an article on [TOPIC/TITLE]. As ten weeks have passed without a response to my query or to my follow-ups (dated September 27 and October 10), I have decided to withdraw this article/query from consideration. [In the case of an article submission, I would add, "Please remove this article from your files."]

Sincerely,
Moira Allen

Writers often wonder whether editors are annoyed by follow-ups. The answer is no. As long as you remain professional, following up on a submission will not harm your chances of acceptance.

THE EDITOR RESPONDS

You might imagine there are only two possible responses to a submission: yes or no. Actually, there are many variations. A rejection, for example, might take the form of no response, a form letter, a checklist in which the editor can mark one or more reasons for rejection (e.g., "something similar on file"), or a personal rejection. As I explain below, a personal rejection is good news: it means you impressed an editor enough to merit a direct response. Sometimes a personal rejection will consist of a few words of encouragement ("liked your style, but unfortunately, this wasn't for us"); sometimes it will include feedback on your article, and sometimes (the best news of all), it will include an invitation to submit something else. If this happens, do so!

Acceptance also comes in a variety of flavors. The simplest is either "yes, send the article" in response to a query, or "yes, we'll take it" in response to a manuscript. This acceptance letter may include the amount that will be paid, the rights to be transferred, and possibly a date of publication.

When you send a query, you may receive a direct assignment, which is a guarantee that the editor will buy your article (unless it proves truly dreadful). More often, however, an editor will say "yes on spec," which means "on speculation." This means the editor won't commit to buying it sight unseen, which is common when a writer is new to the publication. Some editors switch to assignments after you've sold two or three pieces; others only work on spec no matter how long you've contributed to the publication.

In some cases, if an editor gives an assignment and decides *not* to accept your article, you may receive a "kill fee"—usually 20 to 30 percent of the amount that would have been paid for the article. Not all publications offer kill fees, however, and there is no kill fee if an editor does not accept a piece submitted on spec.

An editor may also respond to a query or submission with a request for revisions. He may want a shorter piece, or a longer one, or a different focus. While it's appropriate for an editor to ask for changes to an article *proposal*, it's less acceptable to ask for drastic changes to a finished article without a fairly firm commitment to accept the piece once changes have been made. If an editor asks you to revise an article more than once (especially if the revisions are substantial) without committing to an acceptance, think twice before doing the requested work.

Finally, an editor may reject your submission but ask you to write something different. This shows that you've made a strong first impression. Often, it will be a firm assignment, and may lead to others. In this case, don't feel bad that your original piece wasn't accepted; you have your foot in the door!

AFTER THE ACCEPTANCE

The next step is usually the contract. Chapter 14 discusses the types of terms you're likely to see in a contract, and how to negotiate contracts. If you've reviewed a publication's guidelines, its contract should not come as a surprise; however, publications *can* change their terms without notice, so be sure to read *every* contract carefully (including contracts with publications you've already worked with).

While contracts can often be negotiated, this is not the time to ask for more money. For example, if you know that a publication pays five cents per word, don't send an article and then ask for ten cents. It not only won't happen, it's likely to prevent you from working for that publication again!

If a market pays on acceptance, you should receive a check within about thirty days of signing and returning the contract. (Today, contracts are often sent by email, enabling you to sign, scan, and return it the same way; this saves a lot of time!) If you don't get paid within a month, contact the editor and ask politely when you can expect payment. You may also be asked to send the publication an invoice.

If the market pays on publication, you won't see a check until your article is published. While this may not be long when dealing with newspapers or online publications, it can be months (or even years) before a print magazine publishes your article. If possible, therefore, try to get the editor to set a firm publication date. Generally, pay-on-publication markets issue checks within thirty to sixty days of the *issue* date. This means that if a magazine is published in October, checks may not be issued until the end of November, so you may not receive payment until December.

Your work doesn't end just because you've signed the contract and gotten your check. Often, editors file articles until they come up for publication. Then, an editor may ask for more revisions ("please cut 500 words"). You may also be asked to review and correct galley proofs. A galley is a copy of your article, exactly as it will appear in the magazine. (Today, editors often send PDF files of galley proofs by email.) You may now discover that the editor has made drastic changes to the piece. Unless these result in inaccuracies or change the meaning of the article, however, there isn't much you can do at this stage. (Your contract probably states that the editor has the right to edit the article as she sees fit.) Your input on galleys is generally limited to correcting factual errors and typos.

If you feel that an article *must* be changed at this point, call the editor and discuss the issue. I once found that an article of mine had been badly rewritten simply to shorten it. Rather than accept the butchered version, I quickly rewrote the piece to the desired length and the editor was happy to run the new version.

Finally, once your piece has been published, you should receive at least one complimentary copy of the issue in which it appears. Most magazines will provide two (or more) if asked. Newspapers will also generally send a copy of the issue, or the section, in which your article appears, while electronic magazines will send you the URL of the online publication.

SIMULTANEOUS AND MULTIPLE SUBMISSIONS

One source of controversy is whether it's OK to send simultaneous submissions—sending the same query or manuscript to more than one publication at a time. Since a publication can take months to make a decision, many writers feel that simultaneous submissions are a way to bypass these delays.

Most editors, however, do not like simultaneous submissions, and many refuse to accept them. This means one must either limit "simsubs" to publications that *do* accept them, or lie to those that don't. Either way, this can put a writer in the awkward position of having to say "yes" to the *first* offer that comes in, since you can't ask an editor to wait until you hear from other publications. If you do get multiple offers, you won't look good to the editors you have to refuse.

Editors don't object to "simsubs" just to be grouchy. Many don't assign articles until they can fit them into their publication schedule. If an author comes back and says, "Sorry, I sold it somewhere else," this leaves the editor with a hole in an upcoming issue that must be filled—often on a tight deadline. Rather than put editors in this position, I recommend sending submissions to your top markets first. Then, you only have to worry about accepting an offer from a less desirable market if your first choices say no.

"Multiple submissions" means sending more than one submission to an editor at the same time. Some publications don't accept multiple submissions; others place a limit on how many they will review. It's rarely a good idea to send multiple submissions to an editor on your first contact. Later, when you have become an established contributor to a publication, you may be able to do so, though a better option is to send a query with multiple ideas (see chapter 7) rather than a collection of finished articles.

TRACKING SUBMISSIONS

Once you start sending out submissions, you need to keep track of them. Otherwise, it's easy to forget that an editor hasn't responded to your query. While you can buy submission-tracking software, I find that a simple spreadsheet works fine. My spreadsheet includes the title of the submission,

Figure 12–1: Submission Tracking Sheet

ARTICLE TITLE	PUBLICATION	DATE	ACTION	DATE	ACTION	PAY	STATUS
Smithfield Hist.	VA Hist Monthly	1/10/18	Submitted	3/15/18	Accepted	$25	Paid
Writing Synopsis	The Writer	1/30/18	Queried		Pending		
Cancer in Cats	Whole Cat Jrnl	2/15/18	Queried	3/30/18	Rejected		
Victorian Christmas	Victorian Home	2/25/18	Submitted	4/15/18	Accepted	$300	Paid
Herbal Skin Care	Herb Monthly	4/5/18	Submitted	6/10/18	Rejected		
Sea Shell Angels	Country Crafts	5/15/18	Queried	7/25/18	Accepted	$175	Pending
Natural Xmas Decor	Country Sampler	5/15/18	Submitted	6/10/18	Accepted	$250	Paid
Newbie Writer Column	Byline	6/20/18	Proposed	7/15/18	Rejected		
Traveling with Cats	Cats & Kittens	7/30/18	Queried		Pending		

the publication, and the date of submission. Subsequent columns indicate actions taken (accepted, rejected, or waiting for a response), the payment due if any, and whether payment was received. Figure 12–1 shows a sample submission-tracking spreadsheet; yours might include different columns depending on the information you wish to track. Some writers, for example, like to note the rights sold, so that they don't sell the same rights to another publication. This type of system helps you monitor what submissions need follow-up, what articles have been submitted multiple times without acceptance (which may indicate they need reworking), and what actions you need to take (such as following up on payment).

Some writers create tracking sheets for every article they write, recording what publications each piece has been submitted to and the results of each submission. Some do this on spreadsheets; others create a card file to track articles. Here's an example of an individual tracking sheet:

Figure 12–2: Individual Article Tracking Sheet

Article Title: Traveling with Cats

PUBLICATION	DATE	ACTION	DATE	RESPONSE	PAYMENT	STATUS
Catster	6/15/18	Queried	7/15/18	Rejected		
Whole Cat Jrnl	7/20/18	Submitted	8/30/18	Rejected		
Cats & Kittens	9/15/18	Submitted	10/20/18	Accepted	$300	Pending

Another way to track submissions is to keep a pending correspondence folder. Print a copy of every query or cover letter you send out (including email submissions) and place it in this file. Organize the file by date. When you receive a response, pull the appropriate letter and attach it. If further information is needed (such as a contract), put the letter back in the pending folder; otherwise, transfer it to a completed correspondence file (or dispose of the hard copy if you are keeping electronic files). Every so often, go through the pending file and follow up on letters that are still awaiting a response.

COPING WITH REJECTION

Unfortunately, rejection is part of being a writer. Nor is it just part of being a beginning writer; experienced writers get rejected as well. One of the most important steps you can take is to learn how to cope with rejection, understand what it means to your career, and move on.

The first step in handling rejection is to learn how to separate yourself from your work. You may pour your heart and soul into your writing, but you must also establish boundaries between yourself and your creation. Your writing may be like a child to you, but like any child, it must go out into the world to succeed or fail on its own merits. If you can't develop such boundaries, you'll quit. Success is impossible if you cannot bear the pain of failure.

You've probably heard that editors who reject your work aren't rejecting *you*—and that's true. However, they may not even be rejecting your work. Lack of quality is only one reason for rejection. There are many others, including:

- **A similar piece is on file.** "Similar" can simply mean relating to the same topic. For example, if you submit an article on Antigua to a travel magazine, and they have an article on Antigua on hand, they won't accept another even if it's different.
- **A similar piece has been assigned.** Great minds *do* think alike, and you'd be amazed how often multiple writers will query on a similar topic.
- **A similar piece has been published.** Many publications won't repeat a topic for two or three years. Internet publications may *never* repeat a topic if their archives are available online.

Another reason for rejection is the volume of submissions. If an editor can accept five articles per month out of a pile of five hundred, he won't reject only "bad" articles. Perfectly good articles will be rejected as well. Your article may be perfect, but be sent back because it was the sixth choice in the stack from which the editor could accept only five.

"Good" Rejection Slips

Any rejection slip that offers information is good, because it helps you understand the reason for the rejection. Some magazines offer a "checklist" letter, listing common reasons for rejection and checking the one that applies to you. Finding out that someone else had already been assigned to the topic is a lot better than assuming the editor thought your article stank. Even better than checklists, however, are rejections that include a personal note. Even a scribble (or, these days, a short email note) shows the editor thought enough of your piece to respond personally. Treasure those personal rejections; they mean you're making a positive impression.

Even better is the "please try again" note. When an editor asks you to come back with another submission, do it. No editor says this unless he means it. This often happens when a piece can't be accepted for one of the reasons above. Even though the editor can't use *this* piece, he still wants you as a contributor. Whenever you're asked to try again, *try again*!

Let's Be Honest . . .

While there may be dozens of "good" reasons for rejection, a writer must also be willing to ask honestly whether, in fact, the issue was quality. When we write, we often become so involved in a piece that we find it hard to judge it accurately. Often, our work isn't as good as we thought it was, or wasn't what our target market required.

Good writing is a skill, not a gift, and skills are refined over time. The reality of the writing business is that when you start, you think you're pretty good. After a year, you're likely to look back on those first efforts and think that, perhaps, they could stand some improvement. After five years, you may look at those early masterpieces and wonder why you didn't burn them on the spot. This process never ends. As you continue to improve, you'll feel this way twenty years from now. This may sound depressing—but what would be even more depressing is the idea that you *can't* get better!

As writers, we must be able to look at our work and say, honestly, "This is the best I can do." At the same time, we must also be able to say, "I can do better." Both statements are true. What you write today is the best you can do—today. Tomorrow you'll do better—but only if you don't stop writing today. Remember, there is something worse than rejection, and that's never writing (or submitting) anything to be rejected in the first place.

Understanding the submissions process—its pains and its triumphs—is essential to your success. Editors don't want to waste time with people who don't know what they're doing or how the system works. An editor's job is to run a publication, not educate new writers. When you demonstrate that you know how the writing business works, you give an editor confidence that you might be someone he wants to work with, not just once but again and again.

CHAPTER 13

Understanding Rights and Copyright

One of the most common questions new writers ask is "How do I copyright my work?" Before I answer that question, let me point out that this chapter is written for US writers.[9] Every country has its own copyright laws. While certain international copyright conventions are observed by countries that are members of the Berne Copyright Convention, variations still exist from country to country. While American writers can register their copyrights with the Library of Congress, for example, there is no government copyright registry for British authors (though there are private registries). Canadian authors should consult the Canadian Intellectual Property Office (www.cipo.ic.gc.ca) for more information.

Now, on to that burning question. The simple answer is that "copyrighting" your work is simple—because your work is automatically protected by copyright the moment you put it into some tangible (e.g., written) form. Under current law, copyright protects any work you've created since January 1, 1998, for your lifetime plus seventy years.

This means that as long as your work is under that protection, no one else has the right to use it, reprint it, publish it, or pass it off as their own, without your permission. Doing so is an infringement of your intellectual property (IP) rights. You can grant permission by granting or licensing one of many possible "rights" to your work, as we'll discuss below.

---

9   Let me also point out that I am not a copyright lawyer and this chapter should not be regarded as legal advice.

You do not have to register your copyright in a work for it to be protected in this way. However, you *do* have to register a copyright before you can file a lawsuit for infringement. For lawsuit purposes, registration can be made before a piece is published or within five years of publication—but if a piece isn't registered within three months of publication, or prior to the actual infringement, you can't claim statutory damages or attorney's fees. You can only receive an award of actual damages, such as the profits that another person gained by infringing upon your work.

This is a bit more important for writers today, in the Internet age, than it was when most publication occurred in print format. In the "old days," most magazines and newspapers filed a subscription with the Library of Congress. When your article or story was published, it appeared under the "collective copyright" of that magazine, which was considered a form of official registration. Today, collective copyright is not always considered sufficient registration for a work. But more to the point, there are thousands of online publications that do not register with the Copyright Office at all. Even if such a site includes a collective copyright notice (I'll explain that a bit more later), that doesn't mean your work is *registered*. And since online publications are particularly vulnerable to infringement, this creates a greater problem for authors.

WHAT CAN BE PROTECTED, AND HOW?

There isn't room here to go into all the things that can be protected by copyright. Generally speaking, what is protected is some form of creative expression that is set in a tangible format. That term may seem odd in this electronic age, but it has meaning when it comes to copyright registration. If you decide to *register* your copyright in a work, you are required to submit an actual, tangible hard copy—you may not submit the work on CD or DVD. Even if you file online, you are still required to submit a hard copy.

According to the Copyright Office, "Copyright, a form of intellectual property law, protects original works of authorship including literary, dramatic, musical, and artistic works, such as poetry, novels, movies, songs, computer software, and architecture."[10] "Artistic works" includes artwork, photography, and three-dimensional art. It does not protect titles, so someone else can use the same title for a book or article that you've used.

---

10 https://www.copyright.gov/help/faq/.

(Titles can sometimes be trademarked, but not copyrighted.) Names, such as pseudonyms, cannot be copyrighted—though author names are also occasionally trademarked (particularly if a pseudonym is used by more than one author, as in an ongoing series).

Copyright also protects the author's right to create *derivative* works. This not only gives protection to your work as a whole, but restricts the use of certain elements of that work. For example, if you wrote a novel or story that involved a certain set of characters, or a fantasy world that you created, those characters and that world are also protected. Only you have the right to create additional stories or novels using those characters and/ or that world (or to license that right to others). Note that the characters and/or world must be an original creation. Obviously, if you set your story in San Francisco, your setting is not protected—but if you were to create a fictional street or business in that story, it *would* be protected.

The Copyright Office also notes that "Copyright does not protect facts, ideas, systems, or methods of operation, although it may protect the way these things are expressed."[11] A "work" must be definable as a "work." It doesn't have to be complete—your ongoing novel is protected even if you haven't finished it—but it must at least have been begun. A jumble of handwritten notes generally won't qualify for protection.

Ideas are not protected by copyright. This often troubles writers, who are afraid to send article ideas to editors for fear that editors will steal them and pass them off to their "stable" of writers. Writers are often perturbed when they pitch an idea, are rejected—and then see an article on a similar idea published in that very same publication. This actually happens quite often, not because ideas are stolen, but because writers who review the same markets and the same guidelines quite often come up with very similar ideas. Facts, figures, and data are also not protected, though in some cases, a collection of facts (such as a directory) may receive protection.

Again, your work is legally protected as soon as you create it. If you wish to add the additional protection of registration, you can do so by submitting the appropriate forms by mail or online to the Copyright Office. There is a registration fee for each work (lower for online submissions).

It is possible to register a collection of unpublished works for a single registration fee. However, you cannot register a collection of published

---

11   https://www.copyright.gov/help/faq/.

works—such as various articles you've sold—unless they were originally published as a collection. Otherwise, published articles must be registered individually. Again, you are required to submit a hard copy of your work when you register. If you self-publish a book, you will be expected to register the copyright and submit two copies of that book. (Today literally thousands of Kindle books are being generated every day, and I doubt that most of these are ever registered with the Copyright Office. If you publish such a book, it's a good idea to create a printed copy and register it, as Kindle books are also notoriously subject to infringements.)

It is not necessary to post a copyright notice on a submission. An editor knows (or should know) that you own the copyright to that work. Some editors feel that posting a copyright notice is actually the sign of an amateur, though most of us really don't care one way or another. If you post or publish your own work, however, you should definitely include a copyright notice, which should include the copyright symbol (©), the year of publication, and your name (e.g., © 2020 Moira Allen). You can also use the word "Copyright" instead of the symbol. The copyright date should reflect the date of publication, rather than the date that the work was completed. If, for example, you wrote an article in 2015 but posted it for the first time on your blog in 2018, the copyright date should be 2018.

Finally, let's dispel the myth of the "poor man's copyright." This is the notion that if you put a document into an envelope, seal it, and mail it to yourself and never open it, that sealed envelope with its postal stamp is "proof" that you wrote that document prior to the mailing date. The Copyright Office does not acknowledge or give any legitimacy to this type of "copyright proof"—so don't do that.

KNOWING YOUR RIGHTS

"Copyright" refers to your right to claim ownership and authorship of a particular piece of work. It also means that no one can reproduce, sell, or distribute that work without your permission. To authorize the publication of your work by another party, such as a magazine, you need to grant that permission by transferring "usage rights" to the work. This does not mean that you are giving up your copyright (unless you actually transfer copyright through a contract, such as a work-for-hire agreement).

Many authors become confused about the difference between copyright and use rights. "But I still have the copyright!" they say, thinking this means "I can still do anything I want with the work, right?" Wrong. Once you begin transferring usage rights, you need to keep track of what rights you still own and can either use yourself or transfer to someone else, and what rights you have given up either temporarily or permanently.

Rights are generally transferred or licensed through a written contract (see chapter 14). This is important to remember, because writers have been told that a publisher "owns" all the rights to a work simply because they published it. Copyright law specifically states that "In the absence of an express transfer of the copyright or of any rights under it, the owner of copyright in the collective work is presumed to have acquired only the privilege of reproducing and distributing the contribution as part of that particular collective work, any revision of that collective work, and any later collective work in the same series."[12] There is still some controversy over what a "revision" means—if a publisher buys your work for a print magazine, does it then have the right to post it electronically? The publisher *does* have the right to create an electronic facsimile of a print edition—for example, an exact PDF duplicate of the print magazine—but may not necessarily have the right to post your article online separate from the original magazine issue.

Here are the types of rights most often used by periodical publishers:

- **First rights.** This term is usually used in combination with a qualifier, such as a medium, language, or geographical distribution—for example, "first print rights," "first English-language rights," or "First North American Serial Rights." It indicates that a publisher has the *exclusive* right to be the first to publish your work within the specified parameters. You can sometimes sell different sets of first rights to different markets. However, this can lead to difficulties, particularly if you're trying to sell first rights in different media (print vs. electronic) within an overlapping distribution area. However, you can only sell a specific first right *once*, as only one publication can be the "first" to use whatever right they have purchased. Be aware, also, that a purchase of first rights entitles a publisher to hold on to your

---

12 Copyright Law of the United States of America, Circular 92, Section 201c, "Ownership of Copyright," https://www.copyright.gov/title17/92chap2.html#201.

article for as long as it wishes before publishing it. As long as it has the right to be "first," you won't be able to sell it anywhere else until that right has been used (and sometimes, it never is).

- **First North American Serial Rights (FNASR).** This was once the most common term a writer was likely to encounter. It gives a periodical publisher the right to be the first to publish your work within North America and Canada. (The term refers to the distribution or readership of the publication rather than the location of the publisher.) It authorizes a single use and does not allow a publisher to reprint the piece in another publication, such as an anthology. Technically it does not include first electronic rights, though many publishers would argue that point. Though this term is still widely used, publishers are moving toward contracts that give them a broader range of rights.

- **International rights.** In addition to FNASR, you can sell rights to other regions, based either on geographical boundaries or on language. For example, you could offer "First British Rights," "First Japanese Rights," and similar combinations. You can also sell "First German Language Rights" or "First Japanese Language Rights," which limits distribution by language but not by geographical boundaries. (Note that a license of "First English Language Rights" is actually broader than FNASR, as it would include the right to distribute the work in the UK and any other English language–speaking country.)

- **One-time rights.** This grants a publisher the *nonexclusive* right to publish your material. A publisher can use it once, but does not have the right to be "first." This enables you to sell the same piece to more than one publisher at the same time. This type of right is useful when selling reprints, or when selling articles to newspapers or other publications that do not have an overlapping distribution.

- **Second or reprint rights.** Once you've sold first rights in a particular medium or area, your next sale of the same material is regarded as a reprint and thus a use of "second" or "reprint" rights. (Again, reprints are often sold on the basis of "one-time rights.") Second rights are generally *not* associated with a specific medium or location, and are nonexclusive, meaning that you can market second rights to more than one market at a time.

- **Electronic rights.** Many print publications now want some form of electronic rights, generally so that they can post material on a website. Some try to claim that electronic rights are automatically included in FNASR, but this is not true (partly because FNASR is not based only on the location of the publisher but the distribution of its readership—which, online, can be worldwide). Many don't offer additional payment for electronic rights, even though this prevents you from selling "first electronic rights" to an online publication. See below for more details about electronic rights.

- **All rights.** This means everything: first rights, second rights, print rights, electronic rights, anthology rights, even movie rights. Once you've sold all rights to a publication, you've lost all further use of that material. You may not even be entitled to post it on your own website. Many writers argue that one should never sell all rights. Others feel that it is acceptable if the benefits outweigh the cost— for example, the fee is high enough, the material isn't suitable for reprinting, or the publication is prestigious enough that the clip is worth the loss. Some publications that buy all rights will subsequently license back some of those rights to the author.

- **Work-for-hire.** This was a term originally applied to work created as an employee, but now it is often used by publications buying material from freelancers. A work-for-hire agreement transfers not only all rights to your material but the copyright as well. You are no longer legally the author or owner of the work; the publisher can remove or replace your byline, change the material, and do anything it wishes with it. Worse, if you write another substantially similar or derivative piece, you could actually be liable for copyright infringement. In fiction, a work-for-hire contract would remove your right to create derivative works using the same characters, themes, or settings.

Finally, a word about "collective copyright." Many writers (and quite a few editors) are confused about the difference between a collective copyright that applies to a compilation of materials (such as articles or stories) and the individual copyright associated with each individual work within that compilation. Magazines and periodicals, for example, will usually have a collective copyright notice posted in each issue, usually below the masthead. Websites may have a copyright notice at the bottom of every page of the site that indicates that the website itself is copyrighted by the site's owner or publisher.

This type of notice applies to the issue (or website) as a whole, as it is published. It is a notice of the publisher's ownership of that issue (or site) as an entity. In the case of a magazine, for example, that includes the issue as it is printed, including the artwork, ads, layout, and any other elements incorporated into the final published product. It does not give the publisher any additional rights to the materials within that issue, which are covered by whatever agreement the publisher has with its writers and artists.

Unfortunately, there are editors and publishers who don't know this, and who *do* make an attempt to claim that their collective copyright actually means that they own the copyrights to the individual works they have published. This is incorrect, as the Copyright Office states: "Copyright in each separate contribution to a collective work is distinct from copyright in the collective work as a whole, and vests initially in the author of the contribution."[13]

UNDERSTANDING ELECTRONIC RIGHTS

The term "electronic rights" can cover anything relating to electronic publication, including but not limited to publication on a website or blog, inclusion in an online database, publication in CD or DVD format, use in an app or a mobile device, ebook publication, and so on. Today, the term is most commonly associated with online publications (including publications accessed by apps and mobile devices).

Electronic rights are generally considered to be "worldwide," as a publisher usually can't control where an online publication is read or distributed. Terms like FNASR do not apply to online publication, nor are you likely to see a contract that asks for "first British electronic rights" or something similar. You may, however, see the term associated with a language distribution right (e.g., "first Japanese-language electronic publication rights").

Common electronic rights clauses include:

---

13 Copyright Law of the United States of America, Circular 92, Section 201c, "Ownership of Copyright," https://www.copyright.gov/title17/92chap2.html#201c.

- **First (or first worldwide) electronic rights.** This usually applies to some form of online publication, including publication in an email newsletter.
- **One-time electronic rights.** Like one-time print rights, this is a nonexclusive clause generally applied to online publication.
- **Web publication rights.** This specifically indicates that the material will be used online and not in a CD or DVD or as part of an ebook.
- **Archival rights.** This gives a publication the right to archive material (such as back issues of a publication or newsletter) online. Sometimes this will be for a specific period of time, but more often such rights are requested permanently or indefinitely. If a publication is archived in its entirety, it will remain so generally for the lifetime of that publication. If, however, articles are archived separately on a website, the author may have the ability to request that an article be withdrawn after a period of time.
- **Electronic distribution rights.** This gives a publication the right to market or distribute your work to *other* electronic publications. For example, print publications once requested this right so that they could sell their articles to online databases, but this has become a less common practice.
- **All electronic rights.** This transfers all *electronic* rights (usually in any medium) to the purchaser, but leaves the author free to market print rights.

A sale to an electronic publication can be complicated by the fact that though that publication may acquire "first" rights, it's difficult to determine when this exclusive publication right expires. A print magazine or newspaper has a specific life span. A monthly magazine's exclusive right to use your article expires at the end of the publication month, for example, while a daily newspaper's right might expire by the following day. (That doesn't mean you can sell "first" rights again—only that there is a limit to the period of time in which the publication has the exclusive right to be the *only* publication to use your work.) But when an online publication uses a piece, it may remain online indefinitely.

Thus, many electronic rights clauses will also include a specific duration of exclusivity. For example, a website might request "first electronic rights for ninety days." This gives the publication exclusive use of the material for ninety days after it is published. Thereafter, the writer is free to offer second or one-time rights to other online publications. Some publications also specify a time after which a writer may request the removal of the article from the site if they wish to sell it elsewhere. Many clauses may also specify whether they are exclusive or nonexclusive. Online publications generally prefer a period of exclusivity, whereas a print publication that does not currently have an online presence may request nonexclusive rights in case they opt to use the material online in the future. Also, while most print publications today will also ask for some type of electronic rights, most electronic publications will not seek to claim any print rights.

Exclusivity can be a tricky thing. While a nonexclusive contract means that you can offer the same material to other publications, you must be sure that no other publication requires exclusivity. For example, if you sold an article to a site that wanted nonexclusive archival rights, you could not sell the same article to a print publication that wanted any form of *exclusive* electronic rights.

USE VS. PAYMENT

Authors are often confused over what constitutes a use of rights. I often get questions along the lines of "How can a magazine own my rights if they didn't pay me?" or "How can putting something on my website be a use of rights?" The answer lies in the definition of *use*. When you create a written work, you own the copyright to that creation, which means, again, that you own a bundle of rights. You can sell those rights, give them away, or use them yourself.

Authors are also confused by guidelines that claim that "all rights revert to the author after publication." This sounds nice, but simply reflects ignorance on the part of the publisher. If a publisher uses your material, certain rights have been used and are not "returnable." First rights, once used, are gone; they cannot be used again. Those rights are also used whether you are paid for them or not. If you give away an article for free, you are still licensing (and giving up) the applicable rights.

Finally, if you use material yourself, you may also end up using (and thus losing) certain rights. Many publications regard posting an article or story on your website or blog to be a use of first rights, and regard the work as a reprint if you try to sell it. Showcasing unpublished works on your website is a bad idea for a variety of reasons: it can cost you the use of first rights, and it can make you appear desperate. Editors do not surf the web looking for articles to publish, so posting your work online is *not* the way to get it "picked up" by an editor. It's far better to use your site to display clips of published materials, or else write information specifically for your site or blog that you don't intend to publish elsewhere.

RIGHTS AND THE WILD WILD WEB

Years ago, writers often worried that editors would steal their ideas. They were often dismayed to pitch an idea, have it rejected, and then see a similar article in the publication a few months later. This often seemed like proof that an idea had been stolen—but in reality it proves the opposite. Since periodicals (print and electronic) plan content months in advance, the appearance of a "similar" article so quickly indicates that it was already on file long before your idea arrived.

I won't claim that theft never happens, though an editor is more likely to "steal" a complete article than an idea that hasn't been written yet. It is unlikely to happen among professional editors and reputable publications, however, as no editor wants to risk a copyright infringement suit. Besides, if your ideas are good enough to steal, they're good enough to buy—and an editor would rather find a writer he can work with repeatedly than steal one idea and lose the rest of your material forever.

Today's writers, however, face other problems. The Internet abounds with people who either don't know about copyright or don't care. Many people believe that anything posted online is "public domain," because they think this term means "publicly available." The sad truth is that anything posted online is at risk of being sent about in an email or reposted/republished on someone else's blog or website.

Some infringers are more clueless than churlish, and will take a piece down if they're informed that they've broken the law. Others are less apologetic, and either claim that anything online is "free for the taking" or that they are "doing you a favor" by giving your work more exposure.[14]

---

14 For more on this, see my article "Don't Do Us Any 'Favors'—Don't Steal Our Work!" at www.writing-world.com/rights/favors.shtml.

Then there are those who actually steal your work and republish it under their own names. This happens surprisingly often in the academic community. I've had several instances in which Writing-World.com articles have turned up on a university website or in an online course package—under a professor's name! Editors often receive plagiarized submissions, and we're always wary of something that seems too good to be true (a flawless article, for example, accompanied by a cover letter in which every other word is misspelled).

The unfortunate fact is that if you post something online, or if your work is published online, someone is likely to copy it. One step you can take to protect yourself is to periodically search on key phrases from your works. An infringer may remove your name or change your title, but will rarely change the content.

Once you do find an infringement, there are many steps that you can take. The best place to start is to attempt to contact the infringer directly and request that the material be removed. (Some writers are willing to allow the material to remain if it is properly attributed; that's up to you.) This also shows that you've made an effort to resolve the issue. Sometimes, this is sufficient. If the material is posted on a social media site, look for a link that allows you to report a violation. To learn more about the many other steps you can take, visit "Take Action Against Online Copyrights Infringement Using DMCA" at www.orbitingweb.com/blog/reporting-copyrights-infringement.

If you don't actually object to the reuse of your material, you might consider posting a Creative Commons License. This is a bit complicated as well. The basic purpose of such a license (which is not a legal copyright notice and provides no actual protection) is to indicate what rights you're willing to share. Many sites, such as Wikipedia, rely on this type of licensing for their content. There are six different Creative Commons licenses, depending on what rights you are willing to share with others; for more information, visit en.wikipedia.org/wiki/Creative_Commons for more information. Or, you may find it easier to simply post your terms on your website. I allow other sites to reprint my articles from Writing-World.com, but require, among other conditions, that such reprints retain my bio, byline, copyright information, and a link back to my site.

Copyright infringement can range from annoying to downright infuriating. Much of it, however, is the result of ignorance. If you're a writer launching your career, a far greater threat is your own ignorance. Publishers, as a rule, are rarely your friends—and they have a host of legal tricks to play when contracting for your work. Your best defense against losing your rights is to understand exactly what those rights are. Only then can you determine which ones you're willing to lose—and what you expect to gain in exchange.

CHAPTER 14

Negotiating Contracts

A contract does not have to be printed on stiff paper with gilded edges, or packed with legal jargon. A contract can be any form of document that spells out the terms of a sale, including (but not limited to):

- A preprinted legal document, with blanks for the name of the author, the title of the material being sold, and the fee.
- A letter of agreement—an original letter tailored for a particular sale, a standard form letter, or even an email.
- A "fill in the blanks" or "check the boxes" form.

A contract must be negotiated *before* the ownership of the material actually changes hands. In the past, some publishers attempted to claim rights by stamping a rights transfer clause on the back of a writer's check, indicating that by endorsing or depositing the check, the writer was transferring the rights indicated. In 1999, a judge ruled that such a stamp did *not* constitute a legally binding contract. However, other rulings have supported the use of check endorsement stamps, and the legitimacy or enforceability of such a transfer seems to vary from state to state. So if you do receive such a check, in the absence of a written contract that spells out the rights you are granting, it would be wise to send it back and request a written contract and a check that does not include any contractual language.

Contracts are usually sent by mail, fax (less often today), or email. Today, editors frequently send a contract as an attachment to an email. You are asked to print out the document, sign it, and return it by surface mail—or, if you have a scanner, to scan the signed contract and return it as an attachment.

WHAT A CONTRACT ISN'T

Certain things do not constitute a legally binding agreement, including:

- **Writers' guidelines,** whether published in a guide such as *Writer's Market* or distributed by the company itself. Guidelines can be changed without notice, and are superseded by a written contract.

- **Your own notation** on a manuscript indicating the rights you're offering. Many writers like to put a notice at the top of a submission stating "Rights Available: FNASR." This means nothing; it is the market, not you, that determines what rights are to be transferred. You should know what rights a market requires *before* you submit a piece, and if you aren't willing to sell those rights, don't submit.

- **A verbal agreement.** Actually, a verbal agreement *can* be a legal contract—but it's hard to enforce in court. Back up any oral agreement with a letter confirming the terms.

- **An altered document that has not been signed or initialed by both parties**. If you want to change a contract, you must obtain the agreement of the publisher; it isn't enough to simply mark out or revise unwanted clauses.

In addition, certain rights can be transferred *only* through a written agreement. For example, a publication cannot claim all rights, or that your material is "work for hire," without a contract. According to current law, if no contract exists, a publisher can only claim to have acquired first or one-time rights.

Never let a publisher try to bully you into believing that it owns more rights than it does. I once heard from a writer who was informed by his publisher that "collective copyright"—i.e., the copyright applying to a magazine as a whole—meant that the publisher owned the copyright to the individual articles in that publication. It doesn't. Many publications offer contracts for FNASR, then post material online without any additional compensation for the writer. This is a contract violation. If you find that someone has posted your work online in the absence of a contract transferring some form of electronic rights, you're entitled to ask the publication to remove the work or provide additional compensation.

UNDERSTANDING CONTRACT TERMS

An agreement between a writer and a publisher should contain, at a minimum, the following information:

- **The title of the material being purchased.**
- **The rights being purchased**—such as first rights, First North American Serial Rights (FNASR), one-time rights, reprint rights, electronic rights, all rights, and so on.
- **The medium (or media) to which those rights apply** or in which the work will be published. Some rights apply only to print publication (such as FNASR); others apply to electronic publication; others apply to all forms of publication. Watch out for clauses that attempt to give a right more meaning than it customarily or legally has (for example, contracts that claim that FNASR also includes the right to publish material online).
- **Payment,** specifying the exact fee offered for your material and when you can expect to receive it (e.g., within thirty days of acceptance or publication).
- **Your obligations and liabilities**. Some contracts address issues of accuracy, originality, and libel. Make sure that such clauses don't demand assurances you can't reasonably provide. When in doubt, insert the phrase, "to the best of the author's knowledge" after such clauses.

Many contracts also include the following types of clauses:

- **A statement that the magazine is entitled to edit the material.** This is standard, and most editors understand that it means "within reason." A publication typically has the right to do any amount of editing as long as the basic substance and meaning of the article remain unchanged. Some editors take this as a license to rewrite your piece from top to bottom. If this happens, there is generally very little you can do about it. Often, editing may be required to shorten an article (even if it was within the specified word limit).
- **An indemnification statement.** You'll often see a long block of text about indemnification issues. This ensures that if someone wants to file a lawsuit about the article, it is filed against *you* rather than the publisher. Such suits don't happen often, but it's the sort of legal

protection lawyers like. Again, if the statements aren't clear, insert the line, "to the best of the author's knowledge."

- **The right to use the material for promotional purposes.** Most contracts give a publication the right to use some or all of an article for promotional purposes.
- **A statement that the article is original and your property.** This protects the publisher from a lawsuit if someone claims that you stole his article. Again, this doesn't happen very often!

Finally, consider requesting a clause that states that any rights not specifically transferred under the terms of the contract are deemed to be reserved to the writer.

NEGOTIATING CONTRACTS

If you don't like the terms of a contract, it's always appropriate to ask whether negotiation is possible. Be polite and reasonable. Before you attempt to negotiate, be sure you know what you hope to achieve. What do you want out of the negotiation? What are you prepared to offer? Are you willing to sell a larger set of rights for a higher fee? Or are you simply not prepared to give up the requested rights? Don't attempt to negotiate a contract if you don't have a clear goal in mind.

Before you set out to negotiate a contract—or if you're wondering whether to attempt it—it's important to understand your position as a writer. Don't assume, for example, that you *have* to accept what a publication offers or demands. Many new writers feel that their first acceptance is their *one big chance* to make a sale. They don't want to blow that all-important deal by getting picky over a contract. But the reality is that if you're good enough to get this deal, you're good enough to get another. You'll have other chances. You don't have to accept the first offer that comes along, particularly if it's a bad one. This is your first opportunity, not your last!

Don't assume that a publication will blacklist you if you try to negotiate a contract—or worse, spread the word that you're a "difficult" writer. Trying to negotiate a contract doesn't make you look unprofessional—unless in doing so, you demonstrate that you had no idea what terms the publication offered before you submitted in the first place. A polite effort to negotiate won't harm you. You may not succeed, but it won't make you look bad.

Never assume that you'll never use a piece again. More than once I've sold all rights to material I was certain I'd never reprint, and I've regretted it every time. Granted, you can always write a new article using the same information, but that's extra work.

Don't hesitate to ask for clarification if you're not sure what rights are being requested. I've seen some weird phrases—like "multiuse rights"—whose meaning is not obvious. Don't worry about appearing ignorant if you don't understand what a contract is requesting. Chances are, the ignorant person is the one who made up the terminology in the first place!

If you choose to negotiate a contract, keep in mind that not every editor has the power to do so. In larger publishing companies, contracts are often drafted by the legal department, and editors have no authority to change them. If this is the case, you're pretty much stuck—but even then, some editors may be willing to arrange for a negotiation, while others won't. Again, it never hurts to ask. But if an editor says no and won't budge, there is no point in pushing. Never hassle an editor or lose your professional cool; this will only result in the loss of a potential market.

If the editor won't negotiate, it's up to you to make a decision. Will you accept a contract you don't like, or will you withdraw the article? Only *you* can make this decision. You'll read lots of articles by writers who urge everyone to walk away from all-rights contracts. That's easily said, but if you're trying to earn a living as a writer, you may find you aren't willing to do so. Your choice is your own; don't let someone else pressure you or make you feel guilty for your decision.

MAKING YOUR OWN CONTRACT

If a publication offers no contract, protect your rights by providing your own letter of agreement. Keep this as simple as possible, spelling out the terms you're willing to offer and nothing more. Such a letter might read something like this:

Dear Editor:

Thank you for accepting my article, (title). I have received your check in the amount of ($), in payment for FNASR. I look forward to seeing my article in the (date) issue.

If no publication date has been confirmed (and especially if payment is contingent on publication), you can use this letter to inquire about the anticipated date of publication. While such a letter may not be as binding as a signed document, it does provide a written record of the terms you have authorized.

Another good time to send your own contract is when you've been promised a contract by an editor, but haven't received one. If the promised contract never materializes, your letter of agreement should stand as the "accepted" contract. If the publisher later tries to disavow that agreement, you can point out that no *signed* contract exists to supersede it.

SOME TRICKY CONTRACT ISSUES

While some contract issues are straightforward, others are more complicated. Here are a few of the more difficult contract questions you may encounter:

Is it ever too late to get a contract?

Many writers ask whether it is too late to get a contract *after* a piece has already been published (and, hopefully, paid for). Technically, the answer is yes. However, in this case, the absence of a contract won't hurt you, and may actually be better for you than having gotten a bad contract. In the absence of a contract, the only rights a publication can claim are "first" or "one-time" rights. Even if a publication *tries* to claim or use additional rights, it has no legal basis for doing so, and you're legally free to reuse or resell your material.

What if the publisher never uses my material?

Many writers wonder whether they have the right to resell a piece if it is paid for but never published. The answer is "it depends"—specifically, on the rights the publisher has bought.

If a publisher has bought all rights to your work, you don't have the right to use it elsewhere, whether the publisher uses it or not. By buying all rights, a publisher has bought the right to *not* publish your piece. Sometimes an editor buys a piece and simply can't find a place for it. Or perhaps a magazine changes editors, and the new editor doesn't care for some of the material purchased by his predecessor. When this happens, there's really nothing you can do.

It's more frustrating when a publisher buys *first* rights, theoretically leaving you free to sell reprint rights—but you can't until that first publication has occurred. If a publisher contracts for your work but has not actually *paid* for it (such as when a publisher pays on publication), you may be able to reclaim it if a significant period of time elapses without publication. Keep in mind that a pay-on-publication market *can* take years to actually print a piece, so don't expect to be able to reclaim your work after a few months. When dealing with pay-on-publication markets, I recommend asking the editor to include a clause that indicates approximately *when* the piece will be published. If the piece is not published by the specified date, you can then ask the editor for a new publication date.

If no publication date has been scheduled and you've waited a year or more for the piece to appear, you may wish to ask to withdraw the article from inventory. Since the publication has not paid you, it has not fulfilled its half of the contract, and you're within your rights to request to have the article back so that you can resell it. Keep in mind that not every publication will say yes, but it's worth a try.

Finally, if the publication was supposed to pay you but hasn't done so, and hasn't published the article, then it has not fulfilled the contract. In that case, you're within your rights to formally withdraw the article.

In many cases, however, the sad fact is that you don't have any recourse when your article isn't published. If you've been paid, and you don't have the right to reuse the article, often the only thing you can do is move on.

Can I get my rights back if a magazine folds?

Once again, it depends. If an independent publication folds, chances are that you can reclaim any rights you originally sold to that publication. A contract ceases to be valid if one party to that contract ceases to exist.

The key, however, is whether the actual owner of those rights has ceased to exist. Many magazines are owned by a larger publisher, such as a media conglomerate. In this case, your contract may not be with the magazine itself, but with the larger publishing company, which continues to exist (and own your rights) even if the magazine has folded. If a magazine folds, therefore, check your contract to see who actually owns your rights—the magazine, or a larger publisher that owned that magazine.

If a publisher has bought all rights to your article, it still owns those rights even if the magazine folds. However, a publisher *may* be willing to return those rights if the article has not been published and the publisher has no plans to launch another publication that might be able to use it. For example, when *Cats Magazine* folded in 2001, its owner, Primedia, gave authors back the rights to any unpublished articles on file. If the article *has* been published, a publisher is more likely to retain those rights, as it might wish to produce a DVD of back issues or something similar.

If a publisher hasn't paid you when a magazine folds, you're in a stronger position to request a return of rights. A publisher is far less likely to want to pay you on behalf of a publication that no longer exists. If the work was to be paid for on publication, and has not yet been published, then the publisher would be unable to fulfill its agreement with you. If the work *was* published, but was not paid for, the publisher would be in violation of its side of the contract, and should either pay you or return your rights.

In any case, the best approach in this type of situation is to *ask*. Many writers are afraid to ask publishers for their rights, for fear that somehow they will be blacklisted in the industry. This simply doesn't happen, and you won't get *anything* from a publisher that you don't ask for!

What happens to my work when a magazine is sold to another company?

Magazines change hands with frightening regularity these days, especially as larger media conglomerates gobble up smaller, independent publications. Sadly, many of these buyers are interested only in the bottom line. When a magazine changes hands, its contributors are often left hanging.

For example, when the online publication Allpets.com was sold in 2002, its new owners informed contributors that they would not be paid for any outstanding invoices. Many columnists were owed for two or three back issues, and were left with no means of collecting payment. The new owners claimed that they had purchased only the *assets* of the publication (the columns that had been published) but not the *liabilities* (the payments due to contributors).

Trying to collect payment when a publication changes hands is virtually impossible. In a situation like this, contributors have no leverage over the new owner. Generally, the amounts involved don't justify taking any sort of legal action (in the Allpets case, for example, I was owed a whopping $50).

The same is true when a publication goes bankrupt (as Themestream did in 2000). Contributors will generally be the *last* "creditors" to get paid, if they even manage to file a claim against the company to begin with. In a bankruptcy case, even if a contributor *does* file a claim, one can hope to gain at best pennies on the dollar.

In cases where a writer needs to take steps to obtain an overdue payment or to regain a set of rights, a contract can be both an enemy and an asset. A bad contract can be nearly impossible to overturn—but at the same time, having *no* contract can make it virtually impossible for a writer to claim a debt. A writer's best protection is to be able to understand and negotiate a contract—and, when necessary, to protect one's assets by writing one's own.

CHAPTER 15

Setting Fees and Getting Paid

One question new freelancers often ask is "How much should I charge?" The short answer is "It's not your choice." While many forms of self-employment enable one to set one's own rates, freelance writing is the exception. In this business, rates are determined by the market, and freelancers have little control over what they are paid. In addition, most markets are notoriously inflexible. If a magazine pays ten cents per word, don't expect to talk them into twenty-five cents per word.

There are other ways, however, to determine your preferred rate of pay, even if you can't convince editors to loosen their purse strings.

BY THE WORD VS. BY THE HOUR

If you've come to freelancing from a "normal" job, you may be used to a paycheck that was based on an hourly rate. As you plan your projects, it's a good idea to keep that hourly rate in mind. By determining the hourly rate you prefer to receive, you can determine what publications to approach, what projects to accept, and how much time to invest in each project.

Determining that rate is a highly individual decision. If you're trying to support yourself entirely through freelancing, you'll need to set it fairly high (especially as you must take into account the hours spent on nonpaying work, such as queries, researching markets, accounting, and administrative tasks). On the other hand, if you're trying to break in and don't need to earn a living wage, you can set a lower rate.

The next step is to determine how long a project is likely to take. In the beginning, this may not be easy; tasks such as interviewing, research, and revision may take longer than you expect. As you become more experienced, however, you'll be able to estimate a project's requirements fairly accurately. Then, setting your rate becomes a simple matter of dividing a magazine's fee by the estimated number of hours to see if it meets your requirement.

Suppose, for example, that a magazine offers $100 per feature article, and you've decided that you want to earn $20 per hour. In that case, you'd only pitch an article idea to this magazine if you were certain you could complete the piece in five hours or less. On the other hand, if a magazine offers $1,000 per feature, you'll be willing to invest considerably more time and effort. Based on your hourly rate calculations, you'll also soon realize that a single $1,000 article usually pays considerably more than ten $100 articles, given the rate of effort per article.

Another way to look at your rate is by averaging it across assignments. Suppose you accept a $100 assignment, but spend ten hours completing the project. You've earned only $10 per hour, or half your goal. On the other hand, another article may bring you $600 for ten hours' work, giving you a total of $60 per hour. On the average, you're now earning $35 per hour, which exceeds your goal (and also helps compensate for all those hours when you aren't earning a penny). Often, "averaging" is a more accurate method of determining how much your time is actually worth.

WHEN TIME ISN'T THE ONLY FACTOR

Money is nice, but it may not be the only consideration when choosing whether to seek or accept a particular assignment. Some factors may be worth more than cash, including:

- **Credentials.** If you're starting out, your first goal may be to build a portfolio of clips. In the early stages of freelancing, getting published is often more important than getting highly paid. A track record of success and acceptance can be more important than the actual fees.
- **Practice.** Some writers believe that every word they write makes them a better writer and is therefore worth the effort. Writing for

lower-paying markets can provide an opportunity to build and hone your skills, and prepare you for the demands of better markets.

- **Love.** Sometimes you may choose to write about a particular subject, or for a particular publication, simply because it's what you want to do. In such cases, passion counts for more than cash. Many writers would rather get paid a little for writing about what they love, than get paid big bucks for writing material of no personal interest.

Conversely, you may also discover that some projects aren't worth doing, no matter how much they pay. Some factors outweigh the potential financial benefits of a piece, including:

- **Difficult editors.** Some editors provide unclear guidelines, then expect a writer to keep revising a piece until the editor finally decides it's "right." Some are impossible to please, even when you provide exactly what was asked for. Some drag out the process by constantly asking for one more thing—more information, another interview, another sidebar, another revision, ad infinitum. Others won't answer your questions, provide clarification, or even return your calls or email. Whatever the problem, a difficult editor can outweigh the benefit of a check.
- **Unacceptable alterations.** Few things are as frustrating as to submit an article, and then find that the published piece bears little or no resemblance to your work. Perhaps it was edited by someone with no concept of basic grammar, resulting in a piece that you'd be ashamed to send out as a clip. Perhaps it was cut to half its length, wasting your work. Or perhaps material has been added that actually contradicts the point of your article. If this happens, it's wise to avoid that market in the future, unless you really don't care what appears under your byline!
- **Unfair terms.** Only you can decide what terms you're willing to accept when negotiating a contract. Keep in mind, however, that even a high rate of pay may not fully compensate for the loss of your rights. Be very sure, when giving up all rights or signing a work-for-hire contract, that you have absolutely no chance of selling that material elsewhere.

- **Damage to your reputation.** Will an article make you look good, or bad? Sometimes the very context in which an article appears may damage your reputation in a particular field. If the publication itself is not reputable within a field in which you hope to sell more work, selling to that publication could damage your career. It's also important to avoid assignments that might cast you in a negative light—for example, articles that present an opinion that you don't agree with. What you say in print will be taken as representing your point of view, even if it doesn't. Your good name is worth more than any paycheck, and losing it can make you "poor indeed."

The "bottom line" for a writer can be influenced by a number of factors, of which money is only one. By considering those factors carefully, you *can* set the rates you desire—rates that not only improve your bank account but also contribute to your ongoing career goals.

WHEN TO ASK FOR MORE MONEY

While publications generally quote a specific payment rate in their guidelines, the reality is that most publications offer a *range* of rates, and the quoted rate is usually at the lowest end. Editors know that most writers will never bother to ask if they can get a higher rate. Many writers, indeed, are *afraid* to ask such a question; they fear it will make them look demanding or unprofessional.

Of course, asking for a raise *can* make you look unprofessional if you do it at the wrong time, or in the wrong way. Here are some *bad* times to ask for more money:

- **When you contribute your first article to a publication.** When you contact a publication, the editor assumes you have reviewed the guidelines and are aware of the pay rates. If the rate isn't what you want, don't write for them! It's not professional to demand a higher rate on your first submission.
- **When your article is due.** As an editor, I've had more than one writer who accepts an assignment—only to call on the due date to ask for more money. Editors have a word for this: blackmail. Essentially, the writer is threatening to hold an article "hostage" for more

pay. A writer may get away with this once if the editor absolutely *has* to have the article (for example, the cover has already been printed with a blurb advertising the piece). However, you can be sure that if you try this approach, you'll never write for that publication again!

- **When you find that an article is taking more work than you expected.** When you agree to write an article, you agree to the terms. If you find that an article is requiring more work than you anticipated, that's your problem, not the editor's. Telling an editor that the article is "harder than you thought" simply looks like bad planning on your part.

The best time to ask about higher pay is after you've sold your second or third article to the same publication. The editor should be familiar with your work, and you may even be considered a regular contributor. If you're a reliable contributor, an editor will generally want to keep you happy, and one way to do so is to increase your rate.

Before you ask for a raise, however, take a look at what happens to your work after you submit it. Are your articles printed just as you write them, or are they substantially revised and edited? If an editor has to invest a lot of work in your contributions—particularly if he needs to clean up grammar, spelling, and punctuation—then he may not be enthusiastic about giving you more money. Editors generally pay higher rates to contributors who need the *least* amount of editorial work.

You also need to know the criteria for different rate levels. Some publications offer higher rates for articles that are more difficult—that involve more research, interviews, or expert knowledge. For example, a publication may pay more for an article that requires interviews with four or five technical experts than for a short, personal piece. If you're writing shorter, easier pieces, start asking for more difficult assignments—and then ask for more money. For example, you might approach the editor with a statement like this:

Thank you for the assignment to write _____. I see that this piece will require considerably more research than some of the previous articles I've written for you. It will involve several interviews and a lot of fact-checking. Consequently, I feel it might be worth a higher rate than you have paid in the past. I note that your pay range is between XXX and XXX—any chance that you could bump this one up a bit on the scale?

Note that you should make this request before you begin the article, not after you've written it—for, again, that may look like you're trying to hold the article "hostage" for more money. If the editor isn't willing to raise the rate, you can then choose whether to complete the assignment at the lower rate, or let the editor know that you don't feel the compensation is sufficient for the amount of work involved.

Another approach is to ask the editor to move you from the "new contributor" pay range to the "established contributor" range:

I notice that your guidelines indicate that you have a pay range from XXX to XXX. I assume that the lower end of this range is the rate you offer new writers. As I've now contributed (X) articles, I'd like to think I've moved up to the status of regular contributor. Any chance that my pay could be adjusted to reflect that?

Yet another approach is to ask what the criteria are for higher payments:

I notice that your guidelines specify a pay range of XXX to XXX. Can you tell me what the criteria are for the higher rates? I'd like to offer you the best possible product, and knowing exactly what you're looking for will help!

Keep in mind that pay rates aren't always controlled by the editor. If a range is specified, however, chances are that the editor has a voice in what writers are paid, and it never hurts to ask. Again, don't let fear stand in the way. The key is "professionalism."

MAKING SURE YOU GET PAID

"Selling" your article is only half the battle. The other half involves getting your check.

Some publications offer payment once they have received a signed contract. Others require an invoice from the writer. I recommend sending an invoice even if it is *not* required. This provides a good record for you, both in case you need to take further action, and also so that you can monitor outstanding payments.

These days, you'll usually be expected to submit an invoice by email, so don't bother picking up invoice blanks at an office supply store. Simply design an invoice in a spreadsheet program such as Excel. This way you can email it (I usually convert it to PDF before doing so), or print it out if necessary—and you retain a copy on your computer.

INVOICE

DATE: (Date of invoice)

TO: (Contact name, publication, address)

FROM: (Your name, address)

FOR: (Article title)

(If the person you're invoicing handles several different publications, you might also wish to list the title of the publication the article has or will appear in, and the issue date.)

AMOUNT DUE: $XXX

(If the payment rate is per-word, include the word count here—for example, "2,000 words @ 5¢/word = $100")

Send the invoice to your editor, who *should* send it to the accounting department on your behalf. If you don't receive payment, contact the editor—who may then tell *you* to send the invoice to accounting. If so, send it again—but remember, it's the editor's responsibility to make sure that contributors are paid.

If you are a first-time contributor to a publication, there is often one more step that must be taken before you can get paid. That is the completion of the W-9 form, or "Request for Taxpayer Identification Number and Certification." This form will provide the publication with your Social Security number and verification that the publisher is not obligated to withhold taxes from your payments. Often this form will be sent to you by email, sometimes in PDF format that enables you to fill in the blanks on your computer and email it directly back. Or, you may receive a form that you need to print out, complete, and then either mail back or scan and return by email. In some cases you may get the form by mail, but this is becoming less common.

What if you don't get paid? If a significant amount of time goes by and you haven't seen a check, start following up. Start with a written request, by email or surface mail. It's important, at this point, to establish a paper trail that demonstrates your efforts to obtain payment. Make sure that you have a contract or a letter of agreement stating what you're supposed to be paid and when, and an invoice indicating that you've made an attempt to collect payment. Save copies of any correspondence you send thereafter. Submit regular invoices to the accounting department, and indicate the amount of time that has elapsed (e.g., thirty days, sixty days, etc.) from the date of the first invoice. If you still receive no response, contact the editor by phone.

The sad truth is that there will be times when, even though you've done everything you can, you will get stiffed. It happens. Sometimes publications change hands, and the new owner refuses to honor the contracts or invoices of previous contributors. Sometimes a publication shuts down or goes bankrupt, and though writers can submit their invoices to the court for collection, they're likely to be the last creditors paid and may receive only pennies on the dollar (if anything). And sometimes you run into a publication that simply doesn't honor its agreements.

When this happens, you may be able to get assistance from a writers' organization such as the National Writers Union (www.nwu.org) or the Authors Guild (www.authorsguild.org). Unfortunately, you have to be a *member* of such an organization before you can turn to their legal department for help, and dues tend to be high. If, however, you're trying to claim a payment of $500 or more, a membership fee may be worth the cost.

Beyond that, there is little you can do. Generally, the amount isn't sufficient to justify hiring a collection agency or filing a lawsuit. The one bright spot is that if a publication fails to pay, it has breached its contract, leaving you free to market the material elsewhere. The best response to nonpayment (after you've exhausted every recourse) is to move on, and don't waste time agonizing over the loss.

Finally, until you're familiar with a market and know that it *does* pay in a timely fashion, never submit a *second* article until you've been paid for the first! I've heard from writers who have submitted five or six articles even though they haven't received payment for their first submission. Having a publisher express interest in your work is great, but make sure that interest is backed up with cash.

CHAPTER 16

Writing and Selling a Column

If you specialize in a particular subject area, or have an area of expertise you'd like to write more about, consider launching a column. A column is a great way to establish yourself as an expert, and offers a steady income. Opportunities for columns can be found in magazines (usually monthly), newspapers (generally weekly but sometimes daily), and websites (typically weekly, monthly, or bimonthly). Today, many online columns appear in the form of a blog.

While magazines offer the best pay rates for columns (from a few hundred dollars to thousands), this market is the most difficult to crack, as space is the most limited. When a column opening comes up, most editors will turn to regular contributors, so the best way to get a shot at a magazine column is to become a contributor. Once you've sold several articles to a magazine, try pitching a column idea. Even if it's not accepted, it will let the editor know that you're interested in doing a column if something opens up in the future. Magazines generally expect exclusive rights to a column.

Newspapers represent the largest market for columns. Even the smallest regional papers generally run a few columns, often by local authors. Larger papers run a mix of local and national syndicated columns. Daily papers usually offer a mix of daily and weekly columns. Weekly papers offer weekly and sometimes monthly columns. Weekend editions often have their own set of columns, often covering reviews, local events, and entertainment.

Newspapers also offer the widest variety of content opportunities, as they may have sections covering health, cooking, lifestyles, women's issues, fashion, entertainment, sports, business, real estate, home décor, and more. Papers may also use columns of specific regional interest. The downside is that the pay scale tends to be lower (anywhere from $10 to $50 in smaller papers). However, you can often self-syndicate a column to more than one regional paper. (Most national papers buy exclusive rights, but also offer a much higher fee.)

Electronic publications offer excellent opportunities for columnists, as they have fewer space constraints. A web-based publication could have any number of regular columns. An email newsletter, on the other hand, will tend to have only one per issue, as most email newsletters limit their length to avoid getting trashed as spam. (A newsletter might, however, feature links to additional columns on a website.) Many commercial and "catalog" sites use columnists to offer material intended to attract customers, and often pay more than an independent "zine." And, again, many electronic publications feature columns in the forms of blogs.

Electronic columns are usually archived, so readers can access not only your current column but all previous columns. Most electronic publications want exclusive rights, or at least exclusive *first electronic* rights, making it less likely that you'll be able to market the same column to more than one online publication. Most electronic markets pay less than print markets, except for those affiliated with commercial enterprises, print publications, or other media.

CHOOSING A COLUMN TOPIC

Magazine columns generally follow the same principles that apply to articles, with how-to and informational columns being the most common. Personal experience columns may also be used if they fit the magazine's content. For example, the British publication *Country Living* once featured a column on "life in a country village." When that columnist quit, they followed up with a column on how to live the "country" life in the city.

Thus, the easiest way to determine what type of column to pitch to a magazine is to look at its regular content and choose a topic that could be covered on a monthly basis. Magazines may also feature editorial/opinion columns, news roundups, review columns, and regional coverage (e.g., local restaurants, night spots, entertainment, events, personalities, etc.). Another popular type of column is the "advice" format, in which the columnist answers questions from the magazine's readership. A pet magazine, for example, might have a medical or behavioral advice column, while a women's magazine might have an advice column on relationships, parenting, or family finance.

To write a magazine how-to column, you need to have expertise in the field. Unlike a single feature article, where you can interview experts, a monthly column will be drawing on *your* knowledge of a subject, and a successful pitch will be based on your credentials. Don't try to pitch a gardening column if you don't know a rake from a hoe! Similarly, if you want to pitch an advice column, you'll need to demonstrate that you have the credentials to *answer* the questions readers will ask.

Newspapers may offer a similar array of columns, but focus more on a general readership than on the subject-specific readership of a magazine. Since daily newspapers often offer a different special-interest section each day, these offer a wide range of column possibilities. If your expertise is real estate, consider pitching a column about tips on buying and selling homes, or dealing with your local real estate market. If you have business expertise, consider pitching a column for the business section—and so on.

Newspapers also generally offer a variety of op-ed and personal columns. Op-ed columns (so called because they appear on the page "opposite the editorial") typically focus on a specific perspective or viewpoint—liberal, conservative, feminine, minority, and so on. To pitch an op-ed column, you'll need to persuade the editor that your opinion is worth hearing— and that it will interest a substantial portion of the newspaper's audience. Personal columns tend to focus on a "slice of life" approach, again often addressing local issues or lifestyle topics that will appeal to a large portion of the readership. "Slice of life" columns may be humorous or serious.

Newspapers also use review columns, covering movies, books, products, new technologies, entertainment, local events, restaurants, nightlife, and more. A newspaper's travel section might include reviews of travel destinations and accommodations. The best way to break in with this type of column is to pick a topic that isn't already being reviewed, and offer a convincing argument as to why the paper should cover it. This type of column often requires no special expertise or credentials (though if you're going to review something like computer equipment, you'll need to convince an editor that you understand technology). Such columns often blur the line between information and entertainment; review columns are often chosen as much for the writer's style and voice as for the reviews themselves. The bad news is that for this very reason, review columns are often the first thing amateur writers try to pitch. To earn a space, you'll have to demonstrate that your column rises above the competition.

A review column doesn't necessarily mean free tickets to movies, free dinners, free travel, or free books. I get lots of letters from writers who want to know how to get on a publisher's list for free books to review. Publishers, however, rarely send books to individual reviewers. Instead, they send them to *publications,* which pass them along to established reviewers.

Newspapers also run humor columns, but these tend to be few and nationally syndicated (think Dave Barry). This type of column is very difficult to sell, because the market for humor is limited—partly because a lot of people aren't as funny as they think they are, and partly because newspapers devote a limited amount of space to this type of column.

PITCHING YOUR COLUMN

Once you've chosen a topic, you need to develop a proposal that includes the following elements:

- **A catchy title.** Keep in mind that the editor may *change* that title once the column is accepted, but you still need to develop one that will get an editor's attention.
- **An overview of the column's general subject area.** Explain what the column will cover over time, why you feel that this coverage is important for the publication, and what the general purpose of the column will be.
- **A list of topics.** If you're pitching a monthly column, you'll need to provide at least six months of topics; if you're pitching a weekly column, try to develop topics for two to three months.
- **Three to six sample columns.**
- **A list of your credentials**. These should include an author bio and a photo. You may also include your publications list and, if appropriate, your resume or curriculum vitae.

While it *is* possible to pitch a column by email, the best approach is still a physical package sent by surface mail, especially if you're pitching to a magazine. Most columnists recommend assembling these materials in a pocket folder, with a label bearing the name of the proposed column, and your name, on the cover.

Your package should include a basic query letter, structured much like an article query. However, instead of proposing a single piece, you're proposing an ongoing series, so the goal of your query is to present a rationale for why the target publication would want to cover your subject on a regular basis. Instead of going into detail about any single column, your query should present an overview of the nature and purpose of the entire column. Describe the subject, and explain why this subject is of sufficient importance or interest to merit ongoing coverage.

Any of the types of hooks mentioned in chapter 7 will also work for a column. For example, if you were proposing a column on natural health alternatives to a general-interest women's magazine, you might try any of the following hooks:

- **Problem/solution:** "Many women today are becoming increasingly frustrated with the limitations of 'traditional medicine.' Often, traditional techniques—or harried HMO doctors with not enough time—just don't seem to answer women's questions or meet their needs. More and more women are seeking alternatives—and seeking accurate, helpful information to guide them toward those alternatives."
- **Informative**: "Natural remedies have become big business. No longer confined to strip-mall 'health stores,' they now line the pharmacy shelves of every supermarket. Now, more than ever, women are in need of accurate, reliable information on the products competing for their health dollars—and on how to safely incorporate natural health care into their lives."
- **Question:** "Are you bewildered by the array of natural products on your local supermarket shelves? Do you wonder whether these products are safe, whether they can actually meet their claims, or how to choose between them? If so, you're not alone; thousands of women face the same decisions every day."
- **Personal experience/anecdote:** "When I had my first baby, I wasn't prepared for the violent reaction I would have to XXX drug. Yet it was all my doctors could offer. The next time, I vowed to be

prepared; I studied alternatives, and found natural solutions that eased my pain without ruining my health. Since then, I've talked to many women who wished they had the same options. . . ."

- **Attention grabber:** "Nature can be the death of you—even when it's attractively bottled in a supposedly 'safe' product on your supermarket shelf. While natural remedies offer a host of helpful alternatives to traditional health care, it's vital to know what you're doing—what's in that bottle, how much you can safely take, whether it actually works, and how it might react with other natural products."

Your hook should lead directly into your pitch, which will include not only the title of the column, but its length and frequency (unless this is defined by the frequency of the publication). If you're pitching to a newspaper, mention the section in which you believe your column should appear. A good pitch to follow the hooks above might read:

I'd like to offer you a [monthly, weekly] column covering the many facets of natural health care. Titled "Natural Health," this column would fit well within your "To Your Health" section. It would run between 750 and 1,000 words, and cover such topics as:

Follow this with the body of your query, in which you'll list a selection of topics to be covered in the column. A bullet list often works well for this:

- Traditional home remedies: which ones work, and why.
- How to read and understand the labels of "natural" products.
- Why "natural" doesn't necessarily mean "safe," and how to use such products safely.
- Understanding the health claims of natural products: what they're based on, whether they're true.
- Product interactions: knowing which natural products can be taken together, and which can be harmful.
- Teas, tisanes, and distillations: how to best prepare a natural remedy.
- Natural remedies for pregnancy and childbirth problems.

Finally, close with your credentials: the skills, expertise, education, job experience, and any other factors that qualify you to write this column or dispense advice to readers. Since an inaccurate column can damage the credibility of the entire publication, an editor will want to be sure you're the right person for the job.

The final, closing paragraph of your query should offer a potential start date for your column, and may also be the place to specify your terms—the rights you're offering, and, if appropriate, the fee you would like to receive. Unless you're self-syndicating the column, however (see below), you'll generally leave these items for subsequent negotiation.

While you'll be sending sample columns with your proposal, you may also wish to include relevant clips that support your credentials and demonstrate your ability to write on the chosen topic. Be sure to mention any articles you've written for the publication you're pitching to! Clips from professional or academic journals can help establish your expertise and experience writing on your chosen topic, but they may not reflect the style you'd use for a consumer publication, so balance them with clips that show your ability to write for a more general audience. A published book also makes an excellent credential. Send copies of one or two relevant chapters and a page of excerpts from favorable reviews.

Again, you'll generally submit this package by surface mail. If you're submitting a proposal to an electronic publication, however, you may need to put these materials into an email. If so, find out from the editor whether you can send attachments (such as your resume, publications list, and sample columns), or whether you need to place everything in the body of an email. If you must put everything in a single email, limit that email to a basic query, a list of topics, and *one* sample column, and offer to send the editor additional materials on request.

SELF-SYNDICATING YOUR COLUMN

Since newspaper readership is generally based on geography rather than subject matter, it is often possible to "self-syndicate" a newspaper column to more than one publication. You can sell the same column to newspapers in different states (provided that the subject is applicable), or even to papers in different counties or cities in the same state, as long as those papers have little or no reader overlap.

Reader overlap is not necessarily determined by location. It is also determined by the size and distribution of a paper. While readers of a local paper in one town or county may not read a similar paper that is published in the next town or county, they *may* read a larger city paper that is distributed to *both* towns. For example, residents of Olympia, Washington, may read the local *Olympian* but aren't likely to read a local paper published in nearby Tumwater. However, residents of Olympia *and* Tumwater are likely to read the larger Tacoma *News Tribune* or *Seattle Times*.

To self-syndicate your column, you must have a topic that travels well. You're not likely to be able to syndicate a local review column, for example. Nor would you be able to syndicate a column that might have regional appeal—for example, gardening in the Pacific Northwest—that won't be useful to readers in a completely different climate. Columns on more universal topics, such as home décor, real estate, parenting, health, fitness, or cooking can be distributed to a wide range of papers. Your column must also offer something unique. While you may be the only person writing about parenting for your hometown paper, thousands of other writers cover this topic in other regions, so your column would have to offer something special to compete.

Finding Markets

You can locate newspapers through one of more than a dozen electronic newsstands on the web. Many of these, however, simply provide a title and URL; you'll have to dig deeper to locate the names of appropriate editors, and their address or email. Nor do most of these sites offer information on a paper's distribution area or circulation. Some don't even state whether a paper is daily, weekly, or monthly. (Visit www.writing-world.com/links/magazines.shtml for a list of online newsstands.)

The *Gale Directory of Publications and Broadcast Media*, which you'll find in the reference section of any library, offers information about newspapers' circulation, frequency, and staff. If, for example, you've decided you want to target daily newspapers with a circulation of over 20,000, try the *Gale Directory*. You don't want to waste time submitting to weekly shoppers, or to papers with no budget for freelance material.

If a region is served by several local papers and a larger state or big-city newspaper, you'll need to decide which to target first. This decision may not be as easy as it sounds. While a big-city paper may pay more (and will reach a larger audience), it is also likely to demand more rights or even all rights). It is also more likely to want to post your material on its website, which can further limit your ability to distribute that column elsewhere. Smaller papers, though offering lower pay, may demand fewer rights and may not post columns online.

Protecting Your Rights

Rights are a key issue in self-syndicating a column. Start thinking about rights when you sell your very first column to your very first paper. Don't assume you'll never wish to expand. More and more publications want writers to sign over all rights to their columns, or even produce them as "work-for-hire" (which means giving up your copyright). Publications that pay as little as $10 to $50 per column may still expect you to fork over all rights.

If you hope to sell your work elsewhere, you must retain the rights to do so. Typically, you will want to offer a newspaper "one-time nonexclusive rights" to your column, perhaps with the guarantee that the column will not appear in a competing publication. An alternative is to offer "exclusive regional rights," and define "region" as narrowly as possible. The region should be limited to the area of the newspaper's general readership. If the paper is read only in Yakima, Washington, for example, don't let it prevent you from selling the same column to a paper in Seattle or Tacoma.

In some cases, a newspaper will want first rights. This may work if your first column sale is to your local paper, because it still gives you the ability to resell that column a week later to all your other markets. Since only one publication can ever be first, however, think carefully before granting this option.

Don't be tempted to accept more money for all rights. The goal of self-syndication is not to earn a huge amount from any single publication, but to gain the widest possible distribution for your piece. Payment for columns is always fairly limited; you're not likely to get more than $500 from even the largest paper. If you can sell the same piece to twenty newspapers that offer $50 apiece, you've already doubled that figure, and more than doubled your readership as well. If you have hopes of moving on to national syndication, readership figures will be vital to your success. It is better to be read not just by a large number of people, but by a large number of people distributed across a wide range of markets.

Watch out for papers owned by a larger conglomerate. I've heard from more than one columnist who has discovered that a column that was intended for one paper has been distributed by the paper's "parent company" to dozens of other newspapers without permission or any extra pay.

Finally, determine the minimum rate you're willing to accept. Some small newspapers offer as little as $10 per column, but that can add up quickly if you can sell your column to several papers. Some columnists set a fee based on circulation, such as 50¢ per 1,000 subscribers.

Preparing Your Package

Self-syndication has one downside: expense. Most newspapers still prefer to receive column proposals by surface mail. This means that to pitch your idea to multiple markets, you'll have to invest in postage, printing, and envelopes.

Your submission package will be much the same as that described above, including a cover or query letter, three to six sample columns, a list of topics, your credentials, clips, and a SASE or a self-addressed, stamped postcard with check boxes for an editor's response. Newspaper editors often prefer a postcard to a SASE, as it enables them to check the appropriate response rather than having to write an acceptance letter. Your postcard might read something like this:

Date: _____

Dear (Your Name):

Thank you for submitting your proposal for a column titled "Natural Health Tips for Seniors."

_____ We would like to use this column on a weekly basis. We will pay you a fee of $_____ for one-time, nonexclusive rights (per your guarantee that the column will not appear in a directly competing publication).

_____ We regret that we cannot use your column.

(Signed) _____

Editor's Name: _____

If you plan to submit your column to a large number of newspapers, you'll probably want to have your materials printed in bulk. Have your cover letter printed on a good-quality paper stock; your clips and column samples can be printed on plain 20-pound bond. Most print shops will also be able to print your return postcard. To save costs, print clips double sided.

It *is* possible, though more difficult, to pitch a newspaper column by email. First, you'll have to build a list of email contacts. As with pitching a regular column, you won't be able to send as many materials as you would by surface mail. Usually, you'll be limited to a *short* query letter, a brief list of topics, a description of your credentials, and one sample column. Offer the editor the opportunity to receive more materials either by mail or email.

Don't be surprised if you never hear anything from the majority of the editors you query. Most newspaper editors don't bother with rejections; they respond only if they are interested in a submission. While you can follow up on nonresponders, this may not produce a response either. If you don't hear from a market, just drop it from your list and move on.

When an editor *does* respond, don't be surprised if he wants to modify your terms, perhaps by suggesting a different word count or a lower price. It's up to you to decide whether to accept changes. If you're distributing your column to a large number of publications, it's usually easier to send the same column to everyone and let individual editors make their own changes or cuts, rather than tailor several versions for different markets. On the other hand, if you're working with only a few editors, this can be a good way to build a better relationship with them and possibly gain assignments in the future.

Self-syndication is a wonderful way to build your portfolio. Be sure to ask for copies of the issues in which your column appears, or at least a tear sheet of your column. If your column is published online, keep a record of the links to each installment. You can also "print to PDF" to capture your column exactly as it appears on the publisher's website and use it as a future clip.

Once you have a regular column with a local paper (even if it's not local to *you*), you can list yourself as a contributor or stringer to that publication. This may be just the stepping-stone you need to propel your column into the big leagues—such as national syndication![15]

---

15 This chapter is excerpted from *The Writer's Guide to Queries, Pitches and Proposals* (Allworth Press, 2010).

CHAPTER 17

Writing for Newspapers

by Sue Fagalde Lick

Any writer who is serious about writing, selling their work, and communicating with readers needs to consider newspapers as a possible market. Here's why:

1. **Most people read at least one newspaper regularly.** According to the Pew Research Center, just over 1,300 daily newspapers were published in the United States as of 2014 (the most recent year for which data were available as of this writing).[16] This doesn't count the many weeklies, monthlies, and special-interest papers also being produced. According to the Newspaper Association of America, 69 percent of adults read a newspaper in print or online at least once a week, or access it via a mobile device at least once a month.[17]

2. **There are more newspapers than magazines, and they come out more often, so they require more content.** On daily and weekly general-interest papers, staff writers cover most of the news and many of the main features. The Associated Press and other wire services provide national and world news. But there are many stories the staff and wire services don't cover. That's where freelancers come in. Smaller newspapers generally have smaller staffs. How do they survive? Freelance writers!

---

16 Michael Barthel, "Newspapers: Fact Sheet," in *State of the News Media 2016*, Pew Research Center, June 15, 2016, http://www.journalism.org/2016/06/15/newspapers-fact-sheet/.

17 Jim Conaghan, "Across Platforms, 7 in 10 Adults Access Content from Newspaper Media Each Week," News Media Alliance, March 25, 2013, https://www.newsmediaalliance.org /research_tools/across-platforms-7-10-adults-access-content-newspaper-media-week/.

3. **Special-interest papers are everywhere.** Go out for coffee, and you'll probably see a rack with entertainment newspapers and papers put out by special-interest groups: the LGBTQ community, Hispanics, coffee aficionados, and others. Go to the library, and you'll find even more papers. Visit an antiques store, and you'll find newspapers on antiques. You may receive a church newspaper. Most religions have local, regional, or national publications. And don't overlook newspapers aimed at particular industries, such as *CD Computing News* or *Real Estate Weekly News*.

HOW DO MAGAZINE AND NEWSPAPER WRITING DIFFER?

Many of the tasks involved in writing for newspapers and magazines are the same. But there are differences.

1. **Mission.** The mission of many general-interest newspapers is to be the place readers look for news and features about their area. Remember the slogan "location, location, location?" For newspapers, it's "local, local, local." If there's no local angle, they don't want it, no matter how fascinating or well written it might be.

   Other papers center on a particular group or interest. The newspaper put out by the Catholic Archdiocese of Chicago may run some wire stories about Catholics outside of Chicago, but it won't run anything about Methodists. I used to work for a Hispanic newspaper called *El Observador*. The editors made it very clear that if the subject did not have a connection to the Hispanic community, it would not get in.

2. **News peg.** Timeliness is often a factor in getting an article published. Editors ask, "Why write this story now?" A feature on an artist is more likely to sell if it can be tied to an upcoming gallery show. A school program may be deemed worthy of a feature if it's new, being considered for budget cuts, or just won an award. Stories that can be tied to holidays or anniversaries of major events have more chance of getting published. Stories on chocolate sell for Valentine's Day, religious stories abound as Easter approaches, skiing sells in January.

3. **Timing.** While most magazines are put together at least two months in advance, news and sports sections of the newspaper are written, edited, and laid out less than twenty-four hours before publication. Feature sections are generally planned a little further ahead. This may be a week or, in the case of holidays or other special events, a month or two. For weekly newspapers, get your queries in at least two weeks ahead, and for monthlies, allow at least two months.

4. **Pay.** Many newspapers pay less than magazines. I have seen local papers that pay less than a penny a word, while five to ten cents a word is more common for community weeklies. This won't make you rich, but can help if you need experience and clips. The big dailies generally pay at least $100 for columns and opinion pieces, and as much as $500 for feature articles. The *Chicago Tribune* pays up to $500 for travel pieces. The *Christian Science Monitor* rates start at $250 per article.

5. **Writing style.** Most of us have heard of the "inverted pyramid," the traditional style for newspaper stories. In essence, you start with the most important information and work your way down to the least important so that if the story is too long, the editor can cut it from the bottom. If you wind up writing news stories, you will need to employ the inverted pyramid. However, most freelancers write features (non-news stories) where the style is similar to that of magazine articles.

6. **Words vs. inches.** Some editors will ask for a number of inches rather than words. You can ask them how many words or characters that includes, or you can figure it out for yourself. With a ruler, measure an inch of type. Count how many lines there are per inch, most commonly six, then determine the average number of words per line and multiply that by the number of lines. Do this for several column inches to come up with an approximate number of words per inch. Some editors use the number of characters to determine column inches. Some computer programs will give you the character count as well as the word count.

FINDING FREELANCE OPPORTUNITIES

Now the fun begins. Gather up all the newspapers you can. Set aside the ones that don't interest you, because you don't want to write for a publication you don't want to read. (Trust me.) Now start reading. Go for the big paper first.

If you don't subscribe, buy one at a newsstand or go to the library. You should go there anyway; you'll find newspapers you didn't know existed.

You're looking for two things: sections with articles written by freelancers, and subjects that seem to fit the paper's mission but aren't being covered. For example, if your daily newspaper rarely touches on your neighborhood, maybe they need a freelance correspondent. If nobody seems to be covering your city council or school board—or your local churches, artists, or sports teams—there's an opening for you.

For most dailies, the feature sections are your most likely freelance outlets. These include sections on food, home and garden, travel, entertainment, arts and books, religion, and business. There is also generally a "living," "community," or "our town" section. There may be a special Sunday magazine or feature section. Big papers covering large areas may have weekly sections focusing on particular neighborhoods. Read these sections especially carefully. Look at the bylines at the end of stories. Are the writers identified as staff writers or are they listed as "special writers" or some other category that lets you know they're not part of the staff? Those are freelancers.

Look in the paper for names of the editors. Each section usually has a separate editor. You can often find them on the editorial page. Sometimes newspapers run lists of editors in the front or local section. If you can't find the name in the paper, don't give up. Most papers have websites now. One way to find a newspaper online is to search for its title through a search engine; another is to use one of the many newspaper-list sites (for a list of newspaper directories, visit writing-world.com/links/magazines.shtml). Worst case, make a phone call and ask for the name of the editor. Make sure you also ask how to spell it. If it's unclear from the name whether the editor is male or female, ask if that's Mr. or Ms.

The same method goes for specialty newspapers. Read the paper, look at the masthead, look at the bylines, look for blurbs in the paper asking for submissions. Or, call the newspaper. Ask if they use freelancers and whom you should address material to. The worst they can say is no.

TYPES OF NEWSPAPER ARTICLES

Just like magazines, newspapers thrive on a variety of types of material. Many of these are similar to the types of features you find in magazines, only they generally require a local and/or timely slant.

- **Personality profiles** are standard in newspapers as well as in magazines. You interview someone of interest to the local community or special-interest group because of what he does or his history. A profile may include research from other sources, including interviews of friends, family, and coworkers.

- **Human interest stories**—Jill Dick, author of *Freelancing for Newspapers*, writes, "Study the 'ordinary' stories told by 'ordinary' folk and you'll soon realize . . . that there is a huge depth of warm-hearted humanity that doesn't make the front pages and is often obscured by the constant daily dirge of evil, death, and destruction man everywhere wreaks on his fellow man. Thousands of 'good' stories are just waiting to be told—and when they are, they touch many hearts."

- **Business features** are big in local papers, partially because they help sell advertising, but they also let the community know what's available. Look for a news peg, such as a business just opening, selling a new product, moving to a new location, or planning to close. Maybe your favorite lunch place is about to start serving dinner. Time for a story.

- **Reviews** come in many forms. The bigger newspapers may run reviews of books, plays, concerts, restaurants, movies, or computer software. See who writes these stories. If you don't see reviews of the thing you're interested in, query and see if they'll let you do it. It helps to have some sample reviews ready. Try one just for fun.

- **Roundup pieces** are popular with many editors. I have written everything from where to get a good hamburger to a survey of services offered by local funeral parlors. Travel sections may run "best cruises" or "best playgrounds to take the kids." The food section might do a roundup of local wineries or culinary schools or places to eat pancakes. In the spring, papers look at wedding-related topics, such as the most romantic places to get married or the best places to hold a reception. These are not terribly creative to write, but they are lucrative, and editors love them.

- **How-to** articles help a reader solve a problem, whether it's how to build a birdhouse, how to clean the scum off the bathroom floor, or how to buy a digital camera. You don't always need to be an expert on the subject. You just need to interview someone who is.

- **Opinion pieces** allow you to sound off on a subject. These usually go on what is called the op-ed page, meaning it's the page opposite the one with the staff editorials. Dailies sometimes run a whole opinion section on Sundays. These are rarely just one writer's opinion with nothing to back it up. Such pieces require some research or knowledge, a bit like the essays you wrote in high school or college.
- **Personal experience** articles appear in many feature sections, especially travel stories. Here, using the first person, you tell of something that happened to you, using sights, sounds, smells, colors, moods, and physical description to help the reader experience what you have experienced. A news peg would help you get it published. Your experience as a temporary Santa Claus would be perfect at Christmas.
- **Investigative articles** delve into a subject, ferreting out information that has not been made public before. Often they unmask government wrongdoing, expose a health issue, or look into a crime or disaster. These require a lot of work, using multiple sources to go below the surface and tell a complete story. Usually staff writers do the investigative pieces, but it is possible in some markets for freelancers to contribute.
- **News stories** are covered by staff and wire services on large newspapers, but community newspapers may hire stringers to cover city council, school board, special events, and other news. The term "stringer" comes from the old custom of using a string to measure the number of inches a writer should get paid for. In many cases, you'll have less than twenty-four hours to attend the event and write the story. It's a rush, but it is exciting to be there when news is happening and present it to the readers right away.

DO YOU NEED PICTURES?

Editors also look for "art," the newspaper name for photos, drawings, maps, charts, or any other entity that can dress up the page. Without art, your story may wind up below a less interesting story that has pictures. Larger newspapers usually use their own photographers, but if you're an artist or a good photographer and can provide your own art, you have a huge advantage when writing for small- and medium-size publications. Not only will editors be more inclined to buy your stories, but you will also get paid extra for every photo or drawing.

Not long ago, freelancers had to worry about whether a newspaper wanted black-and-white photos, color slides, or digital media. This is not an issue anymore. Digital photos are the norm, and are usually emailed to the editor along with the article.

QUERYING A NEWSPAPER

Magazine and newspaper queries are virtually identical, so check chapter 7 for details on how to write a query. The real difference lies in how (and when) editors *respond*. Newspapers are notorious for the nonresponse. This also applies to email queries.

The delay at newspapers stems from the extreme workload most editors have. If your manuscript arrives while editors are on deadline, they probably won't see it for a few days. By then, it might be completely buried in an avalanche of letters, faxes, and emails. This means you need to be gently proactive. Wait two weeks, then contact the editor.

Follow up with a short note or telephone call, or email the editor. Do not drop in at the office. Chances are the editor will be busy or not even there, and she will definitely resent the intrusion. A mailed note runs the risk of getting buried along with your query. A telephone call is direct and often works best. In fact, it could open up a dialogue that leads to other things. However, do not expect the editor to remember your piece or know where it is. Chances are she will have to make a note and get back to you.

Before you call, find out the best times to talk to the editor. Usually that's shortly after the paper comes out. For a daily morning newspaper, editors start work in the afternoons, finishing late at night. The best time to call is early in the afternoon before the deadline crunch hits. For an afternoon paper, reverse the process. For a weekly paper, or for weekly sections of a daily paper, call the editor after the paper goes to press. Sometimes this is the day before publication; sometimes it's several days before. Check the paper for deadlines—if not for copy, then for advertising. Assume that's when the editor will *not* want to talk to you.

However you approach it, be polite; don't whine and don't be critical. Try to be as helpful as possible. "I mailed you a story idea about warts on

June 3, and I was wondering if you had decided yet." If the editor says no, don't throw a hissy fit and don't push. Say "Thank you very much for your time." You might calmly ask what you might have done to make the idea more likely to be used, but don't press too hard.

If you still want to write for that newspaper, come up with another idea and get it out there. You might even mention it while you're calling about the first idea. Chances are the editor will ask for something in writing, but it wouldn't hurt to say, "Would you be interested in a story on . . . the new bakery that makes donuts without holes?"

SIMULTANEOUS SUBMISSIONS

While it's never a good idea to send the same stories to *competing* newspapers—newspapers that serve the same market area—you can often sell the same story to *noncompeting* papers. For example, newspapers published in Florida and New York may have completely different readers and contents. Papers that are owned by the same newspaper chain, such as Gannett or Tribune Media Services, often share stories. This can be a boon for the writer if their story is chosen not only by the local daily or weekly but also by its counterparts in the same company.

You're safe offering the same story to noncompeting newspapers as long as it fits their mission in some way. Travel articles are particularly adaptable to multiple sales because they're not tied as tightly to the local area. Columns, how-tos, roundup pieces, and features of national or international interest can be submitted to multiple publications. It is also possible to reslant the same idea, taking the same basic facts and connecting them with a local person, place, or organization. If the newspapers are in completely different markets, I wouldn't mention your multiple queries, unless you have actually sold the article. Then you may need to give credit to the paper where it appears first.

Ideally you want to sell only first serial rights or one-time rights (see chapter 13 for more information). That means you can resell the article again and again. Some publications will buy the rights to a story for a specified time, such as six months or a year. Some papers will insist on buying all rights. Then you need to decide whether the pay and exposure are worth it. Sometimes they are. Often editors of smaller papers don't have a firm policy about rights and will let you keep them for the asking. Know what you're selling. Get it in writing. If the editor doesn't send you a contract, send the editor a letter or email describing the assignment and your understanding as to the rights you're licensing. Also find out if the paper is going to publish your story online as well as in print. Ask how long it will be there, and whether you will be paid extra for this.

WRITING THE ARTICLE

We've all heard the saying "Just the facts, ma'am," but if all we provided were facts, our stories would be so dry no one would want to read them. Like fishermen, we need to hook the readers and keep them reading.

Consider your audience when writing your article. Are your readers young, old, or a mixture of all ages? Are they college educated or not educated at all? Do they live in the city or the country? Are they rich, poor or somewhere in between? Are they likely to know anything about your topic or must everything be explained?

Keep in mind that you're writing for the masses, for your families, your friends, for doctors, lawyers, construction workers, and the teenager who bags your groceries. We don't need to "write down," but we do need to make sure no one is left behind. That means we cannot assume readers know things most people would not know.

Writing the Lead

Start with a headline, probably the same one you used for your query. This is your theme and your story should never stray too far from it. Then move into your "lead paragraph." In a news story, the duty of the lead is to tell us in a nutshell what happened. An easy way to develop this paragraph is to think of what you would tell your spouse or your best friend if you had to quickly summarize what this is all about. You rush in excited about what you just found out and say: "A boat just ran aground at Lost Creek. That's the third one this month. Luckily nobody was hurt this time" (a true story that happened practically outside my door) or "Wow, did you know that whales eat five hundred tons of food a day?"

In a news lead, it is important to spill the most important facts immediately, moving down the story to the more minor elements. For a feature story, you have more leeway. You definitely need to get to the point soon, preferably by the third paragraph, but you can start in many ways, such as:

- **A startling statistic:** "Last year, 10,000 junior high school boys brought knives to school despite increased security and the installation of metal detectors." (I made that up.)
- **A scene:** "Jake Barnes leaned against a bale of hay, tore off a wad of chewing tobacco with his teeth, and stared out at the sun setting over the cow pasture, ignoring the government officials standing by the road talking about running a freeway right through his ranch. "Ah, I heard all that before," Jake said.
- **A quote:** "Up until I adopted Charlie, I didn't think I ever wanted kids. One look at his big blue eyes changed everything."
- **An anecdote:** "Peter will never forget the day he caught his first fish. . . ."

After the Lead

The lead should draw the reader in. It should also set you on the path for the rest of your article. Your second or third paragraph grounds the reader by explaining what's going on. "Now that I have your attention, here's what I want to talk about." The statistics on kids and weapons would probably lead to a paragraph introducing the main topic of your article, such as how school security programs have failed. The ranch scene might move into a paragraph about how this time it was really happening and the new freeway would disrupt a way of life for Jake and others like him. The adoption quote could move into a story on unusual adoptions. The fishing story could move into a feature on Peter's work as a commercial fisherman or his crusade to save his favorite fishing spot.

With any luck, from here, the story should flow from one point to another, until you have covered each topic in your outline. In a feature, you will want to complete the circle by harking back to the quote, the scene, the statistic, or your thesis statement used in the beginning.

You may want to close with information on how to contact the person you're profiling, places to find more information, where to make reservations, and so on. Check the newspaper to see how they format this information and plug in the names, phone numbers, email addresses, or websites.

Quote Correctly

Newspaper articles use lots of quotes from people or printed sources. Number one rule: write it the way they say it. It's okay to correct minor grammar errors, but in general you need to transmit exactly what your source said. If quotes are too jumbled or awkward, paraphrase them, giving the source credit for the thought if not the exact words. Don't take things out of context just to make your story work better. Our job is to write the truth, even when it's clumsy.

With written material, you need to give credit to the source. Newspaper articles don't come with footnotes, so incorporate the attribution into your prose, as in, "As Roger Wilco wrote on December 12 in *The New York Times . . .*" or "*The Webster's New Collegiate Dictionary* says. . . ." Try not to use a lot of quotes from written material (and if you must, paraphrase as much as possible rather than quoting directly.) Getting someone to actually say it is much more convincing.

Beware of making statements without attribution. If you say the sun rises in the east and sets in the west, no one will challenge you. If you say man is going to land on Jupiter by 2022, you'd better have a source to back that up. Anything odd, startling, or that claims to be the best, biggest, first, last, or only needs to be attributed to a source.

Stylistic Considerations

Newspapers have their own style, which can be very different from that of magazine feature articles. Here are some stylistic issues to consider:

- **Point of view:** Most newspaper articles are written in the third person, which means you never say "I" (except in columns and opinion pieces") or "you" (except in how-tos). Check other articles in the paper to see how they handle voice and do likewise.
- **Tense:** Most newspaper articles are written in past tense. Use "said" instead of "says," "walked" instead of "walk," and so on.
- **Newspaper style:** Most newspapers use *The Associated Press Stylebook* for issues of capitalization, hyphenation, dates, times, addresses, and other picky matters. If you don't have the book, at least study the newspaper you're writing for to see if you can detect trends. For example, do they write out percent or use %? Are dates Dec. 25, December 25, or 25 December? These styles enable editors to present more information in less space, and they'll bless you if they don't have to change every date in your story.
- **Short paragraphs:** Looking at a newspaper page, you can see that the stories are set up in columns, usually five or six to a page. When

forced into that format, a single sentence can take up several lines and a paragraph can go on forever. Therefore, newspaper articles are generally written in short paragraphs. A good rule is that if you've gotten to the fourth line, it's time to think about ending that paragraph and moving on to another.

- **Active language:** Active verbs are much more engaging than passive verbs and generally take up less space. Instead of "The whale was fed dead fish every morning" say "Chuck fed the whale dead fish every morning." Or better, "Every morning, Chuck dumped ten gallons of raw fish into the pool."
- **Include sensory details:** Tell us how it looked, felt, smelled, sounded. Put us in the place and take us beyond mere quotes and facts.
- **Look for questions the editor might have:** Did you define any abbreviations, acronyms, technical terms, or foreign words? Have you double-checked sources' names and titles? If there is something you're not sure of, do some more research or take it out. You should be able to back up every word.

DON'T OVERLOOK THE INTERNET

If you only look at the print version of a newspaper these days, you're missing a big part of what its staff produces. Over the last few years, newspapers have grown thinner and some have gone out of business, while others have moved completely online. Today major newspapers not only publish most of their print content on their websites but also offer a wealth of other material, including news updates, audio and video features, blogs, forums, and endless links. These offer additional opportunities for freelancers to get involved, and they should not be overlooked. In the same way you would study a newspaper, study the website, and pitch your ideas to the appropriate editor. Keep in mind that most online stories are short, include lots of links, and frequently provide a space for readers to comment.

Paying attention to a newspaper's web presence can also help you learn more about the market. These days, editors and reporters from most major daily newspapers and many smaller papers publish blogs. Why? They blog for the same reason they developed web pages and started putting stories online: to compete with broadcast and Internet media that offer instant information. Blogging gives them a way to provide the latest developments on breaking news, to publish on topics that don't fit into the newspaper, and to give their writers space to tell the stories behind the articles they write. It also encourages reader participation.

Newspaper blogs are a gold mine for freelance writers. In reading about the decisions behind the stories, writers learn what editors are looking for. For example, when a reader complained about a show not being reviewed, the *Oregonian* arts editor explained in his blog how he chooses exhibits and performances to review. His answer was much more personal and explicit than the dry guidelines offered on the newspaper's website.

A newspaper's blog opens the window to the newsroom and lets you eavesdrop on discussions that can help you present exactly the stories the editors are looking for. Not only can you listen in but you also can comment and perhaps provide a link to your own blog on that very subject.

Don't let today's focus on smartphones, tablets, and blogs distract you from the main focus of the newspaper market, however. Predictions about how the good old "paper" that we have known for so many years would vanish into the ether have not come true. Pew's latest market survey indicates that print is still the preferred method of delivery for the majority of newspaper readers. And while readers may look up or follow a link to an individual news story online, they rarely stay to read more articles in the same issue. Newspapers, like everything else in the current economic climate, have taken a number of hits in the last few years, but they are not dying—and they still look for news that is fit to *print*.

ONCE YOU HAVE YOUR FOOT IN THE DOOR . . .

Although the world is full of would-be writers, most editors have trouble finding writers who can actually deliver a well-written article on time. If you're one of them, you will soon be golden to those editors.

Follow-up is the key to getting more assignments and becoming a regular contributor. If an editor says no to your first idea, come up with another one. If an editor says yes to your first idea, come up with another one. Once you've sold a couple of articles to the same editor, there's nothing wrong with typing up several ideas and trying to get assignments for them all at once. Over time, you'll develop the kind of relationship where you can secure a go-ahead with a quick phone call or email and where the editor calls you with assignments. Once you make the list of proven freelancers, the editor will turn to you again and again.

If you really want to write for a particular newspaper, the worst thing you can do is disappear. If they encourage you in any way to try again, do it before your name fades from memory.

CHAPTER 18

Selling Reprints

You've probably read articles on the wonders of selling reprints. A lot of them sound something like this: "I've sold the same article 462 times, and netted thousands of dollars!" Such pieces tend to make one feel like a total slouch for having sold a piece only once.

Are reprints really an untapped gold mine for writers? Can you make your fortune reselling work you've already published? The answer often depends on who you ask—and also on what you write.

Publications consider an article to be a reprint if it has already been published and remains substantially unchanged from that previous publication. Many publications do not accept reprints at all. Others pay a lower fee for reprints than for original material. Within these broad guidelines, however, you can find a host of variations and exceptions.

For example, when you sell simultaneous, nonexclusive, or one-time rights to a piece of material, that's not the same as selling a reprint. Reprint terms apply when you're marketing to publications that use first or second rights. When you sell first rights to your article, typically any subsequent sale would be of second or reprint rights. However, in some markets you can sell the same material to several different publications, either simultaneously or sequentially, by offering one-time nonexclusive rights. This gives every publication who buys your work the right to use it once, but not the right to use it "first" and not the right to be the *only* publication to use it. A good example of this type of use would be a column distributed to several newspapers or similar publications.

Once you have sold first rights to an article, you generally cannot offer (or sell) reprint rights until that material has actually appeared in the original publication. "First" rights means the publication has the right to use it first, so if you were to sell reprint rights before the article appears, you could be in violation of your contract. Once the article has appeared in print or online or wherever, you're generally then free to offer reprint or "second" rights to other publications.

CHOOSING AND MARKETING REPRINTS

Some articles have good reprint potential; others don't. If you have tailored an article toward a specific audience and publication, it may be difficult to remarket that material elsewhere without doing a substantial rewrite. If you're writing for a narrow market niche, you may not find many markets for reprints. If a small number of publications are competing for the same market share (as is common, for example, in the pet magazine market), you may find it difficult to find a noncompeting market to buy a reprint.

Time-sensitive articles also don't work well as reprints. If the subject will be old news once the article hits print, if the material is outdated, if things have changed substantially, or if interest in the topic has waned, your chances of reselling the material are low. Similarly, material of purely local interest may be difficult to resell to a different regional market. The focus or slant of your article may also hinder its resale potential.

The most important rule when looking for markets for reprints is to look for noncompeting publications. If two publications serve the same market or audience, neither is likely to accept material that appeared in the other. For example, *The Writer* is not likely to purchase an article that formerly appeared in *Writer's Digest,* and vice versa. The key lies in finding a non-competing market—either a publication that addresses an audience with different interests, or a publication that has a very different regional distribution. You may also find that electronic publications are more willing to accept reprints that first appeared in print magazines on a similar topic.

Many authors do well selling reprints to noncompeting regional publications, such as magazines that serve a single city, county, region, or state. Even though the general focus or content of each magazine might be substantially similar, the audience is limited to a particular region. By the same token, it is often possible to sell reprints of your work overseas.

The first step toward finding reprint markets is to identify likely customers. It's actually a good idea to consider this step before you start writing your article. It's easier to gather additional information for revisions and re-tailored articles while you're researching the original than to have to return to your sources later. Brainstorm the potential markets for your topic, and jot down any ideas that come to mind. For example, if you're writing an article on natural health care for women for a major women's health magazine, consider the potential for reselling the same article (or a retailored article) to other markets, such as:

- Women's healthcare magazines in other countries
- General women's magazines
- Magazines targeting specific age-groups (e.g., teenagers, older women)
- General-interest publications (especially if you can develop a newsworthy slant)
- Local and regional publications (especially if you can link the material to a local source or expert)
- Local, regional, and major metropolitan newspapers (target their "lifestyle" sections)
- Publications that address some subset of the topic, such as herb publications, natural health magazines, or New Age/spiritual magazines
- Online publications in any of the above categories

Once you've developed a list of potential markets, start hunting down information in the latest *Writer's Market* or online. Use an online news-stand or a guidelines database to gather more information about potential markets. If you can't find out from the listing whether a market accepts reprints, send an email to the editor and ask, or make a very brief, courteous phone call. Choose the markets that offer the highest pay potential first, and work your way down the list.

SELLING REPRINT RIGHTS

Whether you can sell a reprint at all depends first and foremost upon the rights you sold to the original article. If you sold all rights or produced an article as "work-for-hire," you cannot sell reprint rights, as you no longer own those rights.

If you sell first rights of any kind (such as First North American Serial Rights, first electronic rights, and so forth), you can then sell second rights to the same type of market (e.g., a North American publication). In some cases you can sell also a different type of first rights to a different market (e.g., you could sell first international rights, or first British rights, to a British publication). If you've sold first print rights, you can still sell first electronic rights, and vice versa. However, you will find that most publications prefer to treat a previously published article as a reprint even if the rights to their specific market area (e.g., electronic vs. print) have not been used.

When selling the reprint itself, you will generally offer nonexclusive second rights or one-time rights. Second serial rights can be sold over and over; the term simply indicates that the publication is no longer "first." Since most reprints are sold nonexclusively, you can sell the same reprint to more than one publication, often at the same time. Sending out simultaneous submissions of reprints is a little more acceptable than it is for an original article; just be sure the reprint isn't going to competing markets.

Keep in mind that the original publication of your article has removed certain rights from the table even if those rights haven't been explicitly licensed. For example, if you have already sold first rights to the piece, you can no longer sell exclusive rights to another publication. Technically, you can't even sell all rights, because first rights is a subset of all rights. You could, possibly, sell all *future* rights to the piece, as long as the new publisher is aware that the piece has been published before.

When offering a reprint overseas, be sure to address issues of regional rights and language rights in your sale. For example, you might want to sell a reprint to a British publication, but hold on to the rights to sell the same material in English to another European country, as well as the rights to sell the material in other languages.

REPRINTS VS. REWRITES

One of the myths that has been traveling around writing circles is that if you rewrite or change an article by a certain percentage, it ceases to be a reprint and becomes a new, original article. The percentage varies, though a commonly quoted number is 20 percent—the premise being that if you change an article by 20 percent, it somehow becomes a new article.

Let's start with the obvious question: 20 percent of *what*? How do you calculate that you've changed 20 percent of your article? Does that mean that 20 percent of the words are different? Does it count if you change the words but are essentially saying the same thing? (For example, if you wrote "many dogs suffer from hip dysplasia" in your first article and rephrase this as "hip dysplasia affects a large number of dogs" in your second, does that actually make it a different article?) If your article is 1,000 words long, and you cut 200 words (thereby reducing the article by 20 percent), does this qualify as a 20 percent change?

Hopefully this little excursion into mathematics shows how ridiculous it would be to assign any sort of numerical formula to what does or does not make an old article new again. Now let's look at the question from the standpoint of an editor, or a reader.

Editors and readers have the same perspective on an article: have they read it before? If you write an article for a writers' magazine titled "How to Craft a Personal Essay," and then send an article to another writers' magazine titled "Tips on Crafting Personal Essays," keep in mind that many readers are likely to subscribe to both publications. If they read each of these articles, will they feel that they are reading the same article in two places, or that they are reading something different in each publication? If the article conveys essentially the same information, rephrasing a few paragraphs isn't going to make the reader feel that the articles are fundamentally different, even if every single word has been altered. (There are, by the way, programs that will do just that; I don't recommend them.)

Trying to turn a piece into a "new" article by rewriting and rephrasing it doesn't elevate it from the status of reprint; it simply turns it into a retread. It's not the *same* article, perhaps, but neither is it a different article. You may be able to avoid getting penalized for selling first rights to a retread, but you're not going to make your editor happy.[18]

For an article to qualify as new rather than a reprint, it must be "substantially" different from the original. There's no real definition of "substantially"—but again, the key is that an editor or reader should be able to read both articles and feel that they have read two different pieces.

Rather than selling reprints per se, many writers prefer to use the same information to write individual articles tailored to different markets. For

---

18 This section, by the way, is a retread of my article, "The 20% Solution: How Much Do You Need to Change an Article to Make it Original?" published in Writing-World.com at www.writing-world.com/business/change.shtml. I don't know what percentage of the piece I've actually changed!

example, if you were writing a piece on relocating to a new city, you could slant one article to a business audience, another to a financial publication, another to a women's magazine, and yet another to a parenting publication. Each piece would have a focus specific to the market you're targeting, each would qualify as original—yet each is drawn from the same pool of information. This is often the best approach, as most publications prefer that material be tailored toward their audience.

SUBMITTING REPRINTS

When submitting reprints, you generally don't need to bother with a query. You have already written the article, so you're not looking for an assignment. One purpose of a query is to help you avoid spending time writing an article before you know it will be accepted. Since a reprint has already been written, it's usually best to send it directly, with a cover letter. Just be sure that the publication accepts reprints, and that your material wasn't originally published in a competing magazine. Be sure to inform a publisher that the article is a reprint and where it was published before. If the reprint has been sold many times, however, it isn't necessary to provide a list of *every* publication that has bought it; mention the first, and any significant markets since then.

Since the publisher will have to format your article for publication if it is accepted, it's generally better to send the original manuscript rather than a clip from the previous publication. If, however, the manuscript was significantly edited by the first publisher, and you believe this improved the piece, you might wish to retype the manuscript as it was published rather than as you originally wrote it. Keep in mind that the next publisher may also edit the manuscript.

If the original article included photos, then it's a good idea to send a copy of the clip as well so that the editor can see the images, without requiring you to actually submit the photos or photo files until the editor accepts the piece.

Many writers spend lots of time marketing reprints; others prefer to concentrate their efforts on original material. The choice is up to you. As you build a collection of material, you'll probably find that some pieces are more appropriate for reprint sales than others. Don't waste a lot of time on those that aren't, and don't waste too much time on those that are! For example, you may not want to invest the same amount of time and money on sample copies for potential reprint markets as you would when researching markets for original articles, because there's less return on your investment.

Reprints can provide a viable source of income. However, to be able to market reprints successfully, you must first build a supply of original published articles. Never spend so much time trying to resell old work that you stop writing new material!

CHAPTER 19

Adding Photos to the Package

It has been said that a picture is worth a thousand words. In the world of publishing, this is the absolute truth. Most publications aren't simply a verbal medium; they are also a visual medium. That means that for every 1,000 great words an editor receives, she may need at least one great picture.

If you have a knack with a camera, you may be able to make your editor's day—and increase your writing income—by offering packages of text and pictures. You don't have to be an experienced photographer to sell your photos. Granted, tourist snapshots of your trip to Rome won't make it into *National Geographic*, but they may be just what a smaller travel publication or your local newspaper travel section needs.

PHOTO "OPS"

Many editors make their purchasing decisions based on whether the author can provide photos, so keep this in mind when you plan future articles. While some articles don't lend themselves to easy illustration, others cry out for photographs, including:

- **Travel articles.** Whenever you travel, take your camera along, and use it. If you are using a film camera, don't worry about the cost of film; just snap every shot that looks remotely worthwhile. If you're using digital, then the issue of cost is irrelevant; snap *everything*! Failed shots don't cost a penny, and the results may surprise you.

While major travel publications accept only top-quality profession-al photos, many smaller publications welcome clear, focused shots that illustrate the sights described in your article.

- **Profiles.** Bring your camera when you go on an interview. Try to get a few candid shots of your subject, with several different types of lighting. If you're interviewing an artist or craftsperson, take pho-tos of the person's work. If your interviewee has special interests, include those in the session. Also, ask your interviewee if he has publicity photos that you could include with your article. (Be sure that your subject is authorized to use this photo for publication. The copyright of a professional or publicity photo is usually owned by the photographer, whose name should be listed in the credit line.)

- **How-to articles.** Suppose you want to pitch an article on adminis-tering first aid to an injured pet. While your words may be vivid, nothing will get the idea across like a series of photos that demon-strate exactly how to apply a bandage, where to apply pressure, and so forth. The next time you prepare a how-to piece, consider setting up a photo shoot in which a friend or family member demonstrates the techniques you're describing, while you take pictures. (Or, if your friend is the better photographer, reverse the process!)

- **Craft projects.** Many magazines decide whether to buy instructions for a craft project based on a photograph of the finished result. Most will want to take their own photos of the finished piece, but your photo may still be the key to selling your idea. You may also be asked to take photographs of the step-by-step process of creating the item.

- **Events.** Photographic coverage of a newsworthy event can make the difference between a sale and a rejection. Try to avoid static "grip and grin" shots (where two people shake hands and smile at the camera), or dull headshots. Instead, try to capture people in mo-tion, with natural poses and expressions. Experiment with different angles and lenses (a telephoto lens, for example, can help you zoom in on individuals or zoom out for crowd shots).

BASIC EQUIPMENT

I won't try to tell you how to take great pictures. To learn more about pho-tography, check with your local photo shop or adult education center; you may easily earn back the price of a class with your first photo sale. There are also a host of excellent photography sites on the web that offer free online classes and instruction in all types of photography. But there is some basic equipment that you'll need to get started.

A Digital Camera

Today, the photography world is going digital. While there are still many publications that use film, these are more likely to be the magazines that require professional, high-end photos. Even those often want images to be *submitted* digitally (more on that later), even if they are captured on film. For the rest of us, converting to a good-quality digital camera is truly the best option.

The key here is "good-quality." There are lots of inexpensive "point and shoot" digital cameras on the market that are great for capturing pictures of your toddler or taking selfies of you and your friends at a wild party (judging, at least, by the ads). But when it comes to taking photos that you can sell, aim for something a bit higher. Keep in mind that in the world of digital photography, size matters—specifically, the file size of your image. A large file is required to produce a photo that can be printed on a magazine cover or as a full-page interior image. The megapixel rate of digital cameras keeps going up, and the larger the file size, the more detail you can capture in an image. However, don't purchase a camera based on image size alone—there are, for example, some twenty-megapixel cameras on the market for as little as $25 that have extremely poor ratings. A big image is important but useless if it is not also a *good* image!

Digital photography offers a host of advantages for those of us for whom photography is a secondary skill. Perhaps the greatest advantage is cost. You don't have to pay for film or to have that film developed, which means you can take as many images as you wish without breaking your budget. When you're traveling, this is a wonderful advantage, because you can't just go back and try again if a shot doesn't come out right the first time. A digital camera gives you the freedom to experiment with different angles, exposures, and ideas that you might not want to play around with if every experiment were costing precious funds.

Digital cameras have another advantage in allowing you to immediately review your shots. You can tell at a glance if you lopped off the top of someone's head, or if someone walked in front of you just as you clicked the shutter, or if that castle is just a wee bit out of focus or out of the frame. And finally, you don't have to worry about carrying film around with you or having enough on hand, or whether it will pass through the airport scanners without being damaged.

You *will* need to make sure that you always have enough batteries on hand, however. There's nothing worse than being at a once-in-a-lifetime destination only to find that your battery has run out and you don't have a replacement. I always keep at least two fully charged batteries in my purse. Using your flash and reviewing your shots will both consume your battery faster than shooting alone. Also make sure that you have either a large memory card (SD or micro SD) in your camera or a spare—or both. (While SD cards come in a variety of sizes, don't assume that the largest size is what you need. Many cameras won't accept an SD card of more than 8GB, and some won't accept cards of more than 4GB.)

Software and Storage

The downside of using a digital camera is that you will need to develop a certain amount of skill with a photo-editing program. You'll need to be able to crop photos, and may need to make adjustments to exposure and color balance. For many years, the industry standard for photographers has been Photoshop. Photoshop Elements is a bit less expensive, and offers pretty much all the functions you're likely to need to handle things like cropping and correcting exposure and color balance. The trouble is, Adobe has now shifted to a subscription model for this and other programs, so if you don't want to pay a monthly fee for Photoshop, you may need to buy an older version (which is getting expensive and hard to find), settle for Elements, or try something else. I recommend starting with one of these options and then deciding whether you need to go for a program that has more bells and whistles.

While you can download your photos directly from your camera to your computer or laptop using a USB cable (and in many cases using wireless), most computers now come with a built-in SD card reader. This enables you to switch out your SD card and use your camera for something else while your photos are downloading. A card reader is also usually much faster than a direct USB link to your camera. If your computer or laptop doesn't have an SD card port, it's easy to find an inexpensive card reader with a USB connector.

If you're traveling and take lots of photos, you'll probably want to take your laptop along so that you can download and quickly review each day's shots. This also ensures that a copy of your photos is stored somewhere other than on your camera at the end of the day. Digital cameras are tempting targets for thieves, and you wouldn't want to lose your entire photo collection if, perchance, you lost your camera. If you have a cloud storage account, you can add an extra level of security by uploading your photos to the cloud after you've transferred them to your laptop.

Once you get home, you'll want to make sure that your photos are stored on your computer, and that you also back them up through your system of choice (see chapter 27). Digital photos can take up a great deal of memory, so keep this in mind when you consider backup systems.

What About Your Cell Phone?

Today, of course, one of the biggest marketing factors associated with cell phones is their ability to take pictures. Many cell phones have two cameras built in, one facing front (the screen) and one facing back. Ads abound showing what glorious photos and movies one can capture using a cell phone.

Despite these glorious examples, my impression is that one has to be a pretty good photographer to get the same quality of photos with a cell phone as with an actual digital camera. Most cell phones offer only "point and shoot" cameras. They don't offer you the ability to make adjustments for lighting or other issues, and many don't have a flash!

A good-quality digital camera offers you a host of features that you won't find on your phone. While you can choose the fully automatic exposure mode, you can also control your images by using the programmable settings for aperture or speed. (For fun, try playing around with adjusting each of these factors while photographing a single scene. A good type of scene for this experiment is a fountain or running stream—you'll quickly grasp what differences you can achieve by changing from low to high speeds, and changing from small to large apertures.) A digital camera will also offer you a "scene selector" menu, which provides helpful settings for specific types of shooting conditions (such as low light, fireworks, indoors, people, landscapes, etc.). It will have a close-up function, and a high-speed shutter function that enables you to capture multiple shots of a fast-moving event or object.

Today's cameras have even more to offer. The range of the optical zoom is getting larger and larger on newer cameras, which means you can truly zoom in on distant objects. (Digital zoom is also expanding but is not terribly useful—it simply enlarges your picture the same way that you would if you enlarged or cropped it on your screen.) Most cameras include a "vibration reduction" (VR) feature that greatly improves the sharpness of pictures taken in low light.

Now, I have no doubt that many people who read this will immediately declare that their smartphone can do all this and more, and walk the dog at the same time. And there's nothing wrong with using your phone to take photos. However, I recommend that if you wish to get serious about adding photography to your freelance writing efforts, you spring for a good-quality digital camera.

Is There a Place for Film?

What about your old film camera—or more importantly, your old photos that were captured on film? Does the age of digital mean that these photos are now worthless? Not at all! Many publications actually prefer film photos (especially slides) that have been converted to digital files. And once you've converted your pictures to digital, you can work with them in Photoshop or any other photo-processing program, just like any other digital images.

It can be a challenge, however, to make this happen. It's easy to scan prints on a flatbed scanner (I don't recommend doing it with a sheetfed scanner if you want marketable results). Slides and negatives are another matter.

There are many inexpensive devices that "convert" your 35mm slides to digital. That word "convert" is important, however. Some of these devices are not actually scanners per se. Rather than making a scan of your slide, they take a digital photograph of it, which can result in a loss of resolution and sharpness. Such converters can be useful if you wish to convert a bunch of family photos for personal viewing, but they may not give you the quality you need to convert your slides to publishable digital images.

It's also possible to get a flatbed scanner with a film-scanning function and plastic templates to hold your slides. Unfortunately, scanning slides on a flatbed scanner is very time-consuming, and if your scanning surface acquires any scratches or flaws, these will show up on your scans. If you do decide to use a flatbed scanner, don't use it for anything *other* than slides until your slide-scanning project is completed. Pacific Image offers a series of dedicated 35mm film scanners ranging from $200 to $400. From there you move into the realm of high-end dedicated scanners that can run anywhere from $800 to $4,000. To get a better idea of the options available if you'd like to scan your slides yourself, I recommend reading "Scanning Film: A Buying Guide," by Bjorn Peterson (www.bhphotovideo.com/explora /photography/buying-guide/film-scanners).

A simpler option may be to send your slides to a scanning service. This may also be the only affordable option if you have medium-format or large-format film. If you choose this approach, be sure to test the service first with a few slides to determine the scanning quality. I used DigMyPics to convert my medium-format slides to digital, and was very pleased with the quality; I tried other services that returned appalling results.

Before you spend time and effort scanning slides, take a good look at them first. An image can look wonderful at 35mm but not so wonderful when it's enlarged enough to publish in a magazine. Invest in an inexpensive light box and a jeweler's loupe, and examine each slide carefully. Is it truly sharp? Is it clean? Does it have scratches or other flaws that would make it unusable? These questions must be answered in any case, whether you're submitting digital images of your slides or the slides themselves.

SUBMITTING PHOTOS

The good news about digital photography is that it has made the process of submitting photos much less expensive. You no longer have to worry about losing your photos, or having them damaged in the mail (or by a careless editor's coffee cup).

That being said, there are some guidelines to be followed when submitting digital photos. Nothing is going to annoy an editor more than receiving an unsolicited article by email with a dozen 2MB "sample" photo files attached. Another way to annoy an editor is to inform him that he will need to go to some obscure online photo-sharing website, create an account, and then individually download your photos. (That being said, a photo-sharing site can be a good way to enable an editor to *preview* the photos you have to offer with an article. Such sites also enable you to specify who can view your photos.)

The first step in submitting digital photos is to contact an editor with your query or article submission, and inform the editor of the *availability* of photos. Let the editor know what sort of images are available. For example, if you're submitting an article on a craft project, do you have photos of the finished project only, or do you have step-by-step photos illustrating how the project is made? If it's a travel article, let the editor know which locations you have images of.

Then, ask the editor how he would prefer to review and/or receive photo files. Some editors may want you to send reduced versions of a selection of sample photos. (This is why it's important to know how to reduce a photo's file size in Photoshop or Photoshop Elements.) Others might prefer to preview your photos on a website or photo-sharing site. Others might prefer to have a selection sent on CD-ROM or flash drive. The same applies when it comes time to actually submit your photos. Some editors will want to receive them as email attachments; others will prefer to receive a CD-ROM or flash drive. Most will *not* want to download them from a photo site or website, but this can be an option.

If you are submitting physical photos, take the following steps to make sure they remain undamaged:

- **Put your name and address on each photo.** The easiest method is to attach a return address label to the back of each print, or to the cardboard mount of each slide.
- **Number each photo.** Do not write on the back of a print with a ballpoint pen or ordinary marker, as the ink can smear (and if you stack prints, it will come off on the face of the photo beneath). Use a permanent marker to number prints (and write small), or create printed labels that include the number of the image and the caption information.
- **Send slides and prints in plastic protective sheets.** These protect your photos from handling and postal damage. Editors can view slides through the sheets, and will only remove those they actually plan to use. Use archival sheets, which are free of acids and chemicals that could damage your photos, thus providing an excellent means of storing them as well.
- **Send proof sheets of black-and-white photos**, rather than making expensive enlargements.
- **Prepare a caption list that corresponds to the numbers of your photos.** Don't worry about inventing clever captions (the editor will do that). Just record essential information, such as the subject of the

photo, and anything else the editor might need to know (such as the location, date, etc.).

- **Obtain model release forms for your photos, if necessary.** This is particularly important when photographing children. Editors are very wary of publishing child photos without a parent's permission. You may need a model release when photographing individuals, or even when photographing private property. For more information on the legal aspects of photography, see *Every Writer's Guide to Copyright Publishing Law*, by Ellen Kozak. You'll also find a useful infographic on photographers' rights and limitations at www. whoishostingthis.com/blog/2016/05/25/privacy-photographers/.
- **Package your photos securely.** Sandwich your plastic sheets of photos between sheets of cardboard. Be sure to include a SASE with enough postage to cover the return of your images.

OBTAINING PHOTOS FROM OTHER SOURCES

If you despair of taking good photos yourself, that doesn't mean you can't offer photos to editors. It simply means that you'll have to find another source.

One approach is to find a photographer you can work with, and sell a package deal to the editor. In this case, you'll have to work out a payment arrangement with the photographer, particularly if the publication offers a single rate for the entire package. It's a good idea to write up a brief contract, so that everyone knows what to expect when the check arrives.

However, you may also find free sources of photos. When I write for pet magazines, for example, I'll often put out a call for photos on topical mailing lists (such as a cat-writing list). Generally, these photos won't be professional quality, and I usually don't offer any payment for them. Sometimes the magazine will use them, sometimes they won't. If payment *is* involved, I simply pass along the name of the photographer to the editor and let the editor handle payment for the photos separately.

If you write travel articles, check with tourist organizations for photos. Many tourist agencies offer free publicity photos, which will enhance your article without costing the editor a penny. In some cases, an agency may send you a DVD of photos that they ask to have returned, so make copies of the images you wish to pass along to the editor.

You may also be able to obtain free photos from online sources. For example, if you're writing an article about a travel destination in Great Britain, you'll find a wide range of images on the BritainonView site at www.gettyimages.com/collections/britain-on-view (owned by VisitBritain, the UK's national tourist agency). Many of these are available free to the travel trade, which means that the publication buying your article may not have to pay for them. You can save your editor time and trouble by selecting appropriate images and sending a list or a collection of "comps" downloaded from the site; the editor can then log in to access the images he wants to use.

Another good source of photos is Wikipedia.org. Most of the images on this site are available either via public domain or through a Creative Commons license, which allows them to be used in other publications. To locate collections of photos on a particular subject, visit Wikimedia Commons.

Finally, you may be able to locate photos on personal websites that can be used with permission. If you find the perfect photo, contact the owner of the site to request permission to use it with your article. Don't download the photo directly from the site; photos posted online are often at a lower resolution than is required for print publication, so ask for a high-resolution copy of the image to submit to your editor. Never submit a photo from a website without permission, as this opens both you and your editor to charges of copyright infringement.

SUBMITTING PHOTOS WITHOUT MANUSCRIPTS

If you can take high-quality photographs, you can also sell them independently, without an accompanying article. Many magazines buy shots of their basic subject matter year-round. For example, pet magazines always need generic photos of veterinarians examining animals, animals involved in various activities, animals interacting with different types of people (seniors, children, etc.), seasonal shots, and so forth.

You don't have to simply guess what editors are looking for. Many magazines offer photographers' guidelines that list upcoming articles and the types of photos that will be required. For example, a pet magazine may list the breeds it will cover over the next six months, plus special issue themes like "puppies" or "senior cats." These guidelines will tell you when photos must be submitted for each issue. By tailoring your photo shoots to these "need" lists, you'll have a better chance of breaking in. (As I mentioned in chapter 6, this makes photographers' guidelines a great asset to writers; never assume that because a magazine is planning a special themed issue on a particular topic, it already has all the articles it needs on that topic!)

You may even make more money by selling your photos separately than if you combine them with an article. While some editors pay the same amount for an article with or without photos (or add only a small bonus for the photos), they also have standard rates for photos alone. Check *Writer's Market* or *Photographer's Market* to find out what magazines are looking for photo submissions and what they pay.

Finally, you may find that a photo submission can lead to an article assignment. If an editor falls in love with your photos, but has nothing on hand to use them with, he may ask you to write a piece to accompany them. Remember, editors think in two media—verbal and visual—so by sending a package that combines both, you stand a better chance of selling your work.

Oh, and if a magazine pays 5¢/word and $50 per photo, one picture really is worth a thousand words!

CHAPTER 20

Writing for Businesses

by Dawn Copeman

Writing for businesses—also known as commercial writing or copywriting—probably isn't the first thing you considered doing as a freelance writer. It certainly wasn't high on my list of priorities when I started out. I wanted to write articles. Yet within months I learned that one way to make steady money as a writer was to write for businesses.

Writing for businesses is an exciting, growing field—and more importantly, a lucrative field that you ignore at your own cost. There will always be a need for copywriters. Commercial writing pays well and is a varied and interesting line of work, particularly if, like most writers, you enjoy learning about new things and working with language.

I've been paid to find out about conservatories, orangeries, sardines, cake sprinkles, tequila, the health benefits of red grapes and cocoa, and top-selling Christmas toys—and to write about these things in press releases, brochures, recipes, company newsletters and sales letters. And once the commercial job is over, I can put this newfound knowledge to use in articles. The fact that I get paid to explore topics I can then apply to magazine articles is just one of the perks of the business. Another is the sheer variety of work available.

WHAT DOES A COPYWRITER DO?

A copywriter, or freelance commercial writer, writes "copy" or text to help businesses communicate with their customers—and more importantly, potential customers. Every advertisement, brochure, catalog, and sales let-ter you've ever read was written by a copywriter, as were the words to all the radio and TV ads you hear, and those fund-raising letters you get from charities.

A copywriter is employed by a client, who may be the business itself or a public relations agency hired to create material for the business. The type of material you can be called upon to write falls into three main areas:

- **Business-to-Business Communications:** Sales letters, reports, or articles for trade magazines designed to promote the client's prod-ucts or services to other businesses.
- **Business-to-Consumer Communications:** Materials designed to draw the consumer's attention to what the business has to offer.
- **In-House Communications:** Materials such as reports and news-letters designed to keep staff up to date regarding the company's news, aims, and intentions.

Within the first two areas, a copywriter may be called upon to write some or all of the following materials:

- Press releases
- Advertisement copy for flyers, leaflets, postcards, and press adver-tisements
- Brochures
- Sales letters
- Catalog descriptions
- Company newsletters
- Website content
- Website advertisements
- Scripts for television/radio advertisements
- Scripts for promotional films
- Scripts for training films
- Direct mail campaigns
- Articles for publication in trade/specialist magazines
- Advertorials—advertisements "disguised" as articles
- Speeches
- Social media marketing

A copywriter working on in-house materials may also be called upon to write:

- Internal corporate newsletters
- Training manuals
- Office procedures
- Operating manuals
- Job advertisements
- Corporate vision statements
- Company reports

Even during a recession, companies still need to advertise their products and services, and using a freelance writer is often the most economical way to do so. And when the economy is good, companies still often prefer to use freelancers rather than employ someone in-house because freelance writers are only paid when working on a specific job, and do not cost the company "overhead" fees (such as health benefits and vacation time).

HOW DO YOU BECOME A COPYWRITER?

To become a copywriter, you need the same supplies as for any other form of freelance writing: a computer, an Internet connection, a printer, a workspace, and a telephone. You will find it easier to start in this field if you also invest in the following resources:

A Swipe File

This is a file of all the direct mail that you, your friends, and family receive, including sales letters, brochures, postcards, and flyers. Some copywriters even advise signing up to receive different catalogs just to receive more (and more varied) types of direct mail.

You will never look at junk mail the same way again. Soon, you will get into the habit of analyzing each piece you receive to see if it works. Does it catch your attention? Does it make you consider using the firm that produced it?

Go over each piece of copy you have in your swipe file and look at how it has been put together and, if it's good, note down why it works. If it's bad, try to rewrite it so that it works. This is a great way to learn how to write postcards, flyers and brochures, and sales letters.

A Website

Most copywriters have a website to advertise their services and showcase their writing skills. This can cost you as little as $20 for web hosting and $25 or less for a domain name. If you have little or no experience with web design or HTML, look for a host that offers templates, or for an easy-to-use web creation program (see chapter 24 for more information).

Your website should include a brief description of your experience and the services you offer. Ensure that this is grammatically correct and has no spelling mistakes. Simply state who you are and what you offer, and your experience if relevant. Do not, however, list your rates. This marks you as an amateur, as seasoned copywriters know there's no such thing as a typical project with a typical fee. (See chapter 22, "Commercial Freelancing: Where's the Money?")

Your site should also include samples of your work. These can be real samples or ones you've made up. Many beginning copywriters start by making sample brochures, press releases, and flyers for imaginary companies. On my first site, I used samples of work I'd done in previous jobs: course content, training handbooks, and political campaign material (which was written by me, for me, and won me a seat on the local council). You could also volunteer to do some copywriting for a local church, charity, or non-profit and use this as a sample. This gives you practice in listening to and meeting a client's needs, and shows a prospective client that you have done work for others.

Business Cards

Have some business cards printed with your name and the title "Freelance Copywriter" or "Freelance Commercial Writer." You can obtain business cards very reasonably online (check sites like PSPrint and VistaPrint for discounts and sales). These sites have templates that enable you to design your own card quickly and easily.

Don't fall into the trap of putting too much information on your card. Some people get double-sided cards that include their name and contact details on one side and all the services they offer on the other. This can make you appear to be a jack-of-all-trades (and master of none). I prefer single-sided cards that refer companies to my website for further information.

GETTING THE WORK

This is the part that often fills writers with fear. You know how to write a query letter, but how do you find commercial assignments? In fact, getting copywriting work can be much easier than finding a home for an article. Here are some of the best methods:

- **Word of mouth.** Simply tell people that you are a copywriter. Tell your friends, bank manager, family, people you meet socially, people you meet in elevators and in restaurants, people you meet on vacation. You never know when someone *you* meet will meet someone who is looking for a copywriter. Hand out your business cards whenever you can. I've picked up many jobs through this method.
- **Website.** Your website's job is to sell your services twenty-four hours a day, seven days a week. Ensure that you have the words "copywriting, copywriter, commercial writer, business writer" and your hometown entered as tag words. This will help search engines locate you when someone searches for a copywriter in your area.
- **Memberships.** Join local or national freelance groups. One of the first inquiries I received came about because I was listed on the Freelancers in the UK site as a copywriter and editor. Most of these organizations are free or have a nominal fee. Consider joining organizations that relate to the subject matter in which you have expertise. If, for example, you love to write about gardening, join a regional gardening society, and you may start picking up jobs from local nurseries and other gardening-related businesses.
- **Cold-calling.** This involves telephoning local businesses to ask if they need a copywriter. To cold-call, you need to work out your script (see the sidebar by Peter Bowerman). Then you need to work out whom to call. You could look through your local phone book, or get a list of local companies from your chamber of commerce. Don't overlook any potential client. Don't always think big; many smaller companies also need copywriting. Don't forget to contact local marketing companies and PR firms. Finally, keep a record of whom you have called and when, and whether you have been asked to call back. Be sure that your website is set up so that you can refer potential clients to it. You must also be prepared to mail out a portfolio

(a physical copy of your samples, along with a brief introductory letter and two business cards, within a pocket folder). To succeed in cold-calling, you must be persistent and prepared for rejection—but hey, you're a writer, you're used to that!

- **Social networking.** Many freelancers now get work via social networking sites such as LinkedIn, Twitter, and Facebook. Just like your website, your profile on a social networking site can be working for you 24/7. Just make sure you update it regularly and check your profile daily to ensure you're not missing out on any work. (See chapter 25 for more information on now to use social networking effectively.)

- **Freelance work sites.** Many sites and newsletters that list freelance writing jobs also list calls for copywriters. You can also pay to join job-bidding sites such as Upwork.com, where you can maintain a profile that potential clients can view, and bid for a variety of copywriting jobs. The pay for these jobs, however, can be significantly lower than those found through other means.

The Cold Call
by Peter Bowerman

Peter Bowerman, author of *The Well-Fed Writer* and one of the leading experts on freelance copywriting, is a firm believer in contacting clients through the cold call. "If people aren't expecting your correspondence, chances are excellent it'll go into the trash unopened. You really need to establish that connection with someone so that they know what your package is when it shows up on their desk," he notes. Here's his approach to the cold call:

Your Script. Know exactly what you're going to say when your prospect answers the phone. Write it out word-for-word on a 3x5 card and keep it in front of you. Always say it, and never say anything but. In my opinion, this is a critical secret to staying focused during prospecting, while removing one potential source of anxiety from the process. Keep it brief (fifteen seconds or less), simple and to the point.

My basic version goes like this: "Good morning, my name is Peter Bowerman, and I'm a freelance writer, making contact with local banks, to determine whether you have any ongoing or occasional needs for a good freelance writer to help create marketing collateral material: brochures, newsletters, ads, and so on. Who might be the best person to talk with?" The word "collateral" is industry standard. Use it and you'll fit in.

Ideally, you'll have a name, but if not, this'll do and it's always enough to get some reaction, which then drives the rest of the call. Hopefully, you know what to say if they respond, "Great! Your timing couldn't be better." It happens.

How to Talk. Slowly, clearly, and evenly. When you get someone on the phone, don't just chat away like you normally would. Adjust to accommodate people who don't know you and weren't expecting your call. Make it easy for them to switch gears.

What Not to Say. Refrain from cuteness like an ultra-cheerful, "How are you today!?" unless they ask you first. This fairly screams "Salesman Butter-Up Line!!" If they ask, it can be like a cool drink of water. Simply reply politely, "Very well, thank you. Yourself?" Resist the urge to jump all over them with dirty paws like a golden retriever greeting its master after a two-week absence.

KEYS TO SUCCESSFUL COPYWRITING

To become a successful copywriter, you need to know how to get the client to tell you exactly what he wants, which isn't always easy. Then you need to know how to transform those wants into a clear, easy-to-read format that will generate interest and sales. To accomplish these tasks, it's helpful to keep these three things in mind:

- The target consumer—who is going to buy the product
- The golden nugget—the fact that will help you to create your sales material
- The USP—the unique selling point of the product or service you are writing about

Finding the answers to these questions can be the trickiest part of the job, but there are steps you can take to make it happen.

1. Listen to the Client

Many clients are vague about what they want you to do. They have a rough idea of what they want to achieve, but you will need to work hard to get them to communicate their ideas to you.

Take your time. Ask the client to explain what he wants you to do. Take notes and ask questions. Ask him in detail about the new product or service. Don't be afraid of looking stupid; if you don't understand the product, how can you explain it to others?

Don't rush this phase. When I was contacted to write web content and brochures for a conservatory company, I followed the managing director as he took me for a walk around the showroom. I asked about the different styles, how long it takes to build a conservatory, methods of construction, planning permission, security, uses of conservatories, heating, guarantees, and even how to clean them. By the end of the visit, I knew what I needed to explain the world of conservatories to the general public.

Here are some questions you should put to a potential client:

- What is special about this new product/service?
- What is its Unique Selling Point (USP)?
- Who is the target consumer for this product?
- What type of marketing approach are you considering?
- Will there be any samples or photos available for journalists to use?
- Are you willing to offer a discount to generate interest?

Finally, ask the client for copies of any previous sales letters, brochures, flyers, or press releases to see what approaches have been tried before. Ask which had the best and worst results, so you don't inadvertently go down the same path as a previous copywriter.

2. Research

If you're going to write about a product, you need to know it inside out. You need to learn everything there is to know about this particular product and the company producing it, as you never know what will prove to be the precious nugget you can use to help sell the product. Don't rush this step.

Copywriters must be inquisitive and thorough. They must go beyond the information provided by the client to ensure their work is the best it can be. Here are some ways to approach your research:

- **Review company materials.** Look at any and all materials the company can give you. By reading the brochures and leaflets of the conservatory company, for example, I found that they'd won several design competitions and a prestigious award—useful information the company hadn't thought of mentioning!
- **Look at the website.** When I was asked to create a press release for a new brand of cocoa, I discovered from the company website that some of their profits went to community projects in a Third World country. One phone call later, I learned that in the past year they'd built a school. This was a golden nugget that would help sell the product.
- **Look at competitors' websites.** By reviewing the competition, you can get an idea of what is and isn't working in this particular trade, and you may also discover USPs for your client. By looking at the websites of other conservatory companies, for example, I found that my client offered a much longer guarantee than any of its competitors—a definite USP!
- **Find out about the target consumer.** Ask the client who the product is aimed at. If they are breaking into a new market, whom are they hoping to attract? Many businesses will have a "media card," which contains information about the typical age, gender, and income of their target consumer. If they don't, ask what type of magazines they think their target consumer will read, and visit those magazines' websites and check their media cards. This will help you write copy in a tone that will appeal to the target consumer.
- **Use the Internet.** This is most useful when you are looking for extra facts to help spice up your copy, especially if you are writing a press release and need something newsworthy to grab the attention of journalists. While writing a press release for the cocoa company, I came across a new piece of scientific research suggesting that drinking cocoa could help prevent Alzheimer's disease. This, combined with the information on the company's Third World projects, provided me with all the information I needed to create a successful press release.

WRITING GREAT COPY

Once you've gathered your facts, it's time to sit down and write. Just as in article writing, there are specific rules to follow:

- **Put yourself in the target consumer's shoes.** Your copy must be written in a way that will appeal to the consumer. Is the product aimed at the elderly or the young? At working moms, family men, singles, office administrators, doctors? For each type of market, you need to find a tone that will appeal to the target audience. To find that tone, you must put yourself in the shoes of the target consumer. If you're trying to sell a new type of life insurance for blue-collar family men, think like one. What would push your buttons? What would make you read further? What would make you throw the letter in the trash?

- **Write as you speak.** When you're talking to different people, you use different words. You don't talk to your boss the way you talk to your friends. When you've worked out what tone would be best for your target consumer, imagine you are sitting next to them and having a conversation. What words would you use to describe the product? How would you get them interested? If you write as you would speak in this situation, your copy will be more natural and appealing.

Perhaps most importantly, you must "remember the power of *you*." Successful sales literature may be written in a multitude of styles, but it has one thing in common: it appeals directly to the reader. As I wrote in my press release on cocoa, "You won't only be helping your brain; you will be helping others too." Ensure that your copy is liberally sprinkled with the word "you." Bad copy goes on and on about the company or product; good copy rephrases this information to focus the emphasis on the benefits for the consumer.

Consider this statement:

"We have twenty years' experience in the field of building conservatories. We only employ the best skilled craftsmen and we guarantee our conservatories for ten years."

Okay, but what's in it for me? Let's rewrite it with "the power of you."

"With over twenty years of experience, our expert team will design and install the perfect orangery or conservatory to meet your needs, your lifestyle, your budget, and your home. You can rest assured of a quality service from start to finish, because unlike many of our competitors, we employ all our own craftsmen, from builders to plasterers, electricians to installers, carpenters to heating engineers."

By using "you," you are instantly creating rapport with readers and getting them interested in what the client can do for them.

Discuss Benefits, Not Features

A common mistake is to simply take the information the client provides and reproduce it. When a client creates a new product or service, they get very excited about the features. Consumers, however, don't care about features. They care about benefits. What it will do for them, how it will make their lives easier, how it will make them feel better?

For example, here are some features of a hypothetical writing software called WriteWorld:

- British-English, American-English, and Australian-English Spell Checkers.
- British-English, American-English, and Australian-English Thesaurus.
- Chicago and AP Style Guides built in.

Now, let's write these as benefits:

- You'll never have to worry about misspelling words again. Simply select the destination language and WriteWorld will automatically change all your spellings. Color will become colour and vice versa at the click of a mouse, making it easier for you to sell your work to international markets.
- Avoid confusing readers! With our built-in thesaurus, WriteWorld will scan your text for words that have different meanings in the destination country, and offer you a choice of more appropriate

words, so that your text retains its original meaning and your article is more likely to find a home in an overseas publication.

- Do you need to write in AP style but don't know how? Simply choose AP from the menu and at the click of a button it will advise you where to make changes so that your text is AP style. It does the same for Chicago style too, meaning you need never miss out on a freelance opportunity again.

Note that writing about benefits takes more words than writing about features. That's OK; your job is to communicate those benefits to the reader.

While these tasks apply to most forms of copywriting, some tasks require a different approach.

DIRECT SALES LETTERS

Direct mail, also known as junk mail, is a surprisingly effective means of generating sales, especially in the charity sector. You'll need to do all the research steps above, but also ask to see any previous sales letters and find out what response they generated. This can save you from wasting hours on a format that has already been tried.

When writing your letter, keep all the rules above in mind, but also add the following: picture, promise, price, and action. You paint a *picture* of the consumer's life with the new product; you make a *promise* (your life will be easier with this, you will be helping orphans to a better life); you close with the *price* and the call to *action* (buy the item, take a test drive, sign up to support the charity).

Imagine, for example, that you are writing a sales letter to generate more sponsors for a charity that educates children in Bangladesh. Here's how to put picture, promise, price, and action into the letter:

- **Picture:** Paint a picture in words about the life of seven-year-old Patha—how she has to work twelve hours a day to help support the family, and cannot go to school. Good story pictures appeal to the emotions of the target consumer.
- **Promise:** Now, paint a picture of how Patha's life would be different if only "you," the target consumer, would sponsor her. Show the reader how every cent of her donation goes to help Patha and her family.

- **Price:** Now and only now, state the price for giving someone the chance of a new life.
- **Call to Action:** Reply today! Every day we wait for your reply means another day without schooling for Patha.

PRESS RELEASES

As a copywriter, you'll often be called upon to write press releases, which are one of the most effective means of business advertising. A press release is a one- or two-page announcement of a new product, trend, business premise, or anything that can be described as newsworthy. Well-written press releases are loved by journalists and editors, as they provide much-needed content, either as short news items or items that can be developed into longer articles. Press releases are effective because they don't look like advertising, and if done well, they can generate lots of publicity for the client.

It is estimated that between 3,000 and 10,000 press releases are written every day. Only the best will be published. If your press release is going to make the news, you need to know how to write it effectively. The first step is to understand the layout:

Company Name or Logo

Press Release (in 10- or 12-point font)

Date it can be used (this is either "For Immediate Use" or "Not to Be Used Before a Specific Date.")

Title of Press Release (keep to one line)

Body of Press Release. Interesting Hook. Opening paragraph.

Paragraph

Paragraph

If the press release runs longer than one page, type "1 of 2" and "conts" at the bottom of the first page. At the end of the press release, type the word "ENDS" at the bottom of the page.

(Continued)

> **Notes to Editors**
>
> This section contains fact-checking material to support any claims made in the text, such as details of surveys, opinion polls, or references to scientific studies. It normally appears on a separate page if the release is one page, or underneath the content if the release is two pages. This section should list whether photos or samples are available. All notes should be numbered. This section should also contain the email address, URL, telephone numbers, and contact details for the person within the company whom journalists can contact for more information.

Press releases are short but must be well written. Just like articles, they require an attractive hook, followed by paragraphs that flow and are written in an engaging, easy-to-read style with facts sprinkled lightly through the text. Finally, they must finish with a good ending. Often, you don't have much time to accomplish all this. When I worked for a food public relations agency, I often received details around 8:30 a.m. and was expected to submit my press release by midday or 4 p.m. at the latest.

How do you write a release that is newsworthy and grabs the attention of journalists and editors? The first thing to do is learn as much as you can about the product or item. Think creatively, and take all the steps described earlier: ask the client questions, get them to send you details or samples of the product, check their website, and hit the Internet for further research.

For the cocoa press release mentioned above, for example, I combined the health benefits of cocoa with an appeal to its traditional drinkers, the elderly, to create the headline: "A Cup of Cocoa a Day Keeps Alzheimer's at Bay." This was followed by a hook: "Our grandparents know more than they are letting on when they tuck into their nightly cocoa; not only does it give them a good night's sleep, it is helping them keep their brains healthy too." The rest of the article flowed with scientific facts about the known and newly proven health benefits of cocoa, plus information on why the reader should buy this particular brand: "It has a higher proportion of flavonoids—the health-giving aspect of cocoa—than most other brands." Finally, I ended with, ". . . X not only keeps your brain healthy, it helps others, too."

This particular press release ran, in many cases exactly as I wrote it, in several UK daily papers and many local newspapers—a great result for the client and a great sense of satisfaction for me!

Once you've completed your press release, submit it to the client for approval, then submit it to press release sites or by email or fax to local newspapers. Some press release sites will distribute your press release for free; others have a sliding scale of charges. While a paid service will get your release into more inboxes, it still won't guarantee that journalists will read or act on the release; only you can do that by making it interesting. Here are some press release distribution sites:

- Daryl Wilcox Publishing—www.dwpub.com (sign up to the Response Source service to receive press releases in your chosen areas—great for research!)
- PR.Com—www.pr.com/rss-feeds
- PR Log—www.prlog.org
- 24/7 Press Release—www.24-7pressrelease.com
- PR Fire—www.prfire.co.uk

A final word of warning: not every corporate client is easy to work with. A bad customer can waste your time, and in the business of corporate freelancing, time is money. Don't spend time dealing with clients who don't know what they want and are never satisfied with what you give them. Don't let such clients deter you; just finish the job and move on. There are lots of other prospects available; use your newly gained clips and go after them!

Writing copy for businesses and nonprofits may not be the most glamorous form of freelancing, and since you will rarely see your own byline on what you write, it's one in which you definitely may feel like an unsung hero. But if your goal is to pay the rent and keep food on the table, it is one of the most lucrative writing avenues you can pursue, with far better chances of stable and repeated business and fat paychecks than most other forms of freelancing.

Social Media Marketing for Businesses

by Dawn Copeman

Another area of copywriting that is becoming increasingly open to freelancers is social media marketing. If you're working for a small- or medium-size client, you may be asked to manage their social media. As of 2015 there were over 2.3 billion active social media users worldwide. Businesses, understandably, want to gain access to this large pool of potential clients. On Facebook alone there are over 40 million active small business pages. They all need someone to create posts for these pages, and that someone is usually a copywriter. Several of my clients have asked me to manage their Twitter account, LinkedIn, and Facebook pages in addition to writing web content and blogs.

Managing social media on behalf of a client can be difficult at first. It is far more time-consuming than maintaining your own social media presence. Every tweet or post must adhere to the tenets of good copywriting; it must attract attention and call to action all within a few lines or 140 characters.

So how do you write compelling copy with so few words? Follow these five steps:

1. Identify the Target Audience.

The first step in creating copy for social media is to find out who exactly the target audience is. Does your client want to attract businesses or consumers? Are the messages aimed at existing clients or to attract new clients? Finally, what exactly do they want you to achieve with your posts or tweets?

The answers to these questions are vitally important in helping you to create social media marketing that works for your client. They will not only help you create the correct content but also dictate when you should post this content for optimum results. Once you know who your target reader is, you can begin the task of writing your copy.

2. Research Content.

Before you write the copy, you need to have something to say. Sometimes this is easy; the client has a new product or service for you to sell, so you can use your copywriting skills to sell it. Usually, however, the client is working with an existing product line, so you have to come up with a way to get the product or service into the minds of the target readers. For this you will need to do some research.

You need to find or create a problem that your client's product can solve. Alternately, you need to find a news story that is somehow linked to your client's product and use that to show how your client's product can make the target reader's life easier. Social media is immediate, and people expect current and relevant information. This means you need to link in to something that is newsworthy right now to get your message across.

For one of my clients based in Australia, I had to write tweets to encourage businesses to use my client's business SMS (Short Message Service). To write relevant tweets and Facebook posts, I subscribed to Australian business newsletters and SMS newsletters, and read the Australian press daily to find stories, case studies, and infographics to help me to create relevant and interesting posts.

For another client specializing in server management, I had news alerts set up for anything to do with servers—viruses, firewall management, data security risks, and so on. I used these to create posts for my client, introducing problems and showing how my client could solve them.

As with any other area of copywriting, such research takes time and it is something you should consider when billing for your services for social media marketing.

3. Write the Copy.

For social media marketing, you will need to create two types of copy: the blog post or web content, and a tweet or post on other social media (Facebook, LinkedIn, Google+) to grab people's attention and get them to click through to the relevant blog post or web page.

You already know how to write the content for the blog post or website, so now you need to focus on writing the social media copy. For posts on Facebook and LinkedIn, you can usually use the first paragraph (or a shortened version of it) from your blog post or web content.

For Twitter, however, you need to be a bit more creative. The easiest method is to approach this as you would any other copywriting project: write a hook, arouse interest and then call to action, which in this case is to persuade the client to click through to find out more. You can write this copy in many ways, but my favorite three methods are:

- AIDA (Attention, Interest, Desire, and Action)
- Problem-Solution
- Picture, Promise, Action.

AIDA (Attention, Interest, Desire, and Action)

AIDA has been used for decades in copywriting for the very good reason that it is effective. You attract Attention, arouse Interest, create a Desire for the product and then call to Action.

Here are a few samples of possible AIDA tweets:

Melbourne doctors report 47% of appointments missed. Yet XXXX surgery has only 8% missed appointments. How do they do it? (Link)

Local restaurant uses SMS to ensure tables aren't empty and no food is wasted. Find out how. (Link)

Problem-Solution

Everyone has problems. This is why copy that offers solutions to problems is usually well received and has a high response rate. These are easier to write if you have a genuine problem that your client's product or service can solve. However, with some careful thinking, you can generally rewrite copy so that it fits the problem-solution mold.

Empty tables midweek? Food going to waste? Get customers for your tables now by following these simple SMS steps. (Link)

Need more server space but only at peak times? Only want to pay for what you use? Check out our secure flexible server share. (Link)

Picture, Promise, Action

This works particularly well if the blog post or web page you are directing the reader to also involves the picture, promise, price, and action style of copywriting described above.

> Patha (7) works 12 hours a day for her family and can't go to school. You could change her life completely. (Link)

It will be tricky at first to get your point across and write compelling copy in 140 characters or less, but as with all areas of writing, the more you do it, the easier it becomes.

I always write out my tweets in Word first so I can check the character count and keep tweaking my copy until I'm happy with it. You can add things like hashtags and keywords prior to publishing using a social media management program.

4. Source Images

Social media posts need images. According to *Adweek*, tweets with an image generate 18 percent more click-throughs, 89 percent more likes, and 150 percent more retweets than posts without.[19] With 500 million tweets sent every day, you need every extra edge to make yours stand out from the crowd.

You will need to use either royalty-free images or join a site that enables you to purchase images to use on social media sites. Be sure to read the terms and conditions of free image sites carefully so you know how and where you can use these images. I use iStockphoto.com and factor the price of membership into the fees I charge my clients. This way I know I've bought the rights to use those images in my clients' posts.

5. Publish Posts

It can be tempting to publish your post as soon as you've written it, but although social media needs to be current and relevant, timing is everything when it comes to social media marketing. Research has shown that if you wish to attract likes, retweets, and click-throughs on Twitter from a business

---

19   Shea Bennett, "Tweets with Images Get 18% More Clicks, 89% More Favorites and 150% More Retweets," *AdWeek*, November 14, 2013, http://www.adweek.com/socialtimes/twitter-images-study/493206.

client, you need to tweet on weekdays. If you want retweets, to get your message to more potential clients, you should post at 5 p.m. in the target readers' local time, but if you want click-throughs, you should post at noon or 6 p.m. If, however, you wish to reach a consumer, then you should tweet on Wednesdays or weekends to gain the most retweets and click-throughs.

If you are posting on Facebook, you need to post on a Thursday or a Friday, regardless of which type of client you are trying to attract, as research has shown that posts published on these two days have the highest engagement in terms of shares and click-throughs.

Ideally you will work with your client to determine when and how often you are going to post on social media for them. Then you can post at the appropriate time to get the best results. With social media you need to post fairly frequently.

However, just because a tweet needs to be posted at 5 p.m. doesn't mean you need to be online at 5 p.m. to do it. Most companies will use a social media management program. For Twitter, most companies use Tweetdeck, which enables multiple account holders to post and schedule tweets for a business account. You will need a Twitter account of your own to be able to use Tweetdeck. For Facebook you will need to be added as an admin user by the company. Again, you will need to have your own Facebook account. Once you are an admin user, you can schedule posts to appear on your client's timeline. Some companies use social media management programs like Buffer to manage all their social media presence in once place. Buffer allows users to schedule posts on Twitter, Facebook, LinkedIn, Instagram, Pinterest, and Google+.

All social media management programs offer features that will suggest keywords, tags, and hashtags relevant to your tweet or post. More importantly, they also enable you and your client to see how well the post was received: how many likes, click-throughs, shares, or retweets it got. This will enable you to see what works and what doesn't with this target audience.

For more information on writing copy for social media, check out the following sites:

- "If Don Draper Tweeted: The 27 Copywriting Formulas That Will Drive Clicks and Engagement on Social Media"—blog.bufferapp .com/copywriting-formulas

- "Five Tips to Master Your Brand's Customer Service on Twitter"—socialmediaexplorer.com/content-sections/tools-and-tips/twitter-customer-service-5-tips/
- "Social Media Copywriting"—www.freelancecopywritersblog.com/4100/social-media-copywriting/

By adding social media marketing to your list of copywriting skills, you greatly increase your value to your existing clients—and your attractiveness to new clients. And that has the potential to greatly increase your bottom line as a freelance writer!

CHAPTER 22

Commercial Freelancing: Where's the Money?

In the previous two chapters, Dawn Copeman has explained the many ways in which commercial freelancing differs from writing and selling articles to periodicals. Commercial freelancing differs from writing for periodicals in one additional, profound respect: it is the one form of freelancing where you can set your own rates. Of course, you need to set rates that clients are willing to pay, but here, at last, you are not held hostage to a magazine's standard "per word" rate.

Setting your commercial rates typically begins by preparing a "bid" for your client. A bid should present your client with the following information:

- What you will do
- How long it will take
- What you will charge

On the surface, that all sounds simple enough! In practice, however, developing an effective bid can be quite a challenge, especially if you're not accustomed to setting your own rates or estimating how long a project will take. The most common "beginner" mistakes include failing to clearly define the project, underestimating the time factor, and setting rates too low. Here are some ways to avoid those mistakes.

DEFINING THE PROJECT

The first step in submitting a bid (or deciding whether to bid in the first place) is to determine exactly what the project involves. If, for example, the client wants a brochure, find out how much information will be provided, how much you'll have to dig up on your own, how it should be presented, and whether you are expected to provide a finished product or just written copy. Determine the goal of the brochure, including its audience and the image the company wishes to project.

Similarly, if you're asked to edit a document, review the material first. Find out what level of editing is desired. Are you expected to proofread for typos, copyedit for grammar and style, or content edit for readability and accuracy? Does the copy need a lot of work, or is it fairly clean?

Once you've determined what is expected of you, spell that out in your bid, in writing. In other words, tell the client what the client has told you. This is your only protection against unexpected demands, changes, or requests for endless revisions.

DETERMINING A TIMELINE

Once you have defined what a project entails, you'll need to determine when it can be delivered. In many cases, the client will set the deadline, whereupon you'll have to decide whether you can meet it. In other cases, however, the client will ask you how long the project will take. You may be required to offer a completion date, an estimated number of hours, or both, depending on how you will be billing the client.

Think carefully before you answer this question! It is easy, especially for beginners, to underestimate how many hours a project will require. Be sure to leave room for unexpected delays, difficulties, changes in direction, and people who don't deliver information or their part of the work on schedule. If you have to submit the project for corporate approval at various stages before completion, remember that this can add significant delays. (You can be sure, for example, that a key person will go on vacation right before the project is due.)

Be sure to consider other projects you have going on at the same time. Can you fit this project into your schedule? Will you have to drop or postpone other projects or clients? Will you be able to take on new projects?

Again, budget extra time for the unexpected. If problems arise in another project, will they delay this project?

Resist the temptation to impress a client with your speed and efficiency by underestimating the amount of time the project will require. This can backfire: too short an estimate can give the impression that your work is hasty and slipshod. Though clients value speed, they also want to know that you're giving their work your full attention.

As a writer, you may be accustomed to thinking only about writing time. As a business writer, however, you'll be billing for all the time you spend on that project, including telephone time, meetings, research, errands, revisions, more revisions, and so on. Be sure to include those hours in your estimate.

SETTING FEES

Writer's Market lists fees for a wide range of writing services such as copyediting, copywriting, speech writing, brochures, and so forth. In some cases, these fees are listed by hour; in others, they're listed by project.

Most of these listings offer a range of fees—usually somewhere between $20 and $100 per hour. Where you should place yourself on that range depends on a variety of factors, including your experience *and* your geographic location. Freelancers based in New York City, Los Angeles, or Silicon Valley will typically charge higher rates than freelancers doing the same work in Kansas or Nebraska.

Don't assume that you have to start at the bottom of the rate scale. Instead, do some research to determine the going rate in your area. Look for copy editors online and contact them to determine their rates.

Just as you shouldn't underbid on hours, you should also avoid underbidding on price. It's tempting to bid low, on the assumption that a client would prefer to hire the cheapest contractor available. In reality, clients tend to avoid contractors who price themselves too cheaply. Just as you might wonder why something is marked down to a bargain price, your client may also wonder why you charge so much less than your competitors. Also, avoid the temptation to underbid the competition. It's wiser to build good relationships with other business freelancers, who may then refer clients to you when they're overloaded.

Once you've determined your hourly rate, you can calculate how much a project is worth. Your final decision is whether to price the project on an hourly basis, a flat rate, or some other rate scale. Each has advantages and disadvantages.

If you are concerned that a client will think your hourly rate is too high, a flat rate may work best. The advantage of a flat rate (i.e., "$300 per brochure") is that you get the same fee even if you put in fewer hours than you estimated—more profit to you! The disadvantage, obviously, is that if the project runs longer than you anticipated, you won't get more money. Some clients like flat rates; others don't. This is something you'll need to determine by working with the client.

An hourly rate has the advantage of being more open ended. If the client wants revisions, makes changes, or adds extra tasks, you just add extra billing hours. The disadvantage is that some clients have no understanding of how long things take and may assume you're padding your bill. Again, it may not be possible to determine the best approach until you've discussed the project with the client.

A third approach is to bill by some other measure, such as per page (which is a good way to charge for editorial services). The way to determine this type of rate is to simply estimate how many pages you can edit in an hour, and then divide your hourly rate by that number. The advantage of this approach is that it is easy to calculate. The client only has to count the number of pages in the project to determine the final cost. Another advantage is that, like the flat rate, you'll get paid the same amount even if the work goes more quickly than expected. The disadvantage, of course, is also the same: if the work goes more slowly than you expected, you get paid less.

The final element you'll need to calculate into your bid is expenses, if any. If you will need to purchase special software to handle the job, or subcontract portions of the job to others (such as artists or designers), be sure to include an estimate of those amounts in your bid. Make sure these items are listed separately from your own billing hours. Try to determine exactly what those costs will be, so you don't surprise the client with an unexpected list of outside expenses.

GET IT IN WRITING

When you bid on a project, submit your bid in writing. Email is often acceptable. Don't be surprised if you have to negotiate before your final bid is accepted. Don't start the project until the client has accepted your bid in writing.

Here's a sample bid letter from Dawn Copeman, offering a variety of copywriting services to a client. Note that each section of the bid includes detailed specifications of the services that will be provided for that portion of the project, including planning meetings, revisions, and sample designs.

Dear [Client]:

Thank you for inviting me to your offices yesterday to discuss your copywriting needs.

As per our discussions yesterday I understand that you would like me to come up with a new look for your website for your website builder to install. You would also like me to write new copy for your website, including any additional pages that we decide you need following our meeting to discuss and approve a web design. Finally, you need content for a new, sixteen-page, A4-sized glossy brochure.

Here is my bid for providing these copywriting services.

Website Design Advice
I will provide you with five different suggestions and mock layouts of your website within two weeks of your go-ahead. My fee for this service will be $400 to include all conceptualization, research, and one planning meeting.

Web Content Writing
My fee for writing the content of the website will be $1,400. This will include two revisions and two planning meetings. The copy will be delivered to you within one week of approval of final web design and agreement of page content. Following our first planning meeting, I shall return any redrafts to you within forty-eight hours, and following our second meeting, the final copy shall be with you within twenty-four hours.

Brochure Content
To write copy for a new sixteen-page, A4-sized brochure, my fee will be $500. This is to cover an initial planning meeting with you, at

(Continued)

which we shall discuss photos to be used and the focus of the brochure, all conceptualization, research, and two sets of revisions. As I understand it, you wish to have the new website up and running before commencing work on the brochure.

Before commencing on the web design conceptualizing and the web content writing, I would require half my fee to be paid in advance, with the remainder to be paid within thirty days of delivery of final approved copy and design. Before commencing work on the brochure I would likewise require half my fee to be paid in advance with the remainder within thirty days of delivery of final approved copy.

If these terms are acceptable to you, please sign and date the agreement below and keep a copy for yourself, returning a copy to me via post or email.

I look forward to working with you,

Sincerely,
Dawn Copeman

I have read and agree to the above terms and payment conditions.
Name: _____
Print Name: _____
Date: _____

And here's a sample "letter of agreement" to provide a newsletter for a business website, also from Dawn Copeman:

Letter of Agreement

Dear [Client]:

Following our recent email conversations, I have agreed to write and edit the newsletter for your site. I will produce one 400- to 500-word article per month on the topic you provide to me. In addition to this I will format and edit the newsletter, inserting links and advertiser promotions and ensuring that all content is grammatically correct and reads well.

My fee for this service is $XX per newsletter, with half the amount to be paid in advance and the remaining half within fifteen days of completion of the project. This fee includes one rewrite per newsletter. Payment is to be made via PayPal to my email address.

I hereby confirm that you will own all rights to the articles and the newsletters, as this is a work-for-hire agreement.

We have both agreed that this agreement is a temporary one valid only for the next three issues of the newsletter. We will both review the situation after delivery of January's newsletter.

I will provide you with the first article by Friday, November 10, 20XX, with the second article by December 5 and the third article by January 5.

If this agreement is acceptable to you, please sign below, keep a copy for yourself, and return this copy to me. (I will accept confirmation via email stating you understand and agree to these terms.)

I look forward to working with you,

Sincerely,
Dawn Copeman

Understood and Agreed
Name: _____
Print Name: _____
Date: _____

You also need to determine when and how you will get paid. If you're undertaking a large job (e.g., more than $500), you may wish to ask for payment in installments. Some writers ask for payment in thirds: one third when the bid is accepted or the contract is signed, one third halfway through the project, and one third on completion. Others ask for half down and half at the end. If you have to buy materials or software to complete the project, request payment for those items in advance. If you need to subcontract part of the work, you'll usually ask for reimbursement of those expenses after the work has been completed.

Business clients expect to be invoiced. Accounting departments are more likely to respect a professional-looking invoice, so it's worth going to the office supply store and buying a pack of preprinted forms. If your client prefers to be invoiced electronically, design a professional-looking electronic invoice and save it as a PDF file before sending it. (You can find some excellent free templates for electronic invoices at invoicehome.com.) Find out whether you need to provide a purchase order number to get paid.

Once you've completed a job, follow up! Find out whether the work was considered satisfactory, and remind the client that you would welcome other projects. Ask the client to refer you to other companies, and ask whether the client is willing to be used as a reference when you contact other prospects.

CHAPTER 23

Writing and Selling a Nonfiction Book

At some point in your writing career, you may say, "Wow, I could write a book about that!" Unfortunately, many writers stop there, intimidated by the prospect of writing something as large as a book—or by horror stories about the difficulties of getting published.

Writing a nonfiction book doesn't have to be intimidating, however. Often, it's a logical next step in your career, and can provide a number of benefits. While articles are often forgotten once a magazine or newspaper hits the recycle bin, people keep books on their shelves for years. A book is a more significant credential than an article. And if a book stays in print, you'll receive royalty checks for years.

The market for nonfiction books is huge. Walk into any bookstore and you'll see that the nonfiction titles vastly outnumber the fiction titles—and that's not counting specialty bookstores. There are more nonfiction publishers than fiction publishers, ranging from huge commercial concerns to smaller "niche" publishers that focus on a particular topic or region. Nor is it that difficult to get a nonfiction book published. It rarely requires an agent, and you can often sell your book before you write it.

Writing a book involves the same basic skills required to write and market nonfiction articles. You need the ability to develop and refine a topic, organize your subject matter, conduct research and interviews, and write and polish your material. It also requires similar credentials. Plus, any articles you've already sold on a topic will help demonstrate your ability to write about that topic.

I don't recommend attempting to *start* your writing career with a book. Even if you've got the perfect book idea, keep it on hold until you've mastered the process of writing (and selling) articles. Don't tackle something as significant as a book project until you're thoroughly comfortable with the writing process, and feel sure that you won't mind spending several months writing and researching a single topic.

WHY WRITE A BOOK?

Writers choose to branch out to book-length manuscripts for a variety of reasons, including:

- **To share your knowledge or expertise.** If you're an expert in a particular subject, chances are you're already writing about it. You may have found, however, that there are only so many articles you can sell, and so much more you want to say. A book may be the ideal way to get this information across.
- **To fill a niche.** Frequently, as you conduct research on a topic, you find a gap just begging to be filled. Your inability to find information on a particular topic could be an incentive to provide that information yourself.
- **To help people.** Many books are written out of a desire to help people with a particular problem. I wrote my first book, *Coping with Sorrow on the Loss of Your Pet*, after discovering through a survey that hundreds of pet owners felt they were "alone" in their grief.
- **To gather your written work together in one place.** Many writers compile collections of columns or articles into a book. Mary Emma Allen, for example, turned her series of columns on Alzheimer's into *When We Become the Parent to Our Parents*. Many of the chapters in this book are based on articles or columns written for other publications.
- **To ensure that an important event or person is not forgotten.** Autobiography, biography, and genealogy are all potential sources of material. Many writers want to ensure that future readers can learn "what happened" or "what life was like when."

One reason I *didn't* list is "to make lots of money." While some nonfiction books earn well, others bring only a few thousand dollars in royalties. Cash is not the best motivation to write a book!

GETTING STARTED

It may seem like a big jump to go from 2,000-word features to a manuscript of 60,000 to 100,000 words. The first step, therefore, is to think of your project as a series of "chapters." Each chapter is equivalent to a 2,000- to 5,000-word article. If you can write an article a week, then you can write a book chapter a week, not counting research time. While a book typically takes from six months to three years to write, most contracts anticipate a delivery time of one year.

Choosing a Topic

Choosing a book topic is similar to choosing a topic for an article. Once again, you may start with a general subject (dogs) and move to a more specific topic (health). Then, begin brainstorming subtopics. The difference is, when you're writing a book, each subtopic may become a chapter.

When you choose a topic, you may find you either have too much information or too little. For example, a subject like "dogs" is too broad for an article *or* a book. A topic like "canine health," while too broad for an article, *could* be turned into a book. Narrowing that topic still further—"natural health care for dogs"—will make your book even more focused, and thus more marketable.

A book that targets a more specific market niche is often more marketable than a more general book. For example, a book focusing on "how to have a healthy dog" might seem to have broad market appeal ("all dog owners"). However, it will also have more competition. A book on health care for older dogs may have a smaller audience, but it is likely to attract a larger percentage of readers within that niche.

Don't narrow your focus too much, however, or you may find that your potential audience is too small and you may not have enough information. A book on "chiropractic care for dogs" might be a bit too narrow, but one on "holistic health care for dogs" that includes a variety of treatments (acupuncture, massage, herbal therapies, etc.) will expand your options *and* your market.

Organizing Your Book

Do you need an outline? Yes—if only because you'll need a chapter-by-chapter outline when preparing your proposal.

Fortunately, the techniques described in chapter 5 apply just as well to books. The difference is that each subtopic is likely to be an entire chapter. For example, if you're using the "logical sequence of events" approach (this happened first, this happened next . . .), each major event might be a chapter. Your introduction and conclusion, instead of being limited to a few paragraphs, will also be separate chapters.

Once you've developed a basic chapter structure, use each chapter heading to organize your research. Many writers set up a file folder for each chapter and use it to store research information. If you find that a chapter has too much information, you can always split it; if a chapter is too short, you might combine it with another chapter.

Should you write your book from beginning to end, or write a chapter here and a chapter there? The answer, of course, is to use whatever method works best for you! Some people like to write easier (or shorter) chapters first, then progress to more difficult ones, and finally tie it all together. Others prefer to write chapters sequentially, particularly when it's important to keep track of what you've already covered.

Write, Then Revise

Don't try to edit and polish your book as you go. Get the basics written first, even if the end result is longer than your allotted word count. Once you have a first draft, it's easier to make cuts or add information. It's also easier to polish a manuscript all at once rather than a piece at a time.

Most writers recommend a "cooling off" period of at least a week before attempting to edit your manuscript. Then, you'll find it easier to approach your words from the perspective of the reader or editor, rather than a writer still in love with her own words. This is particularly important when you discover, for example, that your book is 10,000 words longer than the limit. When you've just finished writing those words, it's hard to imagine giving any of them up. After a break, however, you find that you can part with a paragraph here and a minor concept there, or even a chapter that isn't vital to the whole. You can also cut words by creating contractions (changing "you are" to "you're" and "you will" to "you'll"). You'll also be amazed to find how easy it is to tighten up phrases and paragraphs. If your book contains 2,000 paragraphs, you only need to cut an average of ten words per paragraph to achieve a total reduction of 20,000 words.

FINDING A PUBLISHER

As I said earlier, it's often possible to sell your book before you write it. To accomplish this, you'll need to submit a proposal to a publisher. By this, I mean a *commercial, royalty-paying publisher.* Today, writers are bombarded with information from subsidy print-on-demand publishers who want to convince you they are "real" publishers. Professional writers know that a "real" publisher is one who pays *you*, not one that you pay. If you want to see your book in bookstores and libraries, or reviewed in the press, you need a commercial publisher. Submitting your book to a commercial publisher costs nothing; if it is accepted, you will receive an advance and (eventually) royalties.

That doesn't mean that there is no place for print-on-demand and other forms of subsidy and self-publishing. These can be an option in certain circumstances, as I'll explain below.

The first step in submitting your book to an appropriate commercial publisher is *finding* one. Don't just grab a market directory and look in the index for, say, publishers who handle books on "dogs." Instead, start by looking at actual books.

Begin with your own bookshelf. Who publishes the books *you* refer to on your subject? Would your book fit into their line? Pay special attention to publishers from whom you've bought multiple books, as this indicates a certain meshing of interests.

Then, visit a bookstore. What publishers are offering similar titles or topics? Do you find yourself picking up books by one publisher more than others? While you're browsing, ask yourself some questions:

- **Do you like the look and feel of the publisher's books?** Is the paper high quality? Do you like the cover? Is the font easy to read? Would you like your book to look like this?
- **Does the publisher offer the type of book you're planning?** Do their books have a similar depth of content? If a publisher uses lots of color photos, can you provide them? Conversely, if you intend to include a lot of artwork, does the publisher typically do so?

- **Do the books match your writing style?** If you write in a conversational or informal style, don't pitch to a publisher whose books are highly technical or academic in tone.
- **Are your credentials appropriate?** Does the publisher seem to prefer authors who have specific degrees or professional experience?
- **What is the price range?** Does it match the probable budget of your audience? You might like the idea of having your book published as a glossy coffee-table piece, but will your intended audience shell out $30 or more for it?

Once you've found a publisher (or several) who seems appropriate, your next step is to review that publisher's guidelines. You may find these on the publisher's website, or in *Writer's Market*, or in a guideline database (you'll find a list of book publisher directories at www.writing-world.com/links/bookpubs.shtml). Also, try to find the publisher's current catalog (which is also usually available on their website). This will give you an idea of the books that are currently being offered (and also tell you if the publisher already has something too similar to your idea in stock), as well as what may be coming up in the near future. Make sure you can also determine the publisher's requirements, including length, illustrations, and so on, as well as their payment terms.

Chances are, you'll have found more than one prospective publisher. That's good; you'll want a backup plan if your first choice says no. The question is, can you submit a proposal to more than one publisher at a time? There's no single answer to this. Some publishers still object to simultaneous submissions, but others accept that since it can take many months to review a proposal, it's asking a lot to expect authors to submit sequentially. One option is to submit simultaneous *query* letters. If a publisher invites you to submit a more detailed proposal, ask if it must be exclusive or whether you can submit the material to other publishers at the same time.

PREPARING A PROPOSAL

Once you've found a publisher, you need to develop a professional proposal that includes the following elements:

The Overview

The overview is presented in narrative format, and may include several sections:

Title

A title helps establish the concept of your book. Amy Shojai, author of *New Choices in Natural Healing for Dogs and Cats*, says a title "must not only describe the book and/or concept, but be that elusive thing that editors/agents describe as 'sexy.' The title must strike an instant chord of recognition with the editor." Keep in mind, however, that your title is likely to be changed if the book is accepted.

Content

Offer a summary of the content. Don't go into excessive detail; try to convey the general focus and purpose of your book, including the benefits it will offer to readers.

Rationale

Your overview should explain who will buy your book and why that audience will want to buy it *now*. "Back up the need for the book with stats," says Shojai. "Editors want numbers; don't just say 'everybody who loves pets will buy my book.' Tell them how many owners there are who have dogs who chew used bubblegum and would benefit from *Twelve Steps to De-Gumming Da Dog.*"

When pitching her book on natural healing, Shojai began with broad statistics (the fact that Americans then owned 66.2 million cats and 58 million dogs) to define the potential market. She then narrowed that audience to those who "welcome pets into their hearts and homes as full members of the family." She explained the timeliness of her proposal by noting the "national obsession with health and fitness."

Competition

What books will you be competing against, and *how* will you compete? To answer this question, of course, you must first *research* the competition. Says Shojai, "The competition section is probably the most important part of any proposal. I try to *never* slam the competition, but to put my proposal in a favorable light compared to whatever might be out there. In this case,

I felt that some of the competition was quite good—just way, way out of date."

This section should list specific titles (including author, publisher, and publication date). Then, explain how your book differs from those titles: how it improves, differs from, or goes beyond what has been written before. In general, it's not necessary to list self-published books among your competition, unless they have a significant sales record.

No competition is not necessarily a good thing! If nothing has been published on your topic area, it could indicate that there is no market for your book. Shojai notes, "You *want* books on your topic to be out there and successful; that means you have a ready-made market. Then it's a matter of making your book different enough to make the idea viable."

Format

This section should list the book's title and subtitle, the anticipated number of words, and any other information relevant to the production of the book. Indicate whether it will include graphics (tables, charts, figures, diagrams), illustrations (photos, line drawings), sidebars, appendices, and so forth. Indicate how artwork will be provided; will you be creating it yourself? You should also indicate whether any permissions will be necessary.

Market

Explain how your publisher can reach the book's target audience. List magazines in which the book should be reviewed, organizations and groups that might be interested in the book, specialized bookstores, or other market outlets. Note whether the book could be used as a classroom text. (You'll be asked for this information anyway once your proposal is accepted, so start gathering it now.)

Chapter-by-Chapter Summary

Most publishers expect to receive a list of proposed chapters, with a one- to two-paragraph summary of each. If you haven't written your book, you may not know exactly how many chapters it will contain, but you should be able to create a summary from your outline. You can always change the number of chapters, or their organization, later. There's no "correct" number of chapters; however, a book with too few (e.g., fewer than five) may not seem sufficiently in depth, while one with too many (e.g., more than forty) may seem unwieldy. Some publishers will also ask for sample chapters. If so, find out whether they need to be sequential (e.g., the first three) or whether you can send the most *representative* chapters.

Author Bio

What are your qualifications for writing this book? Answer this question in a single page. Your bio should be written in third person: "John Smith is an award-winning decoy carver who has practiced and taught the craft for more than twenty years." As with magazine publishers, a book publisher is likely to expect credentials in one or more of the following areas: educational background, professional background, personal experience and/or expertise, and previous writing credits.

Be sure you know what credentials are expected of you by the publisher and the market you are attempting to target. If your book focuses on scholarly information, chances are that you'll be expected to have academic credentials. If your book focuses on business or technical information, you may be expected to provide relevant professional experience. If your book addresses more popular how-to or self-help topics, you may be able to market your proposal on the basis of professional *or* personal expertise. The more impact your book might have on a reader's well-being, the more credentials you will be expected to have. While you might sell a book on fly-fishing on the basis of a weekend hobby, you may have trouble selling a book on childcare if your only credential is being a parent.

Writing credits are useful if they are relevant. If you have published other nonfiction books, for example, this demonstrates that you can finish *and* sell a book-length manuscript, even if it's on a completely different topic. Articles also help demonstrate your skill, but publishers often aren't impressed by articles on an unrelated topic. Fiction credits may not impress an editor at all. Keep in mind that you're not just trying to prove that you can write; you're also trying to demonstrate that readers should believe what you say!

Supporting Materials

You may also wish to include the following materials, particularly if you are submitting your proposal by surface mail:

- Resume or curriculum vitae
- Publications list citing *relevant* publications

- Writing samples, if requested
- Business card
- SASE and/or reply postcard

Don't send a photo, testimonials or reviews, irrelevant writing samples, copies of other books you've written, or anything that would appear unprofessional![20]

THE PUBLISHING PROCESS

Selling your proposal is just the beginning. Here's what happens next:

1. **The acceptance negotiation.** If your proposal is accepted, an editor will contact you to let you know that the company either wants or is considering your book. At this point, you'll be told whether to proceed as planned, or whether the publisher wishes to make changes to the project. This may involve some discussion and negotiation before you and the publisher reach a mutually satisfactory agreement.

2. **The contract.** The next step is the contract. Read it carefully. If there is anything you don't understand, ask for clarification. Be sure you know what rights you are giving up (don't sign a "work-for-hire" contract!), what royalties you'll receive, and the basis for those royalties. Some publishers pay royalties on cover price, others on "net" price (after bookstore or distributor discounts). This can make a significant difference; for example, while 10 percent royalties on the *cover price* of a book priced at $15 would be $1.50 per book, 10 percent of *net* on that same book might be as low as sixty cents. Find out what you'll be paid for subsidiary sales, such as electronic or audio editions, translations, or movie rights.

3. **The advance.** Once you've signed and returned the contract, you should receive a portion of your advance. Most publishers pay 50 percent on signing the contract and 50 percent on delivery of an

---

[20] A more detailed explanation of how to write a nonfiction book proposal, along with examples of successful proposals, can be found in *The Writer's Guide to Queries, Pitches and Proposals* (Allworth Press, 2010). This book also explains how to research one's book competition on Amazon.com and how to submit a book to an international publisher.

"acceptable" manuscript. A few pay the advance in thirds. If you fail to deliver the book, or if it is not considered acceptable, you will have to return the advance.

4. **The author questionnaire.** You'll probably receive a lengthy questionnaire asking you to describe possible marketing outlets for the book. The publisher will use this questionnaire to guide the book's promotional campaign, so be as thorough as possible!

5. **The manuscript.** Your contract will specify a delivery date for the manuscript and the form in which it is to be delivered (e.g., hard copy, email, CD, flash drive, etc.). Your publisher will announce a publication date and will begin promoting the book before you deliver the manuscript, so meeting that deadline is important.

6. **First review.** Once you've delivered the manuscript, it must be reviewed by the publisher before you receive the second half of your advance. Often, this takes one to three months, so don't expect a check immediately.

7. **Editing.** First, your book will be reviewed for content issues, and you'll be asked to clarify anything that seems unclear, or perhaps to add or cut information. Next, your book will be copyedited and proofread, and you'll be asked to review and approve suggested changes. You may be given only a few days for each review.

8. **Galley proofs.** Once the book is typeset, you'll be sent "galley proofs" for a final review. Today, these are often sent as PDF files. Your job now is to make sure that no typos or errors have been introduced in the typesetting process; the publisher will *not* appreciate editorial corrections unless you spot a major error. Again, you may have less than a week to review galleys.

9. **Indexing.** At the galley stage, you may be asked to create an index for the book. Don't bother indexing your book using the Microsoft Word "index" function. By the time the publisher is ready for an index, you will be working with a PDF or printed file rather than your original manuscript. I have found that the easiest indexing method is to sit down with a notepad and go through the book page by page, jotting down terms that should be indexed, along with the corresponding page numbers. If you don't want to index the book yourself, the publisher will arrange for indexing, but will usually

charge the cost (which can be several hundred dollars) against your first royalty check.

10. **Printing.** Your book may go to press anywhere from six months to two years after you deliver the manuscript. When it does, you'll receive a number of author copies (usually ten). You'll also have the option of buying more copies at a discount; you will *not* receive royalties on copies you buy.

11. **Royalties.** Most publishers pay royalties twice a year. If your book is published in June, your first royalty period will probably end in December, and you may not see a royalty statement until the following spring. You won't actually receive royalties, however, until your book has sold enough copies to "earn out" your advance.

DOING IT YOURSELF

Many authors, frustrated by the length of time involved in getting a book commercially published, choose the self-publishing route. Scores of articles today urge authors to "take back control" of their books, and extol the joy of being able to interact directly with readers.

That control comes with a price—which is usually a lack of sales. However, there are times when do-it-yourself (DIY) publishing is the best choice. My first book, *Coping with Sorrow on the Loss of Your Pet*, began as a self-published title and sold several thousand copies. I then sold it to a commercial publisher, where it languished for several years until I was able to regain the rights. It is now published through print-on-demand and Kindle formats, and earns me several thousand dollars a year.

DIY publishing isn't appropriate for every book, but can be effective for a well-targeted nonfiction title aimed at a relatively small niche market. The niche needs to be large enough to offer a reasonable sales potential, and should also be a market you have some means of reaching, perhaps through your business, your website, seminars, talks, or other methods. If you can't reach your readers, you won't be able to sell them your book.

There are several forms of DIY publishing, including self-publishing, electronic publishing, subsidy print publishing, and subsidy print-on-demand publishing. Each has pros and cons.

Print Self-Publishing

Though subsidy publishers often refer to their services as "self-publishing," this term has a distinct meaning. When you self-publish, you literally become a publisher. Your ISBN points to you—either to your own name or the name you've set up for your publishing "house." You pay all the expenses, wear all the hats, and reap all the revenue.

This generally means setting up an official business, with a business license in your city or state. You may also need a sales tax license. You may need to set up a "doing business as" statement to enable you to use your publishing house name as an official business name. This will enable you to accept checks in that name (though you may have to open a separate business bank account).

Your book will be produced by a *printer*, which will usually specify a minimum number of copies you can print (at least 200). These will probably be stored in your home as you try to sell them. You pay the full cost of printing, and when you sell a book, the entire revenue belongs to you.

A self-publisher is responsible for every aspect of the job, including editing, proofreading, interior design, cover design, marketing, sending copies to reviewers, and fulfilling orders. Of course, you can (and probably will have to) hire out some of these tasks. You may also choose to hire a fulfillment company to store your books and process orders. Obviously, however, the more services you pay for, the lower your profits will be.

Self-publishing is a great deal of work; however, you're in complete control of every step of the process, and you *own* your book. The costs are yours, but so are the profits. It's not a choice to make lightly, but it can be very rewarding.

Subsidy Print Publishing

In the old days, the only way to produce your own print book without self-publishing was to use a subsidy publisher. For a fee of thousands of dollars, the publisher would print a few hundred copies of your book, store them, and pay you a small royalty if and when it sold. One key difference between subsidy publishing and self-publishing is that you do not *own* your book. Despite the huge sum of money you'll pay to have it printed, it belongs to the publisher. If you want additional copies, you must buy them. You have little control over the book design or quality, and may find yourself locked into a contract that is as rigid as any commercial contract, leaving you no way to get out of it if you found a "real" publisher.

Subsidy publishing firms still exist. They usually advertise with phrases like "new authors wanted!" I have yet to hear from a writer who was pleased with the results. Fortunately, we now have other options.

Subsidy Print-on-Demand Publishing

Print-on-demand (POD) publishing enables you to create a printed book without taking on all the tasks of self-publishing. While there are some *commercial* POD publishers (which review submissions and accept only a limited number of books), most are subsidy publishers who will "publish" nearly any book. You pay the company to produce your book, and receive royalties when the book sells. You do not own the finished book, and the ISBN will generally be in the name of the publisher. (Some publishers, like Lulu.com and Amazon.com's CreateSpace, make it possible for you to set up your own publishing entity using their services but using your own ISBNs.)

With print-on-demand, books are literally printed when ordered. This means you can offer a high-quality book without printing hundreds of copies in advance. Often (though not always) the quality of printing is equal to a commercially published book.

Costs vary widely. Some companies, like Xlibris, iUniverse, or DogEar, require you to purchase a publishing "package" ranging from several hundred to several thousand dollars depending on the services included. Sites like Lulu.com, CreateSpace, and Blurb allow you to do most of the work yourself and pay no up-front fees; these also offer access to service providers such as cover designers, editors, and so on.

The advantage of POD publishing, especially the free services, is that you can get a book to the marketplace with a minimum of fuss and expense—and do so within a few days. Orders are handled directly by the publisher. Some POD publishers will place your title on Amazon; in other cases you'll have to pay extra for this, if the option is available at all. In the case of CreateSpace, your book will be posted automatically to Amazon, Amazon.co.uk, and Amazon.ca.

The downside is that POD titles usually cost more than their mass-produced counterparts. You have much less leeway in offering quantity discounts, and since you don't own the book, you'll have to buy your own copies (usually at the production rather than the retail rate). POD books are generally not returnable, and thus are rarely purchased by bookstores. Most major review sources won't review POD titles, and the burden of marketing rests entirely on you.

Electronic Publishing

A decade ago, the market was flooded with electronic publishers who were convinced this would be the next wave of publishing. Most of them are gone. Today, there are still a host of electronic options, ranging from doing it yourself to the option of using a commercial, royalty-paying e-publisher. Some sites make it possible to e-publish a book for a variety of devices and formats, including Kindles, other tablets, and smartphones. By far the most popular platform today, however, is Amazon's Kindle.

Thanks largely to Kindle, reader interest in ebooks is skyrocketing. Most major publishers now offer Kindle editions of commercially published print books. Unfortunately, Kindle is also flooded with literally millions of poorly written, poorly produced books (and there are many reports of plagiarized books appearing on Kindle). Kindle also offers a wide range of public domain titles, usually harvested from sites like Project Gutenberg or Archive.org.

Kindle offers the DIY publisher an easy, free mechanism to get a book published. The directions are fairly easy to follow, and issues of interior design are less important as Kindle has its own format requirements. You'll still need a good cover, and it's vital to ensure that your book is well written, edited, and proofread.

A disadvantage to Kindle books is the inability to pass them along or give them as gifts. You can give someone an Amazon gift card, but you can't actually "give" someone a specific Kindle title. While there are Kindle programs for libraries, it's not that easy for someone to find your book there. Some writers opt into Amazon's "Kindle Unlimited" program, which provides Amazon Prime members with unlimited access to Kindle titles for a monthly fee and provides a small royalty to participating authors.

It's also possible to self-publish an ebook simply by putting up a website, formatting your book and saving it as a PDF file, and creating a shopping cart through a service like PayPal. You can even set up affiliate programs to encourage readers to market your book. If you offer more than one book, you can create a more complex shopping cart using a service like

Softseller.com, which charges twenty-five cents per transaction (no matter how many titles are included in that transaction). If you prefer not to sell your books directly, you can use a platform like Lulu.com or Smashwords (which offers a wide range of e-publishing formats).

The business side of e-publishing is less demanding than print. You don't have to worry about paying for print runs or storing boxes of books in the garage, or shipping books to customers. You *do* have to worry about customers who buy an ebook and then wonder when it will arrive in the mail! Your transactions will be handled electronically, and since you're not selling a physical product, you generally won't need to register as a business. If you use a service like Kindle, you'll receive royalties.

The downside, of course, is that like any other DIY venue, the burden of marketing your book and attracting readers rests entirely with you. Most ebooks will not be reviewed by major review sources, and of course they won't be found in any bookstore.

Before you venture down the DIY road, be sure you understand what is involved. Becoming your own publisher means becoming more than just a writer. Your job truly begins when the writing ends. You become a business owner, involved in the tasks of marketing, shipping, bookkeeping and much more. Or, you have to pay someone else to handle these tasks. And the more time you spend on publishing, the less time you'll have for actual writing—so if writing is your passion, self-publishing that writing may not be the best option for you.

CHAPTER 24

Establishing Your Online Presence

Let me share a couple of scenarios I've experienced as an editor. Scenario one: I come across an article I'd like to reprint. However, all the author's bio tells me is that he lives in Indiana with his wife and three cats. No problem, I'll just look him up online. Scenario two: I'm putting together my newsletter late at night, and realize I'm missing an author bio. It's too late to get that information by email, so I search for the writer's website, hoping I'll be able to find a bio there.

Only . . . neither of these writers *has* a website! The first writer has a blog with no contact information. The only way I can ask about reprinting his article is by leaving a public comment on a six-month-old blog entry. (I don't.) The second writer has a Facebook page with pictures of her kids and dogs and chatter about her latest book, but . . . no bio.

My instant reaction in each case is that I'm not dealing with a professional. Professional writers have websites.

"But I have a Facebook page!" you say. "I have a Twitter account! I'm on LinkedIn! I have a blog! Isn't that enough?" Lots of articles argue the merits of blogs over websites, telling us that blogs are "active" and "fresh," inviting reader engagement, while websites are "static," "stale," or even "a thing of the past." The implication is that "static" is a bad thing. But in reality, this is an apples vs. oranges argument. There are circumstances in which "active" and "fresh" are useful. There are also circumstances in which a "static" (or rather, reliable and unchanging) source of information is important. Nor are websites and blogs mutually exclusive; you don't have to choose one over the other.

A website is still one of the most important tools in the professional writer's toolbox. It should be at the core of your marketing efforts, both online and offline. Everything else that you do should refer readers to your site.

WHY YOU NEED A WEBSITE

Your website should be the place where anyone, from anywhere, can find vital information about you, your products, or your services. Your goal is not to try to entice readers to keep coming back or leave "feedback." Your goal is to enable readers—and, more importantly, customers and potential clients—to find out what they need to know about you the *first* time they visit. Rather than comparing a website to a blog, think of it as comparable to a resume or a business card. You don't redesign your business card or update your resume every week. These marketing tools are static, but they serve a vital purpose. So does your website.

Laura Pepper Wu, cofounder of 30-Day Books, writes, "I like to think of an author's website as the homebase of their online efforts. It's the hub where, unlike with social media, you are fully in control of the content you can share and the image and brand you project. It's a place that allows you full-on engagement with your readers without distraction."[21]

Your website is the place to provide:

- **Contact information.** In most cases you will only want to provide an email address. If you are running an editing or copywriting business, however, you may also wish to include an address and phone number. In this case, consider renting a mailbox to use as your official business address.
- **Bio and credentials.** This should be concise and written in third person. It's a bio, not an autobiography, so hit the highlights and skip the details. Provide a bit of background (education, experience, etc.) and any major publication credits. In general, unless you're actually a humor writer, avoid trying to be overly cute or funny.

---

21 Laura Pepper Wu, "Is Your Author Website Doing Its Job? 6 Things to Check," JaneFried man.com, October 17, 2012, https://janefriedman.com/author-website-what-to-check/.

- **Sample publications.** Post sample published works directly on your site, or provide links to articles available online. Do not, however, post *unpublished* materials on your site. Besides sending the clear message that you are unpublished, this can also constitute a "first use" of your material. If you try to sell that material later, an editor may treat it as a reprint.

- **Sample book chapters or excerpts.** If you've published a book (or several), your site is the ideal place to post sample chapters or excerpts. If you've self-published your book and own the rights, you can do this easily. If your book is commercially published, be sure you have your publisher's permission before posting large samples.

- **A list of services.** A website is the ideal place to list your editing or copywriting services. In this case you may also wish to list the city and state in which you live, as potential clients may search for someone local. Most experts advise against listing your fees, however.

- **Reviews and testimonials.** If you have received positive reviews of a published book, post them, or excerpts, on your site. Set up a page with a title like "What Reviewers Are Saying . . ." or "What People Are Saying . . . ." If you have received testimonials for your editorial or copywriting services, set up a testimonials page. Update these over time.

- **Information about your books.** A website is an indispensable way to promote your books. Most authors set up a "Books" page that lists the various books they've published, with links leading to more information about each title and, of course, a point of sale (usually Amazon). You may also be able to set up an Amazon affiliate account and earn a small affiliate fee for every copy of your book that you sell through your website link.

Note that all of these things are, in fact, "static." They are important, but they are unchanging. Another, more positive term for this type of information is "evergreen." That means that it's *always* meaningful and fresh, no matter when a reader experiences it. These are not things you will need to update or refresh frequently. Yet their value remains undiminished over time.

You can, of course, do even more with your website. If you are a nonfiction author, it's a good place to establish yourself as a subject-matter expert.

Consider developing a site that includes articles or materials that relate to your topic. Add links to useful sites in your field. Think about other resources that might be useful to potential readers. For example, my pet loss bereavement site, the Pet Loss Support Page (www.pet-loss.net) not only includes articles and book excerpts on pet loss, but a directory of over 1,000 pet loss services such as counselors and pet cemeteries.

If you write fiction, think about what attractions you could add to your site that tie in to your books. If your books are set in a particular period, for example, consider adding material to your site that will help readers learn more about that era. Mystery writer Cleo Coyle, who writes the "coffee house mysteries," offers recipes and coffee tips at her site, www.coffeehousemystery.com. Romance novelist Sandra Hill includes a selection of jokes. Vampire/romance novelist Kerrelyn Sparks offers a page of vampire-related games.

In short, one of the primary advantages of a website is that it can be whatever you make of it. And as you'll discover by exploring the sites of other professional writers, that can be a great deal.

BUILDING YOUR SITE

Many writers are reluctant to set up a website because they believe it will be costly or complicated to maintain. It's true that a website does involve a financial outlay. However, that outlay does not have to be large—and it can have a profound effect upon the professional appearance you present to the world. Think of it as the difference between going to a job interview wearing sweats and sneakers or investing in a business suit for the occasion.

Choose a Domain Name

Begin by obtaining an appropriate domain name. This can cost $15 per year or less, particularly if you pay for multiple years. Many registries offer large discounts for your first year if you sign up for two years or more.

Many writers simply use their own name for their domain—for example, JamesPatterson.com, JKRowling.com. Others use an element from their books, such as Cleo Coyle's Coffeehousemystery.com, or J. K. Rowling's Pottermore.com. Nonfiction writers often choose a domain name that highlights their subject area, such as my own Pet-Loss.net and Victorian Voices.net. Writers who offer copywriting or editorial services often use a business name, such as Manuscriptcritique.com, Bookmagic.ca, or Techni caeditorial.com. And some, like Shannon Hale's Squeetus.com, simply defy categorization.

Having your own domain name enables you to set up a business email that provides you with name recognition whenever you send a message. JohnSmith@TechnicalWritingExperts.com sounds far more professional than JSmith492@yahoo.com! It also has the advantage of letting an editor know that an email is coming from a professional writer, even if the editor doesn't know you.

Choose a Host

Once you've acquired a domain name, the next step is to choose a hosting service. The organization that provided your domain registration (e.g., Go Daddy.com) probably offers hosting services as well, but it's wise to shop around. Each year, *PC Magazine* provides a comparison of the top ten hosting services, and it's worth reviewing not only for pricing but to get an idea of what different services offer.[22]

Most hosting services offer some form of "website builder" that includes tools and templates to enable you to design your own site without needing to understand HTML. Some offer these builders for free; others charge an additional fee. Many experts recommend using a service that offers WordPress hosting, which is a content-management system (CMS) that enables you to build static websites as well as blog sites. It's considered easy to use and offers many free and low-cost templates. Plus, if you do want a blog, it's easy to incorporate one into your site. If your hosting service doesn't offer WordPress directly, you can download it.

Look for a service that offers unlimited storage and bandwidth. Storage refers to the amount of file space allocated to your site. If you have a lot of files, or large downloads, or many images, this can become an issue. Bandwidth refers to amount of data transfer used when people visit your site. Lots of visitors means lots of bandwidth. If your visitor rate exceeds your bandwidth, you'll need to pay a higher fee. Worse, if your bandwidth is exceeded for the month, your site *could* go offline until the following month. "Uptime" is also important; choose a service that has a good reputation for *not* having

---

22 Take a look at the 2017 choices here: http://www.pcmag.com/article2/0,2817,2424725,00. asp.

a lot of time when sites are "down." (This is not just important from a visitor perspective; if your site is down, your email service will be down as well.)

Finally, choose a service that offers live 24/7 technical support, either by phone or chat. In the beginning, you may find that service a lifeline as you try to get your site working!

Website Essentials

Volumes have been written about website design, and there are many excellent articles online that can help you get started. As a first step, however, I recommend searching on the names of various authors that you respect, and look at their sites. Get a feel for what you like and don't like, and what you'd like to achieve on your own site. At the same time, don't get discouraged by sites that were obviously put together by an expensive team of designers. Big-name authors can afford to pay big bucks for web design, but that's not what attracts visitors. What attracts visitors is *your* name and what *you* have to offer—not snazzy design.

There are a few elements that every website needs. The first is an effective, easy-to-follow navigation menu. This tells readers what you have to offer and how to find it. Your navigation menu might be a simple as a line at the top of the page that reads:

Home • About Me • Sample Articles • Books • Reviews • Fun Stuff

Each word or phrase, of course, is hot-linked to the appropriate page. This menu should appear on every page of your site. Some people like to put a menu in the left-hand column. Some put it at the very bottom of the page, but this requires visitors to scroll down to see what you have to offer.

A navigation menu is not the same thing as a table of contents. You might have one or more of those as well. If, for example, you're posting several sample articles, your navigation menu might give a link to the page titled "Articles." Here, you would create a table of contents providing links to, and a description of, each article you've posted.

Another essential is a copyright notice. This should go at the bottom of the page, and can simply read "Copyright © 20XX by [Your Name]. All rights reserved." Update this notice every year so that your site never looks outdated. If you are offering reprints, add a line saying "for reprint permission please contact [your contact info]." A copyright notice provides a bit of legal protection against folks who think it's OK to copy anything they find online and post it in their own blogs.

A third essential is, of course, contact information. You may choose to put this on a page of its own, or you might add a contact link that appears throughout your site. Whichever you choose, it's a good idea to mask your email so that it can't be easily harvested by spam bots. WordPress has a plug-in that will do this automatically. If you're not using WordPress, it's easy to unicode your email address; just go to infinetdesign.com/temp/uni code and enter your email in the top box and the title you'd like to use for your contact information in the second. Don't leave that blank or enter your email there, because the goal is to hide your email address completely. Instead, use your name or "Contact Me" as the title. When a visitor clicks on this link, your email address will typically pop up in their email program.

Although it's not essential, another nice feature is a hit counter that tracks the number of visitors you receive. You can get one for free at www.statcounter.com and tailor it to match your site. Keep in mind as well that your site's admin or "C-panel," which you'll be able to access through your hosting service, will provide site analytics and visitor tracking—usually Awstats, Webalyzer, or both. These provide nearly as much data as you'd get by adding Google Analytics to your site, with no extra work. If you plan to offer a great deal of information on your site, another optional extra is a search box. You can get a nice internal search script from www.javas criptkit.com, which gives visitors the option of searching your site through Google, Yahoo, or MSN.

DO YOU NEED A BLOG?

I hope I've convinced you that to develop a professional image as a freelance writer, you need a website. But that still leaves the question of whether you also need a blog! Many articles tout the virtues of one vs. the other, but just as each has different purposes, neither are they mutually exclusive. There's no reason why you can't have both.

I recommend beginning with a website, and adding a blog later. Once you've set up a site under your own domain, you can usually add a blog directly to your site, making it easy to integrate web content and blog content. If you already have a blog, set up a website and then transfer your blog to your new "home."

Now . . . do you "need" a blog? It depends. If you are working as a business copywriter, potential clients may want you to handle their social media marketing (see chapter 21), so they'll want to see proof that you know how to do this. In this case, not having a blog can hurt your chances of being selected. Your blog doesn't have to be on a topic related to the interests of your potential clients; it simply has to demonstrate that you can do it and do it well.

Periodical editors, on the other hand, are less likely to care whether you have a blog. If they want to review your writing samples before deciding on a query, samples posted on (or linked from) your website will do just fine. Editors don't cruise the web looking for writers, so having a blog isn't likely to bring in article assignments.

If you've published a book and wish to increase your audience, some writers feel a blog is the answer. However, while all of the eighteen top-selling authors for 2016 have websites, only five have blogs. Presumably most felt their time was better spent writing than blogging.

Yes, blogging is writing. But it is not writing for "publication," or for a paycheck. If you're a freelance writer whose goal is to use your writing talents to increase your income, this is an important consideration. You have only so many writing hours in a day—and one decision you must make is how to best use those hours for your writing business.

So Why Blog?

There are a host of reasons why people blog. Writers talk about the desire to be heard, to build community, to post on topics for which they can't find a paying market, to get feedback from readers and fans, to promote a business or book, to increase visibility. . . . However, I can think of only one *good* reason to launch and maintain a blog, and that is "passion."

Passion is probably what got you into writing in the first place. Most of us don't write because we're excited about the mechanical process of stringing words together on a page. We write because there is something we want to say. We want to tell the world about something—or perhaps change the world—and writing is our way of doing that. For many, blogging is an extension of that passion.

My first book (and website) was fueled by my passion to help pet owners deal with the grief of pet loss. I wanted to help pet owners understand that they weren't alone in their grief, that it was shared by thousands. That passion has sustained my pet loss website for more than twenty years, and I expect it to be around for at least another twenty.

So think about your passion. What do you want to talk about? Don't start worrying about what will attract the most readers, or win you the most guest posts on other blogs, or promote your business or book. Think about what you *care* about—because if you start a blog, you're going to need something that you can write about again and again. Perhaps it's gardening. Perhaps it's tips on parenting a child with special needs. Perhaps it's caring for unwanted pets. Perhaps it's writing itself. The subject doesn't really matter, as long as you truly care.

If you truly care, you'll be able to engage your readers, because your sincerity will come across to them. Your desire to help and support people who are dealing with the issue you are writing about—whether it's spots on roses or crafting a query letter—will come across in your blog. Your followers will recognize that you're genuine, not a phony, and not just a self-promoter.

Passion will sustain you when you don't feel like writing. If you blog about something you don't particularly care about, or because you think you ought to, your resolve will flag. Your heart won't be in it, and you will soon feel it's too much effort. You may continue anyway, but your lack of enthusiasm is bound to show. If you end up resenting your blog, or if you're only blogging because you've read that every freelancer ought to, your blog isn't going to serve any worthwhile purpose—and it certainly won't enhance your career.

When you're passionate about a topic, you'll attract readers and followers because your blog is about them and their concerns, not just about you. Readers will recognize that even when you're sharing personal details, you're doing it not just to talk about yourself but to help others. And before you know it, you'll have a platform, not because you set out to *build* a platform but because you pursued your passion.

Some Dos and Don'ts of Blogging

The web is filled with articles listing the top ten, twenty, or thirty things you should or shouldn't do with or on your blog. Search on "blogging tips" or "blogging mistakes" to find out some of the things that you should embrace or avoid. Here are just a few suggestions:

- **DO ensure that your blog showcases your best writing.** You may be writing for free, but that doesn't mean you can skimp on quality.

You never know which post will be read by an editor or a potential client. Hence, every post needs to make a good impression.

- **DO create an effective navigation menu.** Too many blogs keep older posts in archives organized by date. Don't tell the reader there are four posts in January 2017. Help readers find what they're looking for by creating topical archives.

- **DO ensure that readers can find out about you.** Make it easy for readers, editors, and potential clients to contact you directly, not just through a comment form. Include links to your "about" or bio page.

- **DO provide content on a consistent schedule.** The basic premise of a blog is regular posts. If you can't post on a regular schedule, stick to a website and add new material when you can.

- **DO moderate and manage comments on your blog.** Set up your comment section so that comments are delivered to you before they are posted. This ensures that you can prevent the posting of abusive comments, spam and "flamers." It doesn't mean you should suppress negative comments, only that you keep the conversation civil. This doesn't just protect you; it also provides your followers with the confidence that they can comment honestly without being "flamed" by other readers. If you allow guest posts, make sure you protect those contributors from abusive comments as well. Find out more about handling comments at Copyblogger.[23]

- **DO decide in advance whether you wish to respond to all comments.** Some bloggers recommend that you respond to every comment; others recommend that you respond only to those that need a response. (In other words, there's a difference between someone saying "Great post" and someone asking, "But how do you handle . . . ?") Keep in mind that if you have a lot of followers, a single post can generate dozens of comments, and responding to those comments takes time. You may also wish to have a cutoff point after which comments are closed.

- **DO include social media sharing buttons on your blog.** Use "share" buttons to make it easy for followers to share your blog posts on Facebook, Twitter, and other social media platforms. Put them

---

23 Beth Hayden, "7 Ways to Manage Comments on Your Site (Without Losing Your Mind)," August 23, 2013, https://www.copyblogger.com/managing-comments/.

at the top of your page, where they are easily visible. (You can add social media buttons to your website too!)

- **DO back up your blog posts.** Some writers prepare their posts in advance, but others enter them directly onto the blogging platform. If something happens to your site, your posts could be lost forever. Make sure you keep copies on your hard drive. You might also want to keep copies of comments.

- **DON'T get sucked in to the latest "how-to" trends.** There are lots of articles that try to tell you how to craft a blog post. Some will tell you that you should use lots of numbered lists ("15 ways to . . . "), or that you should never exceed a certain word count, or that you must include images. Let your content dictate the format, not the other way around. Don't cut your blog short just because you've exceeded 500 words; say what you want to say, the way it needs to be said.

- **DON'T use your blog as a dumping ground for unpublished works.** Many writers say that a blog is a "great place" to post works they haven't been able to publish anywhere else. There are plenty of reasons why this might not be a good idea, but the most important is that such works were not written specifically for your blog. Hence, they may not be effective in conveying the message and purpose you've designed your blog around. A second reason is that rejected works may have been rejected for a reason—and you might not want to put them out there for future editors to read!

- **DON'T rant.** Remember that your goal is to appear professional at all times. That doesn't mean you can't have opinions; it does mean that as a freelancer, you'll benefit more from expressing those opinions in a professional and appropriate fashion. Encouraging readers to be proactive rather than reactive is far more likely to help you achieve the goals of your blog.

- **DON'T use your blog to criticize clients, customers, or publications.** So an editor didn't pay you or butchered your article, or a client is hard to work with. That's the price of the freelance life. Think about how such a post will look to the next client who is thinking of hiring you. If you give him cause to wonder if he, or his company, might end up skewered on your blog next week, you may also be giving him cause to hire someone else.

- **DON'T use other people's posts or articles without permission.** I've heard from "bloggers" who claim that "it's customary to use other people's posts in your own blog!" Copyright infringement—which includes using someone else's material without permission even if you give them credit for it—is stealing. Nothing will destroy your reputation faster.
- **DON'T list blog posts as publication credits.** Editors do not consider posts on your own blog to be "publications." Guest blog posts carry a bit more weight (and paid posts even more), but editors are far more impressed by published articles than blogs of any sort.

The greatest mistake you can make with your website or blog, however, has nothing to do with design, content, or reader comments. It has to do with time. Developing your online presence is time consuming. If you have a website, there's always the temptation to tweak it, add new elements, improve your menus, try to develop better keywords, add more links, and find new ways to promote it. If you have a blog, it's easy to get lost in the process of writing more posts, responding to comments, and promoting your latest posts on other social media forums.

Before you quite know what has happened, you'll find that hours, days, weeks, and even months have gone by during which your primary "productivity" has been limited to blog posts, web updates, and forays into social media. Websites and blogs are excellent tools for promoting your writing and writing business, but they shouldn't *replace* writing. High-tech procrastination is still procrastination. It's important to make time for promotion—but it's even more important to ensure that you have something to promote!

CHAPTER 25

Social Media for Writers

by Gary McLaren

Writers should be active on social media. We hear this advice a lot. But why? Are there some solid reasons, and do these reasons outweigh the cost, especially in terms of our time? Through this chapter I hope you'll see how social media can play a valuable role in growing your writing business. You will also learn how to avoid the most common mistakes writers make with social media networks.

I have to admit I was rather late getting on social media. I rationalized that I was too busy. I told myself that my computer was for "proper" work only. I had no intention of silly socializing and twittering away my valuable time.

Then one day I took a closer look at Twitter. Imagine my surprise when I discovered that there was a whole world of communication and activity happening, and I was totally missing out on it. I found writers tweeting about their latest projects and discussing future works. I found authors interacting with fans and discussing their characters. I found freelance writers connecting with potential clients. It was a real eye-opener.

It is true that some people post stuff that is not of interest to me. I do not want to know what someone had for dinner or what their dog did last night. But I can control that. I can choose whom I want to follow and whose posts I want to see in my timeline or message stream. The power of social media networks lies in how you use them. I choose to use them for business, so I tend to interact with people who use it the same way.

FIVE REASONS WHY WRITERS SHOULD BE ON SOCIAL MEDIA

First, let's get one thing out of the way. If you think one of the main reasons will be to ask people to buy your book, you're wrong. In fact, that's not even on my list.

With marketing posing such a challenge for many writers, it seems such an easy solution to tweet "Buy my book" to thousands of followers. That doesn't work. Online social networks should form part of your *long-term* marketing strategy. They are not places to try and make a quick sale. You'll turn people off, and they will probably stop reading your posts.

Now, let's get into the reasons:

1. **Keep up with industry news and developments.** Have you ever seen a well-trained dog that fetches the newspaper for its owner every morning? Well, my Twitter stream is exactly like that. Like the dog, though, it had to be trained. I have my Twitter feed set up so that I can watch a steady stream of tweets from expert sources. I have learned about many major publishing developments through my Twitter stream. I'll explain how I do this below.

2. **Connect with readers and fans.** Twenty years ago, before we had the Internet and social media networks, it was not as easy to connect with readers. Sure, there were book signings and letters from your fans. Today, if you are an established author, your fans are probably already looking for you on social media networks. Social media enables you to easily engage with your readers, from saying "Hi" to seeing what they think about a new idea for your next book.

3. **Grow your brand and author platform.** As your following grows on social media, your platform grows too. In the traditional publishing world, *platform* was used to describe a person's public visibility or reputation and therefore how much demand there may be for their next book. These days a writer's platform also takes into account their online visibility and reputation. How many people are visiting their website or reading their blog? How many people are following them through social networks like Facebook, Twitter, and Google+?

The most important word in "social media networks" is "social." By being social and *engaging with others*, you will be able to grow your readership, connect with others in the industry, and build your brand and author platform. Professional writing consultants can use social media to identify and connect with existing clients, potential customers, sources, subject-matter experts, editors, graphic designers, and photographers. Authors can engage with readers and fans, as well as with other writers, bloggers, book reviewers, editors, cover designers, agents, and publishers.

4. **A solution for shy writers.** Are you shy in person? Do you get nervous when meeting people face-to-face? Many writers would rather communicate with written words than talking in person. If this sounds like you, then online social networks may be a good way for you to engage with fans and industry contacts from the relative comfort and safety of home.

5. **Make new friends.** Writers tend to be alone for much of their working time. One of the neatest things I see on social media networks is writers connecting with others in the industry. They encourage one another, give and receive feedback, and forge new friendships. This kind of activity can make a big difference to your career satisfaction and to whether you enjoy your life as a writer.

Now here are a couple of add-on benefits:

6. **The celebrity factor.** Imagine the exposure you could get if your posts came to the attention of a famous person or celebrity? Imagine if they were to pick up on something brilliant or witty you have written and then rebroadcast it to their followers. I just love it when I make connections with influential leaders in our industry.

    With online social media, you can go beyond geographical boundaries and limitations. I live in New Zealand now. Before this, I was in Asia for eighteen years. I usually miss out on the big industry conferences for writers in North America or Europe, but through social media I have an opportunity to connect with experts and leaders from around the world.

7. **Going viral.** With social media, you never know when something you have written might go viral. A post you have written spreads

like crazy as people rebroadcast it. There's possibly more luck than design in whether this happens to one of your posts.

There are also a few pitfalls that you should watch out for with social media. The biggest, of course, is being distracted from your work. Another is reading something that negatively impacts your mood and motivation. If you take control and manage your social media activity carefully, however, you can easily stay on top of these issues.

THE BEST SOCIAL MEDIA NETWORKS FOR WRITERS

Today, there are hundreds of social media networks. In this section, I will highlight the social networks that are the most useful for writers. These are the networks that will be most helpful for growing your audience and connecting with readers, clients, and other people in the industry. What may be surprising is that some of these social networks have been designed primarily for sharing visual art such as images and videos, yet writers are using these to grow their audiences. Here they are:

Twitter

Twitter is a website providing a social networking and microblogging service. It enables users to send and read small messages called "tweets." A tweet is a brief text message of up to 140 characters. Although 140 characters may not seem like much, the brevity of Twitter can work in your favor when you are trying to engage in social networks without spending too much time.

With Twitter, everything you post is public, unless you lock your account. Tweets can also include images and video. In your Twitter timeline, you see the latest tweets of the people you have chosen to follow. Those who follow you will be able to see your tweets in their timeline. As of September 2016, there were 313 million active monthly users of Twitter.[24]

The key to successful social engagement on Twitter is to *keep your activity on topic*. As with other social networks, your aim should be to have the right audience following you, whether that be readers, clients, or other industry contacts. Follow people in the same niche or with similar interests.

---

24 Statistics in this section come from *Statista, The Statistics Portal,* September 2016, https://www.statista.com/statistics/272014/global-social-networks-ranked-by-number-of-users/.

Some of them will follow you back. When you read something useful or inspiring, retweet it. Other people will retweet your posts too, and your audience will grow.

More people will find you and your posts if you use *hashtags* in your tweets. Hashtags are keywords starting with the # character, placed in tweets, which make it easy to find and follow threads on particular topics. People searching for those topics will be able to find your tweets more easily.

Facebook

Facebook is the leading social network by size, with 1.7 billion active monthly users. The two main ways to use Facebook are with either:

1. **Facebook profile**: you connect with "friends" and pages (see below) who can "like" your posts.
2. **Facebook page**: designed more for businesses and brands. You can follow other pages, and they can follow you. People can "like" your posts.

I recommend using a Facebook page for your writing business and career, which means you can reserve your Facebook profile for private communication with your family and friends. However, keep in mind that one disadvantage of a Facebook page is that Facebook only shows your posts to a small percentage of people who follow your page. Facebook likes businesses to pay to have their posts seen by more people. You must have a personal Facebook profile before you can set up a Facebook page. You can, however, have more than one Facebook page, which can be useful if you have more than one writing business.

Google Plus

Google Plus, also called Google+, is an excellent social network for posting quality content, including full articles, links to blog posts, infographics, and photography. While the number of active members is lower than Facebook and Twitter, I find that the *quality* of the posts, at least by writers, tends to be high.

According to Statista, there were 300 million active monthly users of Google Plus in 2015. According to a 2015 study by Stone Temple Consulting, the number of active Google users is much lower. Around 16 million people post to Google Plus each month, and 1.93 million users made ten or more public posts in the thirty-day period studied.

On Google+, you can add people, and they can add you, to their "circles." People who have you in their circles will see what you post publicly or to a circle that contains them. Your circles are a useful way to group or "segment" people in a way that you cannot do on many other social networks. Whenever you publish a post, you can decide whether to publish it publicly to everyone or only to a limited group of individuals or circles. With Google+, you can also set up Google Pages under your profile.

LinkedIn

LinkedIn is a business-oriented service. It is used mainly for professional networking and has 106 million active monthly users. LinkedIn is excellent if you want to look for jobs, find people to hire, or discover business opportunities. As a user you can:

- Create a profile and invite people to become a connection.
- Follow companies that interest you.
- Seek introductions to the connections of connections.
- Receive a feed of the latest recommended articles in your areas of interest at LinkedIn Pulse.
- Use LinkedIn's search to find potential clients, literary agents, publishers, editors, illustrators. You'll be able to see mutual connections and shared interests, which will make it easier to introduce yourself and make the connection.
- Create a detailed profile at LinkedIn that will help people *to find you.*

Goodreads

Goodreads is the world's largest site for readers and book recommendations, with 40 million members. The site launched in 2007 and was acquired by Amazon in 2013. Readers can track what they have read and want to read, see which books their friends are reading, receive personalized book recommendations, and write book reviews. Authors can:

- publicize upcoming events, such as book signings and speaking engagements
- share book excerpts and other writing

- write a quiz about their books or related topics
- post videos

YouTube

YouTube is a popular video-sharing website started in 2005 by three former PayPal employees. It is now owned by Google. Writers can use YouTube to create and publish videos for book trailers, how-to tutorials, author interviews, and more. YouTube has excellent, built-in video editing and management tools. If you want to create video screen captures of your computer, however, you may also need to use some software like Camtasia.

Instagram

Instagram is an online mobile photo sharing, video sharing, and social networking service owned by Facebook. There are around 500 million active monthly users (which is an increase of 2 million from 2015). You can use the Instagram app on your mobile device to take and edit photos and videos (of up to sixty seconds), then post these to Instagram and other networks. Instagram will have you thinking in pictures rather than words. For example, you could share:

- the view during your morning walk
- a photo of your writing desk
- pictures of your pets
- your notebook
- book covers
- inspirational images with quotations,

Unlike other social networks that require writing, Instagram allows you to get away from your desk and connect with your followers by means other than words. Think visually. Appreciate and enjoy the beautiful things around you.

Tumblr

Tumblr is a microblogging platform and social networking website owned by Yahoo. It has around 555 million active monthly users (an increase of over 3 million from 2015). Users can post text, photos, quotes, links, chat, audio, and videos. Tumblr is particularly good for people who are into visual aids rather than lengthy text posts. Posts with visual content such as images are more likely to be liked and reblogged.

Be brief. People tend to scan on Tumblr and long posts might not be read. Ask questions to your followers. Invite people to ask you questions. Show your personality. Do you want your followers to reply to your post? Add a "?" at the end of your post. Tumblr will add the option "Let People Answer"—check the box to enable it.

Pinterest

Pinterest is a social bookmarking site with around 100 million monthly active users (a figure that has doubled since 2015). As of December 2014, 71 percent of Pinterest's users were women. It is essentially an online pinboard and visual bookmarking tool. When users see an image, photo, illustration, graphic, or video that interests them, they can "pin" it to their pinboard. Users can choose to follow their favorite people on Pinterest. Writers can use Pinterest to post blog images, book covers, author photographs, and more.

WHAT WRITERS SHOULD (AND SHOULDN'T) DO ON SOCIAL NETWORKS

As a writer on social media you should aim to:

- **Inform:** Post useful and interesting information for your followers. Make sure your profile clearly informs people who you are and what you write about.
- **Curate:** Rebroadcast the best posts from others that you follow, or other useful information that you find online.
- **Engage:** Engage with people who follow you on the network by asking questions, answering their questions, and thanking them for following you and rebroadcasting your posts. Engage with people who don't follow you yet by commenting on, rebroadcasting, or liking their posts.

To build a strong audience of people who will share your posts, find people who reshare or retweet the type of information in your topic niche, and then engage with those people.

Here are some activities you should avoid on social media:

- **Don't post "Buy my book" over and over again.** It doesn't work.
- **Don't get off topic.** If you post too much about what you ate today or why you're mad at your best friend, you run the risk of losing followers. An occasional off-topic tweet is OK, but 90 percent of your posts should be on topic or relevant.
- **Don't nitpick others' posts.** Did you see a spelling mistake? Bad grammar? Sometimes writers abbreviate their words on social media, especially on Twitter. If you see something that's not quite right, relax; I can assure you the sky won't fall in.
- **Don't lose your temper.** Do not display your anger publicly unless you want the whole world to see you lose your cool.
- **Don't spend all day on Twitter.** Or Facebook. Or another social network. Get back to your writing.

Here are a few tips for working smarter on social media:

1. **Limit your time.** I recommend spending a maximum of 20 percent of your working time on social media activities, and preferably less.
2. **Don't try to be everywhere.** Concentrate on one or two social networks.
3. **Use lists and circles.** As the number of people you follow grows, it will become difficult to follow everything in your incoming stream of information. Use tools such as Twitter Lists and Google Circles to filter whose posts you want to see.
4. **Use a dashboard tool to manage posts and stream.** Use tools like Hootsuite or Buffer to manage what you want to see. For example, you could have a stream that shows the latest tweets containing hashtags like *#amwriting*, *#writing*, and *#author*. You could have another stream that shows tweets from a carefully curated list of your favorite people.
5. **Use automation, with care.** Some people do not like automation on social media. I believe it's OK if you use it carefully. Since you won't be on your social media accounts 24/7, it's a good idea to schedule some posts in advance. This is easy to do with tools like Hootsuite. Don't let automation take the place of real engagement, however.

You still need to visit your account regularly and engage with your followers.

WHOM SHOULD WRITERS ENGAGE WITH?

The secret to social media is to have the *right audience* following you and engaging with you. Who do you want to reach? Is it readers? Is it book reviewers? Someone else? Now, how can you find those people on that network? What groups might they be members of? What hashtags could they be using? Start engaging and "joining the conversation" with them. Chances are they'll engage with you, and may follow you back.

Finding the right audience depends on the type of writing you do. Here are some suggestions:

- **For novelists:** Engage with readers, other authors, book reviewers, editors, agents, illustrators, cover designers, publishers, leading industry figures.
- **For nonfiction authors:** Engage with readers, other authors, book reviewers, bloggers who cover similar topics, leading experts in your industry or subject, editors, agents, illustrators, cover designers, publishers.
- **For freelance copywriters:** Engage with existing clients, potential customers, subject-matter experts, graphic designers, photographers.
- **For freelance article writers:** Engage with readers, editors, sources, subject-matter experts, photographers.

WHAT TO POST ON SOCIAL MEDIA

When it comes to ideas of what to post on social media, there are many possibilities. Try to:

- **Keep on topic.** Ensure that the majority of your posts are relevant for the audience you are trying to build. If you're promoting a book, focus on providing useful information and entertaining content that's somehow related to your subject matter.

- **Remember it is a conversation.** Social media is not about shouting out your message. It's about engaging, asking questions, and joining the conversation.
- **Remember the 80/20 rule.** Make sure that at least 80 percent of your posts are informational and no more than 20 percent are promotional. Some experts advise that no more than 10 percent of your posts be promotional. If the majority of your posts are interesting, helpful, or entertaining, your followers won't mind the occasional promotional message.
- **Include hashtags** so that people can discover your tweets when they search on topics they are interested in.
- **Think long term.** As I pointed out above, this is part of your long-term plan to build your audience. It is not about posting a message to buy your book in the hope of receiving instant book sales.

You can also engage your audience by doing these:

- Like and +1 good posts by others.
- Rebroadcast good posts by others.
- Thank people for their comments.
- Thank people for resharing your posts.
- On Twitter, consider sending a welcome tweet to your new followers (more practical when you are in the early stages, not so practical when you have hundreds of new followers every day).

THIRTY-FIVE IDEAS FOR WRITERS TO POST ON SOCIAL MEDIA

For All Writers:

1. Post breaking publishing news (major writing prize awarded, news from a writers' festival, death of a favorite author).
2. Post links to good blog posts you have enjoyed or learned from (at Facebook and Google Plus, add a brief explanation of why you liked it).
3. Give comments about a book you are reading.
4. Answer a reader's question.

5. Ask for book recommendations.
6. Recommend another author.
7. Link to posts on your blog.
8. Post quotations about writing.
9. Invite people to sign up for your newsletter.
10. Invite readers to follow you at Goodreads.

When You're Writing or Have Published a Book:

11. Talk about what you're currently working on.
12. Discuss a character's motivations, goals, and other traits.
13. Post excerpts from book testimonials and reviews.
14. Post local news or something interesting about your book's setting or location.
15. Post a quote or excerpt from your book.
16. Announce your book launch (it's OK to have the occasional promotional tweet, especially at times like a book launch).
17. Post your book trailer video.
18. Inform readers when one of your books is free or at a promotional price.

Ask Your Readers Questions Like:

19. Who is your favorite villain of all time?
20. How should the book (yours or another) have ended?
21. What would you like to see in my next book?
22. What would you like to read on my blog?
23. Who'd like to help me name my next hero (or villain)?
24. Who can suggest the best plot twist?

Posts for Freelance Writers and Professional Writing Consultants
The following ideas have a dual purpose. In addition to the direct purpose of the post, they are a subtle way to remind people that you are a professional freelance writer, which might result in some gigs.

25. Post a link to your latest published article.
26. Post a request for sources or information.

27. Ask people about their biggest concerns, questions, loves, hates regarding a particular product or service. This may form the basis of an article, and you'll already have an engaged audience on the topic.

For posts containing photos and videos:

28. Post your book covers.
29. When designing your book cover, post several possible covers and ask readers which they prefer.
30. Post a video of you being interviewed or answering a reader's question.
31. Post photos from your book's setting or location.
32. Post images with motivational quotations or quotes about writing.
33. Post photos of your own, or other authors', book events (launches, signings).
34. Ask readers to post photos of themselves with your book, or in a shot that reflects a theme from your book. Offer a prize for the best photo.
35. Ask readers to post a photo of themselves dressed up as one of the main characters in your book. Offer a prize for the best photo.

In summary, writers everywhere should be embracing social media networks. If you identify your target audience and start connecting with them, you'll soon be engaging with the right people. Maybe you'll find your next big client. In any case, your audience will grow. If you're not using social media yet, choose a network and get started today!

CHAPTER 26

Handling Income and Expenses

The information in this chapter applies to writers who pay US taxes. If you're not a US resident, or liable for US taxes, you'll need to review the tax laws of your country of citizenship or residence for information on how to report your writing income and expenses.

Any income you make as a writer is taxable. This includes income from sales of articles or stories, book royalties, advances, or revenue that you might make as a contractor for another company (e.g., from writing business and sales materials). It is essential, therefore, to understand how to keep accurate records of your income and writing-related expenses, both to protect yourself from the legal consequences of failing to report your income, and to preserve as much as possible of that income for your own use.

Generally, for tax purposes, your income will fall into the category of "self-employment." The exception is if you work as a contractor for another company and receive an actual *salary*, in the form of a paycheck from which taxes are deducted. In that case, you would treat such income as "wages" rather than self-employment income. If you're not sure whether your income falls under the category of wages or self-employment, the simplest test is to determine whether taxes were deducted from that income.[25]

---

25 Most companies and publications that use freelance work or materials will ask you to complete a W-9 form (Request for Taxpayer Identification Number [TIN] and Certification) that certifies that the company is *not* required to withhold taxes from your payment.

IS IT A BUSINESS OR A HOBBY?

One question that may come up as you begin managing business finances is "are you really a business?" Many writers work only part time, and earnings may be small in the early stages of your business. Thus, many writers fear that if they claim to be a business, the IRS will declare that they were never "real businesses," but merely hobbies, and must repay their deductions with penalties and interest.

Also, many new writers harbor doubts about their abilities and worth. Many feel they are simply "dabbling," or are given this impression by unsupportive family and friends. They look at their meager returns and wonder how they can claim to be "businesses." This is more an issue of self-esteem than of business reality. The reality is that *every* type of business goes through rocky beginnings, and the IRS is well aware of this. You are not expected to be successful from day one.

Still, you may be wondering whether you should treat your freelancing as a "hobby," at least until it *does* become more successful. If you make money as a writer, but choose to regard your efforts as a hobby, you will still need to report your writing income to the IRS. You won't need to complete a Schedule C for self-employment income; hobby income is declared on the "Other Income" line of your 1040 (line 21). However, you may find that you aren't able to deduct any of your writing expenses. Some hobby expenses *can* be deducted, but only up to the amount of income that you earn; you can't use expenses to create a loss.[26] Further, your miscellaneous expenses (including hobby expenses) must exceed 2 percent of your Adjusted Gross Income (AGI) before you can deduct *anything*.

This means that if you earned, say, $500 in your first year as a freelance writer, but spent $1,000 in start-up expenses, you would only be able to deduct $500 of those expenses. But since it's unlikely that this would exceed 2 percent of your AGI, you wouldn't actually be able to deduct any expenses at all. Thus, if you declare your work as a hobby, and you're in the 25 percent tax bracket, you could end up handing $125 of that hard-earned $500 to the IRS.

Needless to say, that means it's in the best interest of the IRS to categorize your freelancing as a hobby—but it isn't in yours! If you absolutely do

---

26 The rules governing what types of hobby expenses you can deduct and how you deducted them are complicated; for more details, visit www.irs.gov/newsroom/five-tax-tips-about-hobbies-that-earn-income.

not want to learn how to maintain income and expense records, and don't mind giving money to the IRS that you could otherwise keep, then the hobby option might be right for you. But if your goal as a freelancer is to make a better life for yourself and your family, you need to learn how to handle the business side of freelancing from the very beginning. After all, part of being profitable is learning how to keep your profits for *yourself* instead of letting them slip away!

PROVING YOU'RE A BUSINESS

One of the most commonly cited "tests" of whether an enterprise is a business is whether it earns a profit in three out of five consecutive years. Since the IRS is aware that start-ups are often not immediately profitable, this means you don't actually have to earn a profit in the first two years of your business to still *qualify* as a business.

Keep in mind that there is a difference between "revenue" (or "income") and "profit." Revenue is the gross amount that your business earns. If you sold ten articles in your first year for $100 apiece, your *revenue* for that year was $1,000.

Profit is the difference between what you make (revenue) and what you spend (expenses). So if, in that first year, you spent $500 on writing supplies, guess what? You're already a *profitable* business. If, conversely, you spent $1,500 on business expenses, you have a loss of $500. If you declare yourself as a business and file a Schedule C, that loss can be deducted from your tax liability for the year, so even though you haven't made a profit, you haven't lost as much as you would if you declared as a hobby. Note, also, that being "profitable" doesn't mean making loads of money. It simply means bringing in more than you spend.

From the standpoint of the IRS, however, being a business isn't just about making money. It's also about being business*like*. Thus, failing to earn a profit in your third or fourth year does not mean that the IRS is going to descend upon you and declare that you're not a business. The IRS looks at a variety of factors to determine whether an enterprise qualifies as a business; lack of profit alone will not necessarily put you in the hobby category.

The underlying theme that unites those factors is whether your business is managed in a businesslike fashion. In other words, are *you* treating your business like a business? Can you demonstrate that you take it seriously?

Are you making every effort to run it in a businesslike fashion? Can you show a clear profit motive, even if you are not yet profitable?

Here are some ways to demonstrate that you are making a reasonable effort to make a profit and conduct your business in a professional fashion, regardless of how much income you're earning:

1. Spend a Reasonable Amount of Time at Your Business

Your business does not have to be full time, but you should be producing regular work. That means you should be able to show that you spend a meaningful amount of time, every week, on writing or writing-related tasks. Set a goal for a certain number of hours per week you wish (or are able) to spend on freelancing. It's far better to be able to cite a specific figure ("I spend between five and seven hours per week on my business") than something vague like "a few hours" or "several hours." Keep in mind that any tasks relating to your business count, including market research, composing and submitting queries, conducting interviews, and even maintaining your business and expense records.

It's a good idea to track how much time you spend on business tasks (and even better to track specific types of tasks). A good way to do this is to get a planner in which you can record the hours spent on various tasks and projects. It's also helpful to invest in a timer with a count-up function, so that you can set it when you begin a project or task and determine exactly how long it takes.

2. Actively Market Your Work

One of the factors the IRS looks for in determining whether an activity is a business or a hobby is "profit motive." A hobby is something that a person does primarily for fun, and would probably do even if no money were to be made. The purpose of a business (even if it happens to *be* fun) is to earn revenue.

The best way to show "profit motive" is to demonstrate that you are seeking appropriate markets and submitting to those markets on a regular basis. Even rejection letters are proof that you have been making an active attempt to market your writing. Keep copies of all queries, cover letters, and responses. These are your best evidence that you are making a serious, businesslike effort to conduct a freelance writing business. If you are seeking markets for your professional writing services, such as editing or copywriting, be sure to keep a log of the contacts as you look for assignments.

By the same token, don't spend a lot of time on nonpaying opportunities. Nonpaying markets can offer certain advantages (as described in chapter 1), but spending a lot of time on such markets can dilute the appearance of "profit motive." This also means that you shouldn't spend a great deal of your "business" hours writing for a personal blog, unless you can demonstrate that your blog genuinely contributes to your business efforts.

3. Keep Accurate and Professional Records

One question the IRS asks about a business is whether it *looks* like a business. A freelancer who dumps receipts into a shoebox in the closet is going to look far less professional than one who organizes them in a meaningful fashion and records daily expenses and revenues in a ledger or spreadsheet.

This means keeping your files in order, whether those files are paper or electronic. (See chapter 27 for tips on handling both.) There's no single correct way to keep a file of expense receipts, but whatever method you choose should show some indication of actually *being* a method. Tracking your income and expenses on a spreadsheet gives you the ability to monitor your business on a daily, weekly, monthly, and annual basis, which is essential in determining how well that business is progressing and what you might need to change to improve it. The IRS will not be impressed by someone who has no idea how much she has made (or spent) in the last week, month, or year!

Even if you are making no money whatsoever today, these are good habits to get into, because they will protect you and your business once you *do* begin earning an income!

KEEPING PROFESSIONAL RECORDS

In writing or any other business, the key to professionalism is good records. Good record keeping enables you to track the work you've done, the time you spent doing it, and the income and expenses that resulted from that work.

Tracking your work means keeping copies of all your submissions, queries, cover letters, and responses. It's a good idea to keep a submission log that indicates when a submission went out, what it was (e.g., query or article), where it went and to whom, when (or if) a response was received, and what that response was. Some people like to track submissions by date, often using a spreadsheet to keep track of when things went out and whether a response is overdue. (See Figure 12–1 on page 145 for an example of a submission tracker.)

Other writers prefer to track submissions by article. A good way to do this is to set up a card file, with a separate card for every article or work; you then record each time that piece was sent out, where it was sent, and what the response was (See Figure 12–2 on page 146). One advantage of this method is that it gives you a good indication of whether a piece is selling or being consistently rejected (which may mean you either need to rework the piece or try a different type of market).

Tracking your income and expenses begins with keeping these separate from your personal finances and supplies. This means getting into a few simple habits:

- **Purchase writing supplies (such as paper, printer cartridges, and postage) separately from other supplies.** If you're making business and personal purchases at the same time, pay for them separately. If you're buying them online, again, place separate orders for business and personal items. It's not a bad idea to have a separate credit or debit card just for business expenses.

- **Store business receipts separately from personal receipts.** When most of my receipts were on paper, my method was to stuff each month's receipts, canceled checks (remember those?), and payment stubs into an envelope in a file drawer. When the month was over, I closed the envelope, labeled it, and moved it to the back of the drawer. If I needed a receipt, I knew where to find it. At the end of the year, I would move that year's envelopes to a box in the closet and start a new set. Now most of my receipts are electronic, but I follow a similar procedure in terms of electronic folders.

- **Store writing supplies separately from business supplies.** Granted, you're not going to swap out the ink cartridge in your printer, or switch from "business" paper to "personal" paper, just because you're writing a letter to your sister. But be realistic. If you're claiming the expense of five reams of paper, and haven't actually sent a single hardcopy submission, this could raise some eyebrows in an audit.

- **Consider investing in a separate phone for business use.** In the old days, I'd have said "a separate phone line," but today it's simpler to just get a cell phone that you use exclusively for business. This is helpful if you do editorial or corporate work that will involve a lot of phone discussions with clients, or if you conduct a number of interviews. Otherwise, it probably won't be necessary. If you do invest in a business phone, consider an inexpensive no-contract phone, such as TracFone, rather than paying for services you may not need. Needless to say, because this *is* a business phone, don't load it up with games apps and movies!

- **Maintain an ongoing record of income and expenses.** This can be as simple as a handwritten ledger, though I recommend using a spreadsheet program, or a program such as QuickBooks. (Quicken is for personal accounting; QuickBooks is for business.) There are also a number of free income/expense software programs; however, I've never needed anything more complicated than a spreadsheet. At a minimum, your entry system should include four basic categories: date, item, income, and expense. Whenever money goes in or out, enter the amount in the appropriate category. If you'd rather save time and effort at tax time, it's helpful to include columns that correspond to the numbered categories on the Schedule C that you expect to use. In this case, it's best to double enter your expenses: once under a generic "expense" column, which will give you a running total of your expenses, and once under the appropriate category (such as "office" or "utilities"), which will enable you to track totals in each category (See Figure 26–1 on page 318).
- **Keep your records for at least three years.** Some sources recommend keeping records for seven or ten years, but three is the minimum. While the IRS technically won't go back more than three years unless they suspect fraud, keep in mind that an audit may not be initiated until a year or more after a return is filed. As I discuss in chapter 27, however, you don't need to keep hard copies of your records; scans are acceptable (and you can store those on your hard drive forever).

Your Business Bank Account

Ten years ago, the standard advice on managing one's bank account was simple: open a separate, business-related checking account. But things have changed. Today, you may never need to write an actual *check* for your business. Most transactions are likely to be handled electronically, online, or using a debit card.

It's still a good idea to have a separate account for your business. This account should never be used for personal expenses. When you receive a payment, deposit it to this account; when you make a purchase of business supplies, it should be drawn on this account. Obtain a debit card linked to the account and use it for business purchases, both online and in stores. If you wish to withdraw money from the business account for personal use, make a transfer or write a check from the business account to your personal account; don't use the business account to pay a personal bill.

It isn't necessary for this account to be an official "business" account. Business accounts often involve additional fees, and you may be required to have a business license or a "doing business as" statement before you can open one. It's simpler to open a separate personal checking account that charges no fee with a minimum balance. Or, check around to see if you qualify for a local credit union, which generally has no fees or minimum balance requirements.

Once upon a time, a canceled check was considered "proof of payment." Today, banks no longer return canceled checks, assuming you even need to write any. Your monthly statement (which you can download electronically) will give you a list of debits and credits, but little detailed information about either, so it's more important than ever to retain actual receipts to back up your expense claims.

Most writers today also find that they need a PayPal account in addition to a checking account. Many publications prefer to make payments by PayPal, and PayPal is particularly useful if you wish to sell material internationally. If you already have a personal PayPal account, set up a second, business account for your freelancing business. (You will be required to use a different email address for each account.) You can also apply for a debit card associated with your business PayPal account, giving you another, secure method of making business purchases.

WHY ALL THIS TROUBLE?

Why is all this record keeping important? Many of us entered the writing business because we wanted to *write* books, not *keep* them. Some writers like to believe that "words" come from one side of the brain and "figures" from the other, and that those of us who are good with words just don't have a head for figures.[27] That's about as accurate as saying "girls can't do math." Besides, we have computers to do the hard work for us!

Getting into the habit of good bookkeeping is important for several reasons. Here are the top five:

1. **Good bookkeeping can protect you from an audit.** If your tax figures make sense, your return is less likely to raise a "red flag" at the IRS. When you track income and expenses over the course of a year, you can identify areas where your expenses are outstripping your income, and make necessary adjustments. For example, if you're hoping to show a profit, remember that there is no law requiring you to claim all the deductions you're entitled to. (You can also postpone some deductions until the following year.)

2. **Good bookkeeping protects you if you *are* audited.** I know; I've been there. Because I had all the records needed to support my claims, my audit was neither scary nor costly. I didn't have to worry whether the IRS was going to uncover some ghastly accounting error. There's nothing like the confidence good records give you if an audit notice arrives in the mail!

3. **Good bookkeeping can help you determine how successful your various writing ventures are.** By tracking income and related expenses, you can determine which projects are profitable and which are actually costing you money. Good records will also show you areas in which you may be overspending. If you're like me, for example, you may find you're spending a lot of money on books about writing that you don't have time to read.

4. **Good bookkeeping is essential if you need to pay estimated taxes.** This occurs if (a) you have a tax liability (you owe money) and (b) insufficient taxes are deducted from your total family income to cover that liability. (If one member of your family is a wage earner, you can help avoid paying estimated taxes by increasing the amount of tax deducted from that person's paycheck.) Good records will

---

27 For a good overview of the left-brain/right-brain myth, see "Left Brain vs. Right Brain Dominance: The Surprising Truth," by Kendra Cherry, on VeryWell.com, September 6, 2016, www.verywell.com/left-brain-vs-right-brain-2795005.

help you figure out how much money you're likely to receive in a given quarter, and how much tax you're likely to owe.

5. **Good bookkeeping drastically reduces your stress level at tax time.** When you've kept a record of your income and expenses throughout the year, all you have to do is plug the totals into your tax form and you're done. Then you can get back to your real job: writing.

PREPARING YOUR TAXES[28]

When you operate a sole-proprietor business (such as writing), you declare income and expenses on the Schedule C. (If you have no more than $5,000 in business expenses, only one business, no depreciation or amortization, no employees, and do not claim the home office deduction, you may be able to use the Schedule C-EZ.) The Schedule C is remarkably straightforward (for an IRS form); it asks a few basic questions, offers a few categories to fill in, and you're ready to go.

First, you'll be asked to fill in your name, address, Social Security number, and "Principal Business Code." For writers and artists, that's 711510. Your principal "business or profession" is "writing" (or "author"). Your accounting method will be cash; that means you claim expenses when you pay them (by cash, check, or credit card) and income when it is received. Did you "materially participate" in your business? Yes, unless someone is doing your writing for you!

Next you'll list your income, which is all the money you've received from writing during the year. This includes royalties. Don't be confused by line 17 on Form 1040, under income, which lists "Rental real estate, royalties, partnerships, S corporations, trusts, etc." and requires that you attach Schedule E. According to the IRS instructions, "If you are in business as a self-employed writer, inventor, artist, etc., report your royalty income and expenses on Schedule C or C-EZ."[29] (By the way, even TurboTax will mistakenly attempt to persuade you to list author royalties on line 17.)

---

28 I'm not an accountant or a tax attorney. This information is based on my research and experience but should not be considered tax advice!

29 "Instructions for Schedule E (Form 1040)," IRS.gov, December 2015, http://www.irs.gov/pub/irs-pdf/i1040se.pdf, E-6.

You'll almost certainly enter the same amount on lines 1, 3, 5, and 7 of Schedule C; ignore the other lines. By the way, don't assume the IRS doesn't know how much you earned. If you received more than $600 from any single source, that source will file a Form 1099-MISC with the IRS declaring that income. Actually, you'll probably receive a 1099-MISC form from any publisher or company that requested a W-9 form from you earlier, even if you were paid less than $600. Any company that has to file a 1099-MISC form to report its payments to you is *supposed* to send you a copy of that form by January 31 of the tax filing year. However, I've received these as late as March, so don't rely on them as a means of determining what your income actually is. Base your income statement on your own records. These copies are simply for your records; you do not need to file them with your taxes.

If you use a service like TurboTax, it may ask you if you want to declare "1099 income." You don't have to declare 1099 income separately from other freelance income, however. Simply declare your total income.

That raises the question of *how* you should do your taxes. Should you use an accountant? Should you use TurboTax? Should you do it yourself? Obviously an accountant is the most expensive option, while doing it yourself is the least—though it is also the most hazardous. I recommend using an accountant for your first year or two in business, so that you can get all your questions answered and learn the ropes. Then, consider switching to TurboTax. It's inexpensive and easy to use, with all the calculations you'll need built in—which makes it safer (and easier to file) than doing it by yourself.

Deducting Expenses

Now for the fun part: expenses. Fortunately, you can deduct any expense that is directly related to your writing efforts, including (but not limited to) the following:

- **Office supplies,** such as paper, envelopes, postage, printer cartridges, pencils, pens, and computer disks. Deduct these under "office" or "supplies."
- **Printing and photocopying,** such as tear sheets and business cards.
- **The expense of an Internet connection,** if it is used primarily for business. If you "share" your connection with other family members, figure out the percentage of time spent on business and pro-rate the expense accordingly.

- **The cost of a separate business phone line or cell phone.** Such a line should be used exclusively for business purposes, such as calls to editors or interviews with sources. You can also include the costs of business-related extras, such as a distinctive ring for your business line, caller ID, call waiting, etc.
- **Books, magazines, and similar materials** that relate to writing or research. This includes sample magazines for market research, and subscriptions to magazines relevant to your field or to writing (within reason). Books are a tricky issue. If a book is for short-term use (e.g., for research for a one-time project, or an annual such as *Writer's Market*), it can be deducted under "miscellaneous." If, however, you keep the book as part of your permanent professional library, it may have to be amortized.
- **The cost of attending a writer's conference,** including 50 percent of your travel and meal costs.
- **Business fees, bank fees, professional fees** (such as the cost of an accountant or lawyer), fees paid to an agent, and so on. This includes the fees deducted from payments you receive via PayPal. You may also be able to deduct a portion of the fee paid for tax preparation, whether you've paid this to an accountant or for a service like TurboTax.
- **Dues paid to societies and organizations** related to writing, or to an area of expertise that you write about.
- **Taxes,** such as state and local taxes incurred on your writing income, and sales tax on large purchases.
- **Repairs to office equipment,** and rental of office equipment (such as a postage meter).
- **Classes, reference materials, and other resources** designed to *improve* your skills are deductible. Thus, once you have established yourself as a "professional writer" (even if you have no sales), you can deduct the cost of writing classes, reference books, magazine subscriptions, and other resources that help you improve your *existing* skills or knowledge. However, if you have not yet begun to write (and therefore cannot be said to already have the skills necessary to be a professional), you may not be able to deduct the cost of a course designed get you started.

These are the types of deductions you're likely to take as a writer. However, if you look at the categories on a Schedule C, you'll find that your expenses don't necessarily match up well with the established categories. There is, for example, no category for "postage" or "bank fees." I recommend setting up a spreadsheet that matches expense categories to Schedule C categories *to the best of your ability*. Other categories, like postage and bank fees, may need to go under "miscellaneous" on the Schedule C, where you'll need to itemize them in a separate list.

Now let's look at some of the more complicated expenses you may incur:

Mileage

Certain auto expenses are deductible. If you can claim a home office deduction, for example, you can deduct the cost of using your car to drive from that office to, say, the office supply store, or to an interview or a photo shoot. If you don't claim the home office deduction, you can't claim the expense of driving from home to a work-related location, but you may be able to claim the cost of driving from one work-related location to another. For example, if you drive from home to the office supply store, and from there to the post office, and from there to an interview, you could deduct the cost of driving from the store to the post office and from the post office to the interview—but *not* the cost of driving from home to the store, or from the interview back home again. (The drive to and from your home is considered "commute.")

For those mileage costs that you can deduct, you can either deduct "actual expenses" (by prorating the costs of maintenance, gas, etc.) or "mileage." The current per-mile rate changes from year to year. Auto expenses are handled on Form 4562.

Depreciation, Amortization, and Expensing

Some expenses cannot be deducted directly. Items that have a long life span, such as equipment, furniture, or software, must generally be depreciated or amortized. This requires a separate form and some rather complicated calculations (which, fortunately, tax software like TurboTax will handle for you). In brief, some of the types of expenses that must be depreciated include:

- **Computer hardware,** including monitors, keyboards, printers, scanners, modems, and so on.

313

- **Office equipment,** such as fax machines, copiers, telephones, answering machines, and so on.
- **Furniture,** such as chairs, computer desks, carpeting, lamps, and so on.
- **Computer software** (unless it's updated annually, like an electronic market guide).
- **Books** that become a part of your permanent professional library.

The good news is that you may elect to "expense" many of these items rather than depreciate them over the course of three to seven years. You can "expense" up to $17,500 of depreciable equipment (but not items that must be amortized) by using Section 179 of Form 4562. The amount you expense, however, cannot exceed your total writing income.

I've heard varying opinions on whether books should be expensed or amortized. My accountant claims they must be amortized, but others say they can be expensed. When in doubt, discuss the question with an accountant (or two). So far, every accountant I've talked to agrees that computer software *must* be amortized *unless* it is something that you have to replace every year.

While my accountant has assured me that any form of office equipment needs to be "expensed," you may find a different answer if you use TurboTax. If the cost of the equipment is small (less than $200), you may be advised to treat the purchase as an ordinary office expense. Again, if you're not certain, ask an accountant.

Travel

Some travel and entertainment expenses are deductible. However, this deduction is shrinking fast. Also, the IRS frowns on deductions that look like "I took a $5,000 dream vacation to France, and now I'll see if I can sell a $100 article about it." If you're going to deduct travel, it's better to have an assignment in hand before you leave. Then you can claim that you were traveling for business purposes from the beginning, not trying to wring a business deduction out of personal travel.

The Home Office Deduction

Writers are entitled to take the home office deduction, which is the "cost" of the space you use for an office. You can deduct a variety of home-related expenses in this category, including a percentage of utilities, mortgage interest (though not the mortgage itself), repairs, homeowner's insurance, homeowner's fees, and various other expenses. The percentage of the costs that you can deduct is based on the percentage of your home that is dedicated to business use. For example, if your house is 2,000 square feet and your office takes up 100 square feet, your deduction is 5 percent. If you own a home, this deduction may also include a percentage of depreciation on your property.

Taking the home office deduction is *not* an automatic "red flag" for auditors, as many small business owners assume. It can, however, be a complex calculation—and it's not a bad idea to use an accountant the first time you attempt this. To claim this deduction, the following conditions must apply:

- **Your office must be a clearly defined location,** such as an actual room like a bedroom, attic or basement, or a clearly defined space such as a closet or breakfast nook. You can't deduct "a corner of your living room" or "10 percent of the kitchen."
- **Your office must be used exclusively for business purposes.** Pay your personal bills somewhere else, and don't use that space for personal storage. Clean the games off your computer!
- **Your home office deduction cannot be used to create a loss.** For example, if your total deduction were to come to $2,000 per year, but your writing income is only $1,000 and you have $400 in other expenses, the maximum home office deduction you will be able to claim is $600.

If you plan to sell your home, and you have been claiming a portion of it as an office on your taxes, you may have to pay taxes on a portion of the income of your home sale. Once you have declared a portion of your home to be business property, when you sell your home, a corresponding portion of the revenue from the sale is now business income. If you anticipate moving or selling your home, talk to your accountant about this issue before declaring a home office deduction.

There's far more that could be said about expenses and deductions than I have space for here. Fortunately, the web abounds with excellent articles on this topic. One useful site is FreelanceTaxation.com (www.freelancetaxation.com), "taxes for freelancers, artists, writers and psychotherapists."

This site has some excellent information about the pros and cons of the home office deduction, Form 1099s, deductions, and more.

ESTIMATED TAXES

While we all dread April 15, taxes aren't actually due on that date. They are due *when your income is earned*. When you earn a paycheck, your taxes are deducted automatically. When you work for yourself, however, you don't have that advantage—and chances are that you may have to pay estimated taxes both to the IRS and to your state.

You are expected to pay estimated taxes if your tax liability for the coming year is $1,000 or more. For example, if, this April, you will have to pay $1,000 or more in taxes for the previous year (over and above any taxes that have been deducted from your paycheck or your spouse's paycheck), then you will probably be required to file estimated taxes for the current year, *beginning* this April. (In other words, you'll have to file last year's taxes *plus* the first quarter of estimated taxes for this year at the same time.)

Estimated taxes are due quarterly, beginning in April. The problem, of course, is that you must pay them before you actually know what your income will be. As a writer, it's often difficult to predict one's income from one quarter to the next, but that's exactly what you're expected to do. It's better to overestimate than underestimate; refunds are better than penalties. You can also pay your self-employment tax (another cost you'll be hit with when you make a profit) through estimated taxes.

If your writing is not your sole source of support, or if you or someone else in your household is earning a paycheck, one way to reduce your estimated tax liability is to increase the withholding tax on that paycheck. While that may mean slightly less cash now, it can help offset your tax burden later.

SURVIVING AN AUDIT

The thought of an audit seems terrifying, but in fact they are not that common. Audits are more common in some regions than in others (Las Vegas and Los Angeles are high on the list). But due to budget cuts and reductions in personnel, IRS audits are currently at an all-time low. Fewer than 1 percent of all returns were audited in 2014. Chances of an audit are much higher if you make a very large income (in 2014, the IRS audited nearly 11 percent of those who made $1 million or more).[30] In other words, the IRS is far more interested in big fish who might owe big bucks to the government. It is far less concerned about small businesses that, aren't likely to be liable for large sums.

So don't let the fear of an audit prevent you from establishing a writing business. And even if you are audited (as I have been), the event is not as terrifying as you might think. Your best defense is good records.

- Keep all expense receipts; never claim a deduction you can't verify.
- Make sure you know where your receipts are. File receipts by month and by year.
- Keep copies of all writing correspondence, which proves that you are "working."
- Make sure your ledger/spreadsheet numbers are accurate.
- Don't make stupid claims, like huge travel expenses that will get an auditor's attention.
- Don't give an auditor more than he asks for. Simply provide the requested receipts.
- Don't panic!

---

30 "The 8 Most Common Tax Audit Triggers," QuickBooks, undated, http://quickbooks.in tuit.com/r/taxes/8-common-tax-audit-triggers/.

Figure 26–1: Sample Income/Expense Tracking Spreadsheet

DATE	DESCRIPTION	INCOME	EXPENSES	OFF/SUPP	POSTAGE	INTERNET	BOOKS	DUES/PUB	PROMOTION	UTIL	MISC
2-Jan	Web hosting renewal		$100.00			$100.00					
3-Jan	Article: Tuscarora Times	$25.00									
4-Jan	Cats Article	$225.00									
11-Jan	Sample magazines		$13.29					$13.29			
13-Jan	Comcast		$45.95			$45.95					
15-Jan	Business cards		$25.00						$25.00		
17-Jan	Phone bill		$23.62							$23.62	
18-Jan	Lulu Royalties	$18.82									
20-Jan	Writer Article	$400.00									
21-Jan	Cat care book		$17.74				$17.74				
25-Jan	Paper and envelopes		$43.50	$43.50							
28-Jan	Amazon Affiliate	$75.19									
28-Jan	Domain name renewal		$44.00			$44.00					
29-Jan	ETS	$300.00									
28-Feb	Postage		$9.82		$9.82						
INC	$1,044.01										
EXP	$322.92										
P/L	$721.09					(Note: Tracking Profit and Loss by month is optional but useful for keeping track of progress.)					

DATE	DESCRIPTION	INCOME	EXPENSES	OFF/SUPP	POSTAGE	INTERNET	BOOKS	DUES/PUB	PROMOTION	UTIL	MISC
5-Feb	Book		$37.20				$37.20				
10-Feb	Lulu Royalties	$37.52									
12-Feb	Lulu	$6.25									
15-Feb	Computer repair		$80.00								$80.00
16-Feb	Comcast		$45.95			$45.95					
17-Feb	Phone bill		$23.62							$23.62	
21-Feb	Book Royalties	$569.00									
23-Feb	Camera batteries, case, etc		$30.00	$30.00							
24-Feb	Amazon Affiliate	$183.45									
25-Feb	British Heritage	$800.00									
25-Feb	Printer cartridges		$39.95	$39.95							
26-Feb	Bookmarks		$27.76						$27.76		
27-Feb	Postage		$4.99		$4.99						
28-Feb	Google AdSense	$30.85									
		$2,058.69	$2,671.08	$612.39	$113.45	$14.81	$235.90	$54.94	$13.29	$52.76	$47.24	$80.00
2018	PROFIT/LOSS	INCOME	EXPENSES*	Off/Supp	Postage	Internet	Books	Pubs	Promotion	Util	Misc
INC	$1,627.07										
EXP	$289.47										
P/L	$1,337.60										

*(This "check sum" figure totals the subtotals of each column to make sure that they have the same total as the expense column—this cross-checks for entry errors.)

319

Notes on Figure 26–1:

- The categories listed on this spreadsheet are Supplies, Postage, Internet, Utilities, Dues, Books, Promotional, and Misc. You may need different categories. A good rule of thumb is to create a category for any type of expense that exceeds $10 per month. Start with the categories listed on the Schedule C. However, many of these don't apply to writers, and you may also find that many of your expenses (like postage) fall under "miscellaneous." If any subcategory of "miscellaneous" exceeds $50 per year, it's wise to spell out the nature of this category (and maintain a separate spreadsheet column for it) rather than claiming a large and undefined "miscellaneous" deduction.
- Year-end totals are achieved by totaling each column. The Profit/Loss for the year is, of course, the total income minus total expenses.
- It's not necessary to create a subtotal for each month. However, I find this useful for tracking my progress over time.
- I run a "check sum" figure at the end of the spreadsheet. This figure is the sum of the totals of each individual expense column. This ensures that I've entered the information accurately in all the columns; if it doesn't match the total of the main expense column, I've made an entry error.

CHAPTER 27

Keeping Records

Traditionally, the business of writing generates *lots* of paper. Your work will include manuscripts, correspondence, research notes, expense receipts—and, of course, contracts. The good news is that we're a lot closer to the fabled "paperless office" than, say, ten years ago. While a completely paperless office is unlikely, it's possible to run a writing business without slaughtering a forest in the process. This chapter looks at two important aspects of record keeping: what you need to keep, and ways to keep it.

WHAT YOU NEED TO KEEP

Which writing files do you need to keep? Unfortunately, with the exception of rough drafts, the answer is nearly everything. You are running a business, and your files are an important part of that business. You never know when you're going to need something you thought you could discard.

Here are some of the things you'll need to hold on to:

Contracts and Letters of Agreement

Whenever you sell a work, you should have some sort of written agreement with the purchaser. In some cases this will be a formal contract; in other cases, it may be a letter or an email saying, "Thanks for sending this; yes, we'd love to use it." If you don't receive even that, draft your own letter of agreement specifying the terms of the sale, including the name and address of the periodical or buyer, the amount you are to be paid and when, and the rights you are licensing. (See chapter 14 for more information on creating a letter of agreement.) Ask the purchaser to countersign this letter and send it back to you.

In later years, these contracts and agreements could be your only evidence as to what you sold or licensed, or what you were supposed to be paid. If you find your work being used in a way you did not authorize, it will be difficult to prove if you haven't kept your contract.

Keep these contracts *forever*. Keep them even if you decide to give up freelancing. You don't need a fancy filing system; a folder marked "contracts" is sufficient. If you have lots of contracts, consider filing them by publication in an alphabetical pocket folder. Eventually, you'll probably shift them into archival storage—but *don't* get rid of them. Never assume you won't need a copy of a decade-old contract; when magazines began adding websites, stuff of mine began appearing online that I'd sold years before.

Correspondence

A lot of your writing correspondence may look pretty trivial: "Would you like to buy this article?" "No." Even rejection letters are important, however. If nothing else, they demonstrate to the IRS (in case of an audit) that you are conducting a business.

Acceptance letters are even more important. Often, they spell out the terms of a sale. If so, keep copies in your contracts file. Be sure to retain copies of any correspondence with an editor that discusses how an article is to be written, what the editor expects of you, your deadlines, and so forth.

You may also wish to retain correspondence with experts and interviewees, requests for information, and any other business matters. If you become involved in any sort of dispute or legal issue, you would need to keep those materials as well.

Today, much, if not most, of your correspondence will be via email. Once upon a time, I actually printed emails out and filed them. That may sound archaic, but even today, archiving email messages onto your hard drive is not that simple. (See "Printing to PDF" on pages 327–328.)

If you prefer to keep correspondence in hard copy, you don't need a complicated filing system. I recommend using two file folders. One is for "open correspondence"—letters to which you are awaiting a response, such as an answer on a submission or a contract. Once you've received that response, staple all the relevant correspondence on that topic together and file it in the "closed correspondence" folder. At the end of the year, label that second folder with the year and file it in your archives. If you still have open correspondence at year-end, simply store it in the next year's "closed" folder once it is resolved.

Invoices

If you send invoices to editors, you may want to store them separately from your regular correspondence. Again, you may want to use two folders: one for pending invoices and one for paid invoices. If you do a lot of invoicing—as you may if you do corporate copywriting or technical writing—you may wish to file invoices by company.

Clips

Rare is the writer who doesn't preserve copies of everything she ever published! This is your "clip" file, which you can use as a portfolio and as a means of organizing and filing clips to send with future queries.

Once again, you'll want to choose whether to store clips in hard copy, electronically, or a combination of both. You might decide, for example, to keep hard copies of clips of major feature articles, but electronic copies of smaller pieces or pieces sold to less prestigious markets. The only right answer is what works for you.

Today, I store all my clips electronically, but in earlier days I kept the best in plastic sleeves in an attractive leather portfolio. Newspaper articles often don't conform to an 8.5" x 11" format, so it's often best to cut them up, arrange them on a sheet of paper, and then photocopy them before filing them. This also preserves them more efficiently, as actual newspaper does not age well. This also makes it easier to copy them and send them out as clips, or to scan them to save electronically.

You may also want to keep copies of the magazines in which your work appears. I used to ask publications to send *two* complimentary copies. I'd pull clips from one and store the other whole. Eventually, this became too cumbersome, but in the early years of my writing career it was nice to be able to pull out the original magazine and leaf through it.

Many writers like to post clips on their website. This is fine if you still own the electronic rights. If you've sold all rights or all electronic rights, you technically don't have the right to do this without permission. Ask your editor if she has any objection to this type of use; most won't. Keep in mind that even if you own electronic rights to your text, you don't own the rights to any artwork or photos that were added from other sources, so again, ask for permission. The best way to post articles is to scan them and save them as PDF files.

I recommend scanning clips and saving them as PDF files regardless of whether you plan to post them online (see "Scanning Your Files" on page 326 for more information). This means you will always have a copy of your clip even if something happens to the paper file. If you need a copy, you can print one out; you don't have to make another photocopy. It also makes it easier to send clips by email. And eventually you'll have more clips than you actually want to store in hardcopy—yes, this can happen to you!

Manuscripts

Should you keep old manuscripts forever? I once thought there was no need to keep my old, hard-copy manuscripts—until I tried to sell a reprint and found that I only had the published version of the original, which had been butchered by a grammatically challenged editor. I had to reconstruct my reprint from the editor's hatchet job. Fortunately, this isn't really an issue today, as your manuscripts are almost certain to be electronic. Just make sure you back them up, or a crash could wipe out your life's work!

It's also wise to save research notes and interview transcriptions, especially if there is any possibility of a question arising about your facts at some later time. Definitely save these materials until your piece has been published. After that, if a piece is unlikely to cause controversy, there's not much need to keep those notes. If you recorded interviews, keep the recordings for a few years.

Income and Expense Records

Finally, keep copies of all receipts and other materials that relate to your business income and expenses. This includes receipts for any business purchase, whether online or in a brick-and-mortar store, and the stubs of checks you've received as payment.

According to the IRS, "Keep records for 3 years from the date you filed your original return or 2 years from the date you paid the tax, whichever is later, if you file a claim for credit or refund after you file your return. Keep records for 7 years if you file a claim for a loss from worthless securities or bad debt deduction."[31] But you don't have to keep hard copies; you can scan them if you prefer.

---

31 "How Long Should I Keep Records?" IRS, May 13, 2016, https://www.irs.gov/businesses/small-businesses-self-employed/how-long-should-i-keep-records.

There's no need for a complicated filing method. You will only need these receipts if you are audited, and that happens less often than you might think. You can file them by category (e.g., "office supplies," "postage," etc.), or by month. I simply shove them all into a single folder for the year and put that folder into my archival storage once I've filed my taxes.

If you decide to keep your records in hard copy, eventually you'll probably need to move older records out of your office and into some other storage location. When you archive files, label your boxes clearly. There's nothing more annoying than going through a bunch of unmarked boxes because you can't remember where you put a file. Don't use old boxes with lots of scribbles from past storage contents. Pay for new file boxes and label them clearly—for example, "Writing Records 2019." Be sure to store archives in a place that is neither too hot nor too damp. If you live in a damp or humid climate, don't put them in your garage, attic or basement; store them in a part of your home that has climate control. Otherwise, if you *do* need them, you may find they are no longer usable.

GOING PAPERLESS

Many people aren't aware that the IRS accepts scanned copies of receipts and other tax-related documents—and has done so since 1997. Thus, if you'd rather not keep boxes and folders of expense files, you have an alternative. You can scan copies of your receipts, and just about every other bit of paper that your business generates, and keep them as electronic files.

You may also find that a great deal of your "paperwork" never appears on paper at all. Most correspondence will probably be handled by email. Manuscripts are created on your computer and submitted electronically. Though you may prefer to print them out to review and proofread, there's no need to *store* hard copies. Many publications transmit contracts by email, usually as PDF attachments. Some will even send you galley proofs in PDF format.

When you order products for your business online, you will generally receive a receipt by email. If you order something on Amazon, simply go to your orders, select the order in question, and click the blue "Invoice" link in the upper right corner. You can then either print the invoice physically, or print it as a PDF file directly to your computer. Many brick-and-mortar stores, like Staples, also offer the option of sending your receipt by email when you make an in-store purchase.

I used to keep a file folder in my desk drawer for business receipts, which I would scan at the end of the year. Now, however, I have so few paper receipts that I simply scan those I *do* receive as soon as I get them, and save them in the same computer folder as my online receipts.

If the idea of a paperless office appeals to you, it's relatively simple to achieve. However, it will require some organization, some dedication, and a bit of equipment.

Scanning Your Files

If you truly want a paperless office, or as close to it as you can get, you'll need a scanner. Scanners come in two basic types: flatbed and sheetfed. A flatbed scanner is essential if you plan to scan pages from books, or items that are too large to run through a sheetfed scanner, such as pictures or maps. They're also the best choice if you plan to scan photographs, especially for publication. While prints *can* be run through a sheetfed scanner, a flatbed gives you much more control over the process, including the ability to correct colors and other problems.

For sheer speed, however, nothing beats a sheetfed scanner. These allow you to scan individual pages as fast as you can feed them into the scanner. When I digitized my old files, I found that I could scan an entire file box of material in about ninety minutes. A single receipt can be scanned in an instant.

Models of each type begin around $65. Xerox offers a model that combines both functions for about $265. Keep in mind, as you plan your office space, that a flatbed scanner takes up quite a bit of room. The smaller sheetfed scanners, however, take up very little space. You may want to keep one hooked up to your computer at all times so that whenever you have a receipt, you can run it through without having to set up your equipment.

Either type gives you the option of saving a scanned document as a PDF file. Many scanners come bundled with a copy of Adobe Acrobat, which is useful, because if you're using a version of Windows earlier than 10, this will enable you to set up a PDF printer on your system.

I do *not* recommend a handheld "wand" scanner. With these, the quality of the scan depends on how steady you can hold the device. If you plan to do research in the depths of a library where your only other option is to pay for photocopying, this sort of device can be useful; otherwise, its quality is disappointing.

Printing to PDF

In addition to scanned files, you're likely to receive and generate many other electronic files. Again, many stores will send receipts by email, which you'll then need to save as a file in your receipts directory. Publications routinely transmit contracts by email, and expect you to be able to print them out, sign them, scan them, and email them back. When you make a purchase on Amazon.com, you can go to their website and print an invoice from your orders section.

The easiest way to convert online documents like receipts and invoices to electronic files that you can easily store in a directory on your computer is to "print to PDF." If you have Windows 10, this function is built in to the operating system. It's also built in to the Mac operating system. For older versions of Windows, you may need to download software to make this possible.

One option is to obtain a copy of Adobe Acrobat. Many scanners come bundled with Acrobat, in which case simply install that and you'll have what you need. You can also purchase the program, but it's a bit expensive. *Digital Trends* has a good article on free alternatives that will enable you to install a print-to-PDF function.[32]

One reason to have this function is email. Most email programs, whether they are hosted on your computer (like Windows Mail or Outlook) or online (like Gmail or Yahoo Mail) do not enable you to save messages to your hard drive. Outlook, for example, allows you to save emails as .msg files, but these can only be read by Outlook. You can't open a message as an independent document or access it in another program.

Yet it is important for a business to be able to download and save business correspondence. While you can certainly store your business emails in a subfolder on your email system, that doesn't protect it from viruses or crashes. While crashes are rare for a system like Gmail, if you're using an email account associated with your own domain, you're more vulnerable to a server failure.

Your email provider may also automatically delete your emails! Some email providers, including Suddenlink, automatically purge your trash

---

32 Rick Stella, "These Are the Best Ways to Print-to-PDF in Windows 10, Windows 8, and Windows 7," *Digital Trends*, July 24, 2016, http://www.digitaltrends.com/computing/print-pdf-windows/.

folder after a certain number of days, and also purge any unread message from your inbox after a longer period. (My sister just learned this the hard way.) So at the very least, it's vital to transfer your messages to other directories, and to make sure you don't exceed your account's storage limits.

I have found that the easiest way to save my business emails is to print them to PDF and save them to the email folder on my hard drive. Having faced the task of archiving an entire year's emails at once, I now do this daily, backing up any message I want to keep as soon as I receive or send it.

If this seems too complicated, there's always the option of printing out important emails and then scanning them, though it's a bit of a waste of paper!

Protecting Your Files

There is a downside to the paperless office. While most of us think computer storage is a wonderful thing "just in case the house burns down," the reality is that we're far more likely to experience a computer crash, hard drive failure, or computer virus. A paperless office works *only if you are diligent about maintaining backups.* This means ensuring that your files are transferred to a secondary storage device, such as an external drive, flash drive, CDs or DVDs, or the "cloud."

I recommend backing up your work every single day. Make it a habit that the last thing you do before shutting down your computer is to back up the day's work. When you do this on a daily basis, it never becomes an insurmountable task—and you never risk losing something important.

The easiest and least expensive method is to use a combination of an external hard drive and a flash drive. Every month, I back up my entire "documents" folder to an external drive. (Actually, I use two, and store the second in a safe deposit box for added protection.) Between these monthly backups, I use a flash drive to back up daily work.

It's also important to make sure you don't keep your backup device connected to your computer. (This is one reason I make keep a copy in a safe deposit box.) One of the more recent bits of nastiness on the web is "ransomware." Ransomware encrypts the data on your computer, *and* any storage device connected to your computer at the time. You're then asked to literally pay a ransom to get the decryption key. While ransomware is more likely to target companies than individuals (the goal being, after all, to get money), any computer can be hit. The FBI reports a steady rise in attacks, with more than 320,000 incidents in the US in 2016.

Another option is to sign up for a cloud storage service. This will greatly reduce the risk of data being lost to ransomware or any other malware. One advantage of cloud storage over an external drive is that you can usually access your files from any computer, anywhere.

Amazon and Carbonite currently charge $59.99 per year for unlimited storage and backup. Carbonite also offers an automatic file backup program that syncs your files every night, so you don't have to remember what to upload. (Amazon does not.) File syncing programs are nice if you have a small number of files, and don't have lots of large files. If, however, you have lots of files—and you have lots of very large files—syncing can take a long time; it's generally faster and easier to upload your most recent changes manually.

There isn't space here to go into the pros and cons of cloud storage, but be aware that there *are* tradeoffs involved. For example, many cloud storage providers place a cap (e.g., 2GB) on the size of individual files. For most writers, this might not be a problem, but it can be if you have larger files. Uploading and downloading files can also be time consuming, and many people have concerns about security issues with "the cloud." So if you are considering cloud storage, research your options and compare providers carefully.

Keeping good business records isn't just a matter of saving what you're working on today. It's a matter of recognizing that you have no way of knowing what will be important to you *tomorrow*. It can be so tempting to throw out that email, that unsold article, those old letters. But you never know when you're going to need proof that you sold a piece for a particular set of terms. Good records—whether you store them in a file box or on a hard drive—are your best source of protection. When in doubt, *don't* throw it out!

CHAPTER 28

Five Habits of the Effective Freelancer

In chapter 2, I discussed the various tools and supplies needed to launch a freelancing business. Since then we've explored how the writing business works, along with a number of techniques and strategies to help you get started.

However, the most important "tools" that one can bring to a business are not the latest software or apps. When you launch a business—any business—your success isn't based on having the right physical equipment. It's based on having the right *mental* equipment.

What kind of "mental equipment" do you need to ensure your success as a writer? Quite possibly your first thought is, "I guess you need to be a good writer!" Unfortunately, that's not enough. It helps, but I've known many good, even brilliant, writers who never managed to get their careers off the ground. In fact, a "good" writer who lacks the equipment I'm going to describe below actually stands less chance of success than a less "talented" writer who does have it.

WHY BEING "GOOD" CAN BE "BAD"

There's a good chance you've been told you're a "good" writer. Many of us discover this in school. When other kids groaned over an essay assignment, we rejoiced; English class was our place to shine. (Chances are also good that we didn't rejoice quite so much when asked to "solve for X" in algebra.)

Dr. Carol Dweck, in her study that led to the book *Mindset*, discovered that this type of praise may not be helpful. Her study demonstrated that children who were praised for "innate" qualities (e.g., "you're a good writer" or "you're very talented") were at a higher risk for failure later in life than those who were praised for effort and hard work. In a nutshell, it's apparently better to tell a child, "You worked hard for that A; I'm proud of you!" than "You're really good at math!"

According to Dweck, people who learn to believe they have an innate talent for something also tend to believe that "talent" and "hard work" are mutually exclusive. If you have "talent," it means things come easily. If you have to work hard to achieve that same thing, therefore, it means that you must *not* have that talent. Hence, if getting good grades in English came easily, that meant you had a "talent" for writing. If solving for X was difficult, it must have meant you were "no good at math."

Note that the study isn't claiming talent doesn't exist. It's simply indicating that if you believe in "talent"—or worse, that having to work hard for something means you *don't* have talent—you can set yourself up for failure. You may, indeed, be a good—even gifted and talented—writer. But when you embark on a freelance career, you're going to be bombarded with apparent evidence to the contrary. Queries and submissions will be rejected. You'll go for months without hearing from an editor. Before long, you'll start asking yourself why, if you're such a "good" writer, your work is being rejected. If writing is your talent, why is it so difficult? Eventually, you may start thinking, "I guess I'm not as good a writer as I thought I was. I must not have talent after all. And if I don't have talent, obviously I'm in the wrong business."

Fortunately, you'd be wrong. Being able to write well *is* important, but it's not the only quality you need. The good news is that the habits you *do* need to succeed can be developed. You don't have to be born with them; you just need to learn how to build them.

HABIT #1: BELIEVE IN YOURSELF

This is probably the most common piece of writing advice you'll ever hear. But . . . believe in what? What does it mean, exactly? Believing in yourself doesn't mean standing in front of the mirror repeating feel-good affirmations in the hopes they'll stick. Nor is there any benefit in believing anything about yourself that isn't true. For instance, if you have issues with spelling, trying to "believe" you can spell won't help.

On the other hand, believing in negatives—however true they might be—isn't helpful either. Simply believing that you are a "bad speller" won't get you any closer to success. Instead, it's an example of the problem of believing in "innate characteristics" in reverse. Instead of believing that you have an innate talent, you might believe you have an innate *lack* of ability in a particular area—for example, spelling. You may assume that "bad spelling" is part of who you are—a quality that is innate and unchangeable. (Of course, if you're bad at spelling but believe you *aren't*, that's another issue entirely—and also one that is bound to hinder your career.)

Qualities vs. Abilities

To believe in yourself in a manner that will be effective for your writing career, it's a good idea to separate the concept of "qualities" (characteristics that are considered innate and definitive of self) from "abilities" (characteristics that can be acquired or developed). Another way to express this is to separate "I am" statements from "I can" or "I have the ability to" statements.

Try this on something simple. Instead of saying, "I am a good writer," try saying, "I have the ability to craft a marketable article." This shifts your mental focus away from "I *am* this" to "I can *do* this." When obstacles arise (and they will), they are less likely to shake your basis of belief when they no longer threaten your sense of identity. If you base your self-belief on innate qualities, a rejection may make you wonder, "Am I *really* a good writer, or am I just fooling myself?" If you base belief on abilities, however, a rejection is more likely to make you think, "This doesn't mean I can't write a marketable article; it just means I need to work on that ability."

Choose to believe that you *have the ability* to learn how to write a successful query. You *have the ability* to develop marketable ideas. You *have the ability* to improve your spelling or grammar. You *have the ability* to conduct research and interviews.

This type of self-belief doesn't mean you already have the skills needed to be successful. It means you *have the ability* to build and develop those skills. A belief in innate qualities often implies that one doesn't have the *need* to learn—because if you needed to learn something, it wouldn't be a talent, right? This doesn't mean you should *discard* your belief in your talents, but rather, that you use those talents as the starting point for your abilities.

Another approach is to start with a belief in a talent ("I am a good writer") and then start defining that talent in terms of abilities. What makes you a good writer? Perhaps it is the *ability* to make difficult concepts comprehensible to a general readership. Perhaps it is the *ability* to describe a scene or setting so that the reader can experience it. Perhaps it is the *ability* to gather and assemble information into a coherent whole. As you begin to identify these abilities, consider making a list; these are your strengths! Build on them!

You can do the same with perceived innate negative qualities. Rather than telling yourself, "I'm no good at marketing," begin identifying the factors of marketing that you have difficulty with. When you research potential markets, do you find that you can't seem to come up with any viable ideas? Do you feel you don't have the qualifications to approach a potential market? Identifying specific issues gives you a starting point from which to build your *ability* to become a better marketer. Keep in mind that *having an ability* doesn't mean you need to enjoy the task. After over thirty years in the writing business, I still don't enjoy conducting interviews—but it doesn't matter whether I like it. All that matters is being able to *do* it.

And that's really the bottom line. Believing in yourself—in the strengths you have, and the ability you possess to learn and develop new skills—is great. But it means nothing if you don't take action. Don't stop at "believing." Take the steps necessary to turn belief ("I can improve my spelling skills") into reality. Believing you can do something won't help you if you never actually *do* it!

HABIT #2: THINK OF YOURSELF AS A WRITING BUSINESS

One of the most self-sabotaging beliefs that writers entertain is the notion, "I am an *artist*." This generally means one of two things. Sometimes it means "and therefore I am above the ordinary, humdrum stuff of business; I can't taint my art with bean counting!" More often, it means "I have an artistic mindset; I just can't understand that complicated spreadsheet stuff."

Now, I fully agree that writing can be an art. However, if your goal is to launch a freelance *business*, you have made a decision to move beyond "art for art's sake." Your goal is to use your art to generate revenue. That doesn't mean giving up the artistic side of things; it means recognizing that "art" is simply the product your *business* is trying to sell.

If you have—or have had—a "day job," chances are you worked for a company that had many departments. There was a department (or at least a person) to handle accounting, another for HR, yet another for PR and marketing, another for sales, another for IT. The company might have had its own art department, and perhaps a legal department. It probably had a receptionist to handle phones and appointments, and an administrative person to handle, well, nearly everything. There may even have been someone (if not an entire department) whose job was to distribute the mail.

When you start your own business, you are all of the above. And all of the above are *necessary*. Accounting, for example, isn't an annual chore that you can postpone until tax time, when you haul a shoebox full of receipts to an accountant. Managing a business means being aware, on a daily basis, of what is happening in every area of that business— particularly the financial area. You need to know what is coming in and going out every day, which projects are profitable and which aren't, whether a payment is overdue, or whether you're facing a financial dry spell and need to send out a flock of queries to get more work. Messages must be handled promptly. Marketing—including maintaining your online presence—is an ongoing requirement. As for legal issues, at the very least you need to understand the basic rights and contracts terminology that affect you as a writer, or you'll have no way of knowing whether a contract is a blessing or a disaster.

Of course, it may be necessary to outsource certain tasks. Understanding the basics of rights and copyright doesn't make you a lawyer. If your computer breaks down, get a qualified person to repair it. Sometimes, too, you may have more work than you can handle, and need to contract some of it out. You may also find that you can expand your client base by building a stable of reliable subcontractors who can handle tasks like web design and artwork. Software exists to help you with financial issues.

Someone once complained to me, when I was emphasizing the need for responsible accounting practices, that it was fine for me to talk because "this is easy for you." I came up with a host of snappy comebacks several minutes after hanging up the phone. It's too late to share them with that particular individual, so I'll share them with you.

Snappy comeback number one: "So are you telling me that when it comes to running a business, you only want to do the stuff that is *easy* for you? How's that working for you?"

Snappy comeback number two: "Yes, it *is* easy for me. It's easy because *I've been doing it for thirty years*! It wasn't easy when I started. Now, it's second nature. It didn't become easy for me because I liked it; it became easy for me because I *did* it."

When you're starting a business, a lot of things aren't going to *look* easy. However, you may find, when you tackle them, that they're a lot easier than you thought. One reason they don't look easy is that we're often programmed to believe we just "don't have what it takes." Let's be blunt; a lot of us became convinced that "girls" are great at language arts but no good at math. But guess what? We do just *fine* with calculators and spreadsheets!

When you have a day job, someone tells you what to do, and saying "it's not easy" or "it's not fun" won't help. Books that talk about the joys of self-employment list one key "joy" above all others: the fact that you are now your own boss! What they don't always mention, however, is that you are *also* your own employee. Having the best boss in the world won't help if that boss doesn't also have the best *employee* in the world—one who tackles the stuff that isn't easy and isn't fun, and gets it done.

HABIT #3: TRACK YOUR TIME

How long does it take to write a 2,000-word article? How long will it take you to complete that assignment an editor just offered you? Will you be able to get it done by the deadline? What if another assignment comes up in the meantime? Should you take it (you need the money) or say no (not enough time)?

When you're starting out, chances are you have no idea how to answer these questions. But as acceptances and assignments start coming in, knowing the answers will become vital to your business—and your peace of mind. So how can you develop the time management tools that you need before you actually know what you *do* need?

One of my husband's favorite bits of advice is "you can't manage what you can't measure." That applies to time. I recommend that you start by investing in a planner that will help you track your time—not only the time you spend working, but time you spend doing other things.

Start by entering all the nonwriting events coming up in the next few months that will affect your writing time. For example, if you're planning a week-long vacation two months from now, make a note of that. If family members are coming for the holidays, note that. Record appointments with the dentist, the doctor, the vet. Keep in mind that errands involve travel time; your dental appointment may be at 3:00, but if you have to leave at 2:30 to get there, pencil in the full amount of time that will be involved.

This helps you identify events you'll need to work around as you plan your writing schedule. Next, start tracking how much time specific writing tasks or projects require. If you're working on an article, make a note whenever you start and stop work during the day. A timer with count-up function can be helpful here; set it when you start work and pause it or turn it off when you stop.

Don't just track hours on a specific project; track what you *do* in those hours. For example:

- Internet research—2 hours
- Interview one—30 minutes
- Interview one—transcribing notes—45 minutes
- Interview two—10 minutes
- Interview two—transcribing notes—30 minutes
- First draft—2 hours
- Second draft—1 hour
- Total—7 hours

Tracking the components of a project is important, because this will help you estimate the time requirements of future projects. If you've discovered, after two or three articles, that it typically takes you an hour and a half to conduct an interview and write up your notes, then you'll know that a future project involving three interviews will require at least 4.5 hours just for that part of the work.

The results of this tracking will serve you in several ways. First, it will enable you to determine whether a project is worth your time. Let's say you've determined that it takes roughly five hours to research and write 1,000 words (200 words per hour). Once you know this, you'll be able to determine that an assignment that pays you $100 for 500 words ($40 per hour) is worth more than an assignment that pays $150 for 1,000 words ($30 per hour). This will also enable you to bid more accurately on writing projects for business clients, and help you avoid scheduling conflicts. And, of course, it gives you the tools you need to track billable hours for clients.

By tracking nonwriting events on your planner, you'll be able to estimate how much time is available for a project. Then, build in "wiggle room." Expect to experience *unexpected* demands on your time. You never know when you, or another family member, will catch that bug that is floating around. You never know when your car or your computer will end up in the shop. Remember that no editor or client will mind if you turn in a piece *before* your projected delivery date—but getting a reputation for lateness will not improve your bottom line.

HABIT #4: AVOID APPEARING UNPROFESSIONAL

You may be wondering about that heading. The obvious statement would be "always be professional." But that is, indeed, *obvious*. Of course it's essential to behave professionally. Be courteous, even when editors don't treat you courteously. Meet your deadlines. Deliver what you promise. Those are basics.

However, one concern many new writers have is that editors won't take them seriously if they lack experience. This concern is not unfounded. The key is to identify the "clues" that signal a lack of experience. It isn't simply a matter of no clips or publication history. A writer with no clips can still "fool" an editor into believing he is experienced. Conversely, a writer with a hefty portfolio can still come across as anything but a pro.

Back in 2005, I developed a website focusing on historic British travel destinations. A writer sent me an article and I bought it. She sent another and I bought that. I soon discovered she had a knack for writing on nearly any topic I could come up with, so I gave her regular assignments. Within a year she had a regular column on the site. Eventually she became the managing editor of the *Writing World* newsletter—a position she held for seven years. She's also the author of two chapters in this book.

Years later, I discovered that the very first article I'd bought from her was her first professional sale. Yes, she "fooled" me—because her approach had me convinced from the beginning that I was dealing with a professional writer. And, really, I was.

As I said, there are "clues" that editors notice, warning flags that suggest a writer is not a pro. If you know what some of those clues are, you can avoid them. Here are some unprofessional behaviors to avoid:

- **Don't ask a question you should know the answer to.** Don't inquire about information that is covered in the publication's guidelines. If a publication has clearly posted guidelines that specify rights, payment rates, and word lengths, sending an email asking "how much do you pay?" is a clear indication you haven't done your homework.
- **Don't call a submission a query.** I often receive emails with the subject line "query" that actually include the entire article. That's not a query, it's a submission. A professional writer knows this.
- **Don't cite nonprofessional writing credits**. A nonprofessional credit is any publication that does not involve a review process. This includes anything self-published, including materials posted on your own blog, and also such publications as the (thankfully defunct) International Library of Poetry.
- **Don't state that you're unpublished.** Find some other credentials to mention. That doesn't mean we won't pick up on the fact that you're unpublished, but don't draw attention to the fact!
- **Don't bombard an editor with submissions.** If you receive a rejection, it's fine to come back with another idea, and perhaps one more after that. If, however, you are rejected three times in a row, stop. While the problem may not be you, there's also a good chance that somehow you're missing the mark. Editors don't really pay much attention to authors they've rejected once or twice. But if you come back week after week, we *will* notice—and not in a good way. Pretty soon you will cease to be "someone I rejected" and become "someone I *expect* to reject."
- **Don't send submissions in any format other than Word unless asked to do so.** If you do, an editor may not even be able to open your file. Avoid Rich Text (RTF), NotePad, and WordPerfect.
- **Don't confuse an article with a blog post.** Many writers today seem to think anything online is a "blog." In reality, there are blogs, websites, web zines, e-zines, email newsletters, and other formats. If you write to the editor of an e-zine with an offer to "send a blog post," it's clear you haven't checked (or don't understand) the format of your market.
- **Don't say anything that would indicate you haven't reviewed the market.** A writer kept sending travel articles to Writing-World.

com. In vain I protested that we did not publish travel articles. "But you *do*!" he insisted. Turns out, he had looked at our menu—which includes the word "travel" in reference to our articles for travel writers—and had gone no further. He had no idea what the site was about. Similarly, I've received fiction submissions because our menu includes the word "fiction." Don't submit to a publication if you don't know what it's about!

- **Don't rely on your spell-checker.** Proofread your query scrupulously. An editor is more likely to reject a query riddled with spelling or grammatical errors than an actual submission. If we get so far as to read the submission, and it's good, we may overlook the errors—but if we receive a query full of errors, we probably won't bother asking for the article.

- **Don't send out mass form letters—at least without checking them first!** I often receive queries addressed to "Dear Angela." Angela happens to be the editor of another, excellent writing newsletter. When I receive such a query, therefore, I know that either (a) you've already sent the piece to Angela and she's rejected it (not a good sign), or (b) you're sending out simultaneous submissions (also not a good sign). Either way, I'm not impressed.

HABIT #5: STRIVE FOR GROWTH WHILE RECOGNIZING PROGRESS

My first article was published in 1979. It was a lengthy piece on a new recycling center. If I were writing on that same topic today, I suspect I'd have a very different article. But in 1979, it was the best article I could write—and more to the point, it was my first publication credit.

One of the hazards of the writing life is what we tend to call "the inner editor," or "the voice." It's the voice that tells us that a piece is never good enough, that it could be better. It urges us to go over an article one more time, give it one more tweak, try a little harder. It can be a useful voice—but if left unchecked, it can also prevent us from ever getting an article (or even a query) out the door.

The reality of writing is that we are always changing. We are always learning, growing, and improving. This is not a fault or flaw, but rather, a wonderful thing. The writer you are today is not the writer you will be a year from now, or ten years from now. But that doesn't mean you should look down upon the writer you are today. Ten years from now, you know that you'll be a different writer in *another* ten years.

Conversely, the writer you are today is the best writer you can be . . . today. The fact that you *can* do better and *will* do better does not mean that here, today, with this article in front of you, you *should* do better. Today, you are doing the best job you are able to do. You need to recognize that this article is as good as it gets—and it's time to get it out the door.

No one *starts* at the top of their field. Nor do all writers start at the same place. We start where we are. It's very easy to get caught up in the thinking that tells us we "should" be somewhere *other* than where we are. Many of us believe that if it's possible to say, "I *could* be better," that means we *should* be better—and that we've therefore somehow failed because we aren't.

One of the most liberating experiences I've had as a writer was to read an early novel by a writer whose work I enjoyed. I didn't realize it was an early work until I'd gotten a ways into the book and was beginning to wonder why it didn't seem terribly good. Then I checked the publication dates, and realized . . . this writer *wasn't always brilliant*! She had gone through a growth period, and yet she'd gotten this novel published before she had achieved her later success. If she could, so could I. I didn't have to be "perfect" from the start. No matter where I was on my personal growth process, there would always be writers who were far, far better—and writers who weren't nearly as good. Comparing myself to those other writers was pointless; the only work I needed to measure my progress against was my own.

I'm not suggesting that you don't assess yourself and your work from time to time. If you are aware that you need improvement in some specific area—such as spelling or grammar—there's no point in dismissing that by saying, "Well, hey, I'm the best writer I can be right now." That's true, but you also know there's a genuine obstacle preventing you from becoming the best writer you can be tomorrow.

Assessment works the other way as well. If you are making progress, you need to *recognize* that progress. This gets back to believing in yourself. If you fail to recognize your own growth and improvement as a writer, you'll keep on submitting the same material to the same types of markets, perhaps for years, in the mistaken assumption that you aren't "good enough" to aim higher. You may not crack better markets the first time, or the second, or the fifth. But if you don't keep trying, you'll never get there at all. Besides, if you move up to a higher-paying or more prestigious market even once, you realize that you can do it again, and again.

Basketball star Kevin Durant has said that "Hard work beats talent when talent fails to work hard."[33] Having a talent for writing is certainly helpful, if not essential, to a successful freelancing career. It is not, however, sufficient in itself. A successful business involves many factors—and these five habits will take you much further than writing ability alone.

---

33 https://www.goodreads.com/author/quotes/6880671.Kevin_Durant

CHAPTER 29

Full-Time Freelancing: Taking the Plunge

Wouldn't it be great to quit the rat race? To leave bosses and time clocks behind, skip the commute, ditch the heels or tie, and work in the same clothes you wear to weed the garden?

It's called "taking the plunge," and if you're serious about writing, you've probably dreamed about it. But you may also have regarded that dream as an improbable fantasy. Writing may be the career you love, but chances are it's not the career that's keeping food on the table and a roof over your head.

I can't tell you whether you can make that dream a reality. But I can offer a few tips on making the decision to plunge or not to plunge!

WHEN TO PLUNGE—AND WHEN NOT TO

The first question to ask when considering "the plunge" is where is your writing career today?

If the answer is "just getting started," stop right there. If you have only a few clips or no clips at all, you're unlikely to be able to support yourself at your craft.

I hear from many writers who say they would like to quit their jobs and "start writing." To such writers, I say, "Start writing now. Quit your job later." If you haven't started yet—or if you're *just* starting—you won't know enough about this business to earn a living. So start writing. Get your feet wet. Find out what you can and can't do, what you enjoy, what you don't enjoy. Discover your strengths, and identify areas that could use improvement.

Find out whether you really wish to pursue writing as a business, or whether you'd rather pursue it as an avocation.

Writing can be a career or hobby or anything you care to make it. *Writing for a living* is a business, pure and simple. If you wouldn't dream of quitting your day job to run, say, an auto repair shop without training as a mechanic, then don't dream of quitting your day job to become a writer without a comparable level of experience.

But how much experience *is* enough? Should you write for a year, or three, or five? Can writing experience even be measured in terms of years?

I suspect it can't. The real question is "where you are," not how long it has taken you to get there. The following checklist may help you determine whether you may be ready to consider "plunging."

A WRITER'S CHECKLIST

1. **I write more than five hours per week, every week.**
   You have discipline. It's tough to find five hours a week for writing when working a day job. You've already passed one of the biggest hurdles writers face.
2. **I submit at least one new query or article per week.**
   You have a high output. Clearly you don't spend your time re-polishing old material, or stuffing your work in a drawer. You're already "in the marketplace."
3. **More than 50 percent of my queries and/or articles are accepted.**
   You know how to target markets effectively, and you obviously write well enough to impress the majority of the editors to whom you submit. (With that kind of acceptance rate, there's a good chance that your rejections aren't due to poor quality.)
4. **More than 50 percent of my markets pay more than $100 per article.**
   You've found the guts to break out of the low-paying "ghetto." You have confidence that your work is worth more. You won't be held back by self-esteem issues.
5. **I have at least one "regular" market that has accepted several of my articles.**
   You have a steady source of income.

6. **I have at least one "regular" market that gives me assignments generated by the editor.**

   You are reliable and dependable. You meet deadlines and produce quality work. Otherwise, editors wouldn't come to *you* with ideas.

7. **I am familiar with the practices and terminology of the publishing marketplace (e.g., I know what "FNASR" and "SASE" mean, and I know how to format a manuscript).**

   You know the basics, and won't waste precious time "gearing up."

8. **I own at least one current market guide.**

   You know the importance of obtaining the tools of the trade.

9. **I subscribe to two or more writing publications.**

   You keep current with your field.

10. **I know how to cope with rejection.**

    You won't be daunted by the inevitable disappointments of this type of career.

11. **I earned more than $5,000 from writing activities last year.**

    It won't keep a roof over your head, but it's more than many freelancers make in a year. It's one of those invisible lines: if you know how to earn this much, you know how to earn more. Probably the only thing holding you back is lack of time.

12. **I report writing income for tax purposes, and maintain proper business/tax records of income and expenses.**

    You know that "writing" isn't just putting words on a page. It's also a matter of records, accounting and good business practices.

13. **I keep a household budget.**

    You already have an idea of what it will take to support your household—which means you know how close you are to being able to go full time.

While scoring 100 percent on this checklist is no guarantee that you're ready to quit your day job, a low score is a good indication that you need to build up more of a foundation for your writing career before attempting to rely on it for a paycheck.

MAKING A PLAN

So you've scored a perfect thirteen, you're totally fed up with your day job, and you're sure this is what you want to do. What next?

For most writers, the answer is *not* "quit your day job today." The answer is "make a plan." If you hope to become a full-time writer, you'll often need to plan at least six months to a year ahead before actually "taking the plunge." What will you do during that year? Lots! Here are some of the steps you'll need to take before saying farewell to a regular paycheck and "hello" to the joys and uncertainties of the freelance life.

1. Discuss your desire to become a full-time freelancer with everyone in your life who will be affected by that decision (e.g., spouse, significant other, children). Presumably, your desire to write won't be a total surprise. However, family members who supported your "moonlighting" career may not be as enthusiastic about losing a significant chunk of family income. They may not be happy about making adjustments, such as providing extra income themselves or accepting cutbacks and lifestyle changes. Don't be surprised if you encounter resistance or even sabotage. Don't dismiss those concerns as unfeeling. If your decision will affect others, their needs should be a part of the decision-making process.

2. Evaluate your household income requirements. If you don't track your monthly expenses, this is a good time to start. Before you can make an effective plan, you need to know exactly where every penny of your income goes. Try tracking expenses on a simple spreadsheet, with categories such as:

- rent/mortgage
- groceries
- utilities
- insurance
- auto (gas and repairs)
- medical expenses (e.g., insurance)
- household expenses (e.g., maintenance)
- clothes
- children's expenses

- meals and entertainment (e.g., restaurants and movies)
- miscellaneous

It's also wise to break "miscellaneous" into more detailed categories, such as books, music, videos, pets, crafts, subscriptions, and whatever other regular expenses you incur. A good rule of thumb is to establish a separate listing for every category that exceeds $50 (or even $20) per month.

If you're never tracked your expenses in such detail before, you could be in for a shock. You didn't know you spent $100 a month on books? Or that those twelve magazine subscriptions (that you never have time to read) cost more than $500 per year? Your budget may be a rude awakening, but it can also be a welcome one, as certain categories may emerge as ripe for cost cutting.

3. Create a projected budget. It's "trim the fat" time. Go over your current expense list, and determine what you can cut and what you can't. Be realistic. Don't imagine that you can go a year without buying a new book, or without eating out. (By resolving to buy those books used instead of new, however, you may cut those costs in half!) Be sure to budget for unexpected expenses; you can bet that sometime in the next year, the car will need repairs, the dog will get sick, or the roof will leak.

4. Determine the difference between your projected budget and your current contribution to the family income. If, for example, you can trim $10,000 in expenses, and you currently earn $30,000, you'll need to earn $20,000 as a writer to pay the same costs.

5. _Save._ Most writers suggest having a full year of income saved (or at least enough to cover a full year of expenses). You need a cushion to pay those regular bills while waiting for irregular checks. Savings will be easier once you trim the budget, however. For example, if you've determined that you can cut $10,000 in expenses, you can save that over the next year. You can also ramp up your writing (by producing more articles or seeking higher-paying markets), and bank every penny of that income as well. If your shortfall is $20,000, and you save $10,000 in expenses and earn another $10,000 in writing over the next year, you'll have covered the difference.

6. Create a business plan. Determine your existing income sources, and explore ways to increase that income. Should you pitch more articles to your regular customers? Should you seek new, higher-paying markets? Should you focus on a specialty or expand your range?

7. Be realistic. Nothing will sabotage your dream faster than setting impossible or unsatisfying goals. One writer I know attempted to increase her regular workload in order to build up her savings *and* triple her writing output to gain more clients at the same time. Needless to say, this didn't work, and her "plunge" has been postponed indefinitely. Another common cause of failure is "plunging without a net"—with no savings backup. It only takes one missed rent check to get you back behind that office desk.

Your goal is to improve your life, not ruin it. Many writers take the plunge so that they can spend more time with loved ones, so don't create a schedule that shuts those loved ones out of your life! Many also want to find more time to do what they love, so don't create a plan that forces you to give up the types of writing you love in favor of higher-paying projects that bore you to tears. In short, don't sabotage your plan—or your life—in your attempt to make life more rewarding. Writing is a rewarding activity in itself; being able to write for a living can be the icing on the cake.

About the Author

Moira Allen has been writing professionally for over thirty years, and has published several hundred articles and columns in a variety of magazines and newspapers. She is the author of several books on writing, including *The Writer's Guide to Queries, Pitches and Proposals* (Allworth Press, 2nd Edition, 2010), and *Writing to Win: The Colossal Guide to Writing Contests* (CreateSpace, 2010). Since 2001, Allen has hosted Writing-World.com (www.writing-world.com), one of the world's largest and most popular websites for writers. She has served as a magazine editor, business and commercial writer/editor, columnist, and desktop publisher; she is now hard at work on a novel. Allen lives in Maryland with her husband and the obligatory writer's cat.

About the Contributors

Peter Bowerman (chapter 20: sidebar) is a veteran commercial freelancer and business coach, and the author of the award-winning self-published Well-Fed Writer titles, the how-to "standards" on lucrative commercial freelancing writing for businesses (www.wellfedwriter.com). He chronicled his self-publishing success (52,000 copies of his first two books in print and a full-time living for seven-plus years) in the award-winning 2007 release, *The Well-Fed Self-Publisher: How to Turn One Book into a Full-Time Living* (www.wellfedsp.com). He has published hundreds of articles and editorials, and is a professional coach for commercial freelancing and self-publishing start-ups. His Well-Fed Writer Blog was named as a Top 50 Freelance Blog in 2010. Visit his website at wellfedwriter.com.

Dawn Copeman (chapter 20: Writing for Businesses; chapter 21: Social Media Marketing for Businesses) is a freelance and commercial writer who has published more than one hundred articles on travel, history, cookery, health, and writing. As a copywriter Dawn has written press releases, web content, brochures, newsletters, company reports, and articles for trade journals and newspapers. She has also devised recipes for clients to use in press releases.

Sue Fagalde Lick (chapter 17: Writing for Newspapers) is the author of *Freelancing for Newspapers*, published by Quill Driver Books. In addition to many years as a staff reporter and editor, she has published countless freelance articles and three books on Portuguese Americans, including *Stories Grandma Never Told*. Her articles, short stories, and poetry have appeared in many magazines and newspapers, as well as two Cup of Comfort anthologies. She lives with her dog, Annie, on the Oregon Coast. Visit her website at www.suelick.com.

Gary McLaren (chapter 25: Social Media for Writers) is the founder of WorldwideFreelance.com, a website he started in 1999, where freelance writers can search through thousands of writing markets around the world. He is very active on social media and regularly posts helpful tips for writers on Twitter with the username @GaryJMcLaren.

Index

INDEX

Books from Allworth Press

The Author's Toolkit (Fourth Edition)
by Mary Embree (5½ × 8¼, 272 pages, paperback, $16.99)

The Birds and Bees of Words
by Mary Embree (5½ × 8¼, 208 pages, paperback, $14.95)

Business and Legal Forms for Authors and Self-Publishers (Fourth Edition)
by Tad Crawford with Stevie Fitzgerald and Michael Gross (8½ × 11, 176 pages, paperback, $24.99)

The Business of Writing
by Jennifer Lyons with Foreword by Oscar Hijuelos (6 × 9, 304 pages, paperback, $19.95)

The Copyright Guide (Fourth Edition)
by Lee Wilson (6 × 9, 288 pages, hardcover, $24.99)

The Fiction Writer's Guide to Dialogue
by John Hough, Jr. (6 × 9, 144 pages, paperback, $14.95)

The Law (in Plain English)® for Writers (Fifth Edition)
by Leonard D. DuBoff and Sarah J. Tugman (6 × 9, 272 pages, paperback, $19.99)

The Online Writer's Companion
by P. J. Aitken (6 × 9, 344 pages, paperback, $19.99)

Promote Your Book
by Patricia Fry (5½ × 8¼, 224 pages, paperback, $19.95)

Propose Your Book
by Patricia Fry (6 × 9, 288 pages, paperback, $19.99)

Publish Your Book
by Patricia Fry (6 × 9, 264 pages, paperback, $19.95)

Starting Your Career as a Freelance Editor
by Mary Embree (6 × 9, 240 pages, paperback, $19.95)

Starting Your Career as a Professional Blogger
by Jacqueline Bodnar (6 × 9, 192 pages, paperback, $19.95)

Starting Your Career as a Social Media Manager
by Mark Story (6 × 9, 264 pages, paperback, $19.95)

The Writer's Guide to Queries, Pitches and Proposals (Second Edition)
by Moira Allen (6 × 9, 288 pages, paperback, $19.95)

Writing the Great American Romance Novel
by Catherine Lanigan (6 × 9, 224 pages, paperback, $19.99)

Writing What You Know
by Meg Files (6 × 9, 212 pages, paperback, $16.99)

To see our complete catalog or to order online, please visit *www.allworth.com*.